Modern Marriage
and
Its Cost to Women

Modern Marriage
and
Its Cost to Women

A Sociological Look
at Marriage in France

François de Singly

Translated from the French by
Malcolm Bailey

DELAWARE

Newark: University of Delaware Press
London: Associated University Presses

Associated University Presses
440 Forsgate Drive
Cranbury, NJ 08512

Associated University Presses
16 Barter Street
London WC1A 2AH, England

Associated University Presses
P.O. Box 338, Port Credit
Mississauga, Ontario
Canada L5G 4L8

The paper used in this publication meets the requirements of the American National Standard for Permanence of Paper for Printed Library Materials Z39.48-1984.

Library of Congress Cataloging-in-Publication Data

Singly, François de.
  [Fortune et infortune de la femme mariée. English]
  Modern marriage and its cost to women : a sociological look at marriage in France / François de Singly.
      p.   cm.
  Includes bibliographical references and index.
  ISBN 0-87413-572-9 (alk. paper)
  1. Marriage—France—Economic aspects. 2. Wives—France—Economic conditions. 3. Women in the professions—France. I. Title.
HQ624.S5613   1996
306.81'0944—dc20   95-42335
                                                              CIP

Contents

Preface to the American Edition: Marriage, Justice, and Equality

THE women's movement and feminist theories have had a profound effect on our understanding of the family (Thompson and Walker 1989; Ferree 1990). They have forced not only researchers but also ordinary men and women to view their worlds differently in their day-to-day interactions. This raises questions about equality and fairness in assessing the relationships between partners. Does the way the modern family functions perhaps mask processes that, whether we like it or not, strongly contribute to the creation and maintenance of inequality between the sexes?

This book answers those questions by analyzing family life in France during the 1970s. It claims, in fact, that it is possible to understand how family life operates from the point of view of justice, as illustrated by Martha Nussbaum (1992) and Susan Moller Okin (1992), proving it sociologically by pointing out the benefits and costs of family life for both sexes.

Contrary to what might at first appear to be the case, this book is by no means a microeconomic study à la Becker (1981). That particular school of thought claims that both men and women act rationally. With a couple's actions coordinated by the male partner, as the person in charge, no one wins and no one loses. The division of labor between the sexes does not matter; women are not handicapped by it. What really matters is the way the profits are distributed.

The microeconomic point of view is in reality a conjuring trick; it wants the reader to believe that two different statements mean the same thing. "It is in the interest of men and women to become a couple," according to this view, is identical to "It is in the equal interest of men and women to become a couple." Obviously the definition of "equal" is important. A woman's gains within the family structure are not equal to those of her male partner, however, as this book demonstrates with the aid of a number of statistical studies.

7

If women are paid less on the labor market than men even when they have the same qualifications, it is largely due to their family situation. A woman living with a man has difficulty defending the social and economic value of her initial capital—inherited from her parents and acquired through her education—whereas the exact opposite is true for a man.

This inequality is important. But conjugal life has an even more important effect. Women, on the one hand, become socially and economically dependent on their partners, whereas men remain much more independent. Most women invest less in their professional activities because of the extent of their investment in their family lives. When they live with a partner it is quite possible for them not to be aware of how resources are being distributed. But as soon as they split up, as studies on divorce show, they experience a drop in their living standards. Usually only by finding a new partner can they regain the standard of living they had enjoyed previously. The cost of marriage for women resides in their social dependency on their partners, to which is added their emotional dependency (this latter being equally true for men, of course).

Unlike men, women are defined socially by their relationships with their partners. The status of the male partner thus plays a greater role in establishing the status of the female partner than does the reverse. This is what is unjust about marriage: the (albeit implicit) contract in a partnership affects women and men differently. The former are deprived much more than the latter of their right to be themselves. This injustice is all the greater in modern society because of the increasing importance attached to individual autonomy and independence.

The education of girls to a higher level, the greater number of women who now have a career, and the increase in cohabitation have not really had much effect on the fundamental lack of equality between the sexes within the family unit. The postscript to this book describes the cost of marriage for couples in the 1990s. In the twenty years since the 1970s there has been little or no change for women as compared with men.

The statistics have altered very little for both men and women. The division of labor between the sexes, whereby the greatest professional investment is made by men and the greatest investment in the family is made by women, remains more or less unchanged. Thus, in a 1994 national study of the 25 to 35 age group in France, the question "What are the two most important things in your life" resulted in 41 percent of the male respondents choosing "Success in your career," compared with 26 percent of the women. In contrast, 71 percent of the women chose "Having children and sufficient time to look after them," compared with 58 percent for the men (Bozon, Laufer, de Singly, and Villeneuve-Gokalp 1994). Women are more concerned than men (despite some effort on the latter's part) with attending to the material and psychological needs of children. In fact, it is the issue of looking after children (or elderly dependents) that causes stress lines between the concept of justice and equality to appear. To what extent does justice imply equality when equality means sameness? Must women match men on their own terms to be considered their equals (Gilligan 1982; Bubeck 1995)?

In the same way that Charles Taylor (1992) proposes a policy of recognition within a multicultural society, can we not envisage a similar policy between partners who respect their differences without creating divisions or permitting masculine domination? This approach presupposes the possibility of a relationship between partners that can be at the same time affectionate, intimate (Shorter 1975; Giddens 1992), and fair. For that to happen there would have to be a social relationship that respected individual identity and at the same time a creation of something valuable that both partners could share equally.

Two aspects about this book may surprise the reader. The first concerns the linking of research done in the United States with that done in France. In spite of the obvious differences between the two countries with regard to family life, I feel that there are considerable similarities between the United States and France. The research link can be justified first of all from a theoretical point of view. Many analysts of modern society believe that the Western countries—at least as far as the white population is concerned—have experienced a growth in individualism and its effects on private life, in particular a rise in conjugal instability. National differences have less to do with behavior and more to do with the way society and the family deal with the problems arising from this individualism (Lefaucheur 1992; Commaille and de Singly 1995) as well as with the ideological struggle that emphasizes either the defense of the family and of moral values or the defense of individuals, who are defined more by their personal needs than by their attachment to a family unit.

Second, the empirical research in both countries often has comparable aims.[1] Some common themes are: the time parents devote to children (Moen and Dempster-McClain 1987); the division of labor between partners (Hiller and Philliber 1986); unequal investment in careers (Moen and Dempster-McClain 1987; Folk and Beller 1993); the effects of the priority given to male careers during marriage (Korenman and Neumark 1991; Shihadeh 1991) or after the marriage breakup (Weitzman 1985; Kitson and Morgan 1990). The results of these studies all bear out the fact that marriage is an inegalitarian institution.

This inequality is revealed by means of quantitative statistics that show the objective effects of family life on men and women. Women probably have a distorted view of these effects because of their emotional attachment to their husbands and children. To understand how such a distorted picture of an unfair and inegalitarian institution is maintained and perpetuated we need to study the ways in which individuals perceive their situations. Not all women look at the social and economic dependency of marriage in the same way. "Autonomous" women certainly are unhappy about it, for example, and women who see marriage as a state of fusion are reasonably content. For many women these two attitudes coexist, however, and give rise to a number of contradictions.

The second unusual feature in this book is its use of literary references. Novels often have certain passages, in condensed form, that illustrate issues that women face in marriage. Such passages are not accidental. Romantic novels serve principally to feed the female fantasies—women read this kind of book more frequently than men (Garbe 1993)—about men and romantic love (Luhmann 1982); they also, however, refer to disappointment and disillusionment. These references illustrate how the objective significance of marriage—as presented here—is often, in women's experience, split between the desire to exist as an autonomous individual (the justice dimension) and the desire to love and be loved (the emotional dimension).

To what extent can love and justice exist together? We can see why certain justice theories (for example, Rawls 1973) leave the family unit out of their analyses. Certainly one way of getting around the problem is by limiting justice to the public domain. Nor is it enough simply to reintroduce the equality and justice perspective—the aim of this book—into a study of the family, since the question of love is excluded. In both the fantasy and the real world love, justice, and equality between the sexes are inextricably linked, and novels exist to remind us of that fact. Before the "idea that love is about justice, a better world, and transforming relationships that have been damaged by social constraints and inequality between the sexes" (Fraisse 1993, 73; 1992) can be completely integrated into a rational sociological proposition, a great deal of theoretical work remains to be done.

Acknowledgments

Modern Marriage and Its Cost to Women attempts to respond to the question "Why do couples live together?" by elaborating a theory of the advantages of cohabitation—some of them considerable, some less so—for men and women. This theory is now available to English readers, thanks to the translation of Malcolm Bailey and the attentive and meticulous editorial assistance of Elizabeth Reynolds. I am deeply grateful to both of them.

My greatest debt is to Chantal Bourdaud-de Singly, who so ably checked and, where necessary, corrected this sociological appraisal of the cost of marriage.

Introduction

Aɴʏoɴᴇ hoping to find in this book either a diatribe against marriage or an argument defending it might as well close the cover right now, since he or she will be disappointed. It is not through statistical studies based on representative samples that scientific credence can be given to any one particular point of view of what marriage means for women. A few sociologists have already followed that particular path and declared that married women are "happier" than single women (Glenn 1975). Others claim that marriage may have a detrimental effect on women, saying that married women and single men tend to suffer higher rates of depression. Both believers and nonbelievers in the salvation of women through marriage look for conclusive arguments in the statistical arsenal and simply select those that confirm their own point of view.

A Sᴏᴄɪᴏʟᴏɢɪᴄᴀʟ Lᴏᴏᴋ ᴀᴛ Mᴀʀʀɪᴀɢᴇ

The aim of this book is not to present a neutral, objective set of arguments backed up by statistics. Quite to the contrary, I propose instead a sociological account of modern marriage. Like Roland Barthes in *Empire of Signs*, who did not claim to represent or analyze the situation of French women during the nineteen seventies, I can nonetheless identify from within this matrimonial universe "a certain number of characteristics and from these formulate a definite system" (Barthes 1975, 7). This system will describe the consequence of married life for women.

To examine these consequences I have not constructed a scale model or a miniature version of marriage in French society. My plan is to focus on a number of significant traits. Any scientific project is a work of fiction insofar as it is the product of a new conception of reality and is obtained by means of a completely new focus on that reality (Simmel 1981, 87–88):

15

we do not see everything but we do see things differently. To obtain a different view of married life, I have adjusted my sociological microscope in such a way that the element of love that unites married couples remains out of focus. The exclusion of this factor enables us to view a dimension within marriage that is all too often obscured: the social interest at stake within the contemporary family. In this book we are going to see how marriage changes the management of a woman's cultural, economic, and social capital. Do women have to pay a high price for marriage? If so, is it higher, in fact, than that paid by their husbands? Within the institution of marriage are women's interests better served or less well served than men's?

This evaluation of the cost of marriage resides upon a theoretical abstraction. The complexity of individual identity is reduced to four elements: sex, age, married status, and the possession of a "savings account" representing the social worth of the individual. This account is comprised of the total capital that individuals possess, which includes their cultural value in terms of diplomas and degrees, actual financial capital, and social capital (derived from family background). These capital resources, both inherited and acquired, do not lie dormant. They are invested. Marriage is a market, just like the labor market, in which capital changes hands. The choice of a marriage partner is made according to a principle of equivalence between the capital worth of the two partners. Women with university degrees tend to marry men with similar qualifications. The daughters of blue-collar workers tend to fall for blue-collar workers rather than executives. Whether achieved consciously or not, one's selection of a marriage partner is based on social criteria. Marriage constitutes for a woman the public recognition of her value through the capital value of her future husband.

The value of the individual's "savings account" is not permanently fixed. Individuals can increase the worth of their financial holdings, of their cultural wealth by undertaking further educational studies, for example, or of their social worth by acquiring friends who themselves are highly valued. On the other hand, the value of individuals can fall as a result of a change in the way in which their professional (or matrimonial qualities) are assessed. Marriage is affected by these value changes. The way in which a woman is valued after marriage is not the same as she was before it, possibly by giving up working or by marrying a rich husband. The "savings account" now in the name of a married woman is not the same as the one that was in the name of a single woman. The changes in the social value of a woman are an indication of the way in which she is affected by marriage. We can thus see how an institution shapes the individuals it takes into its bosom.

This way of looking at marriage is not usually within sociology. When capital is studied—as in resource theory (Blood and Wolfe 1960)—it is considered as an independent variable. It alters the form married life takes: a highly qualified wife does not take to domesticity in quite the same way as one who is not. Here capital is seen as a dependent variable. The potential value of a woman's qualifications on the labor market is transformed once she is married and has children. Nevertheless, this does not necessarily mean that married life affects all women in the same way. The consequences of marriage cannot be defined without taking into account the social identities of the partners. Even if the institution of marriage imprints its mark upon a woman's material and symbolic possessions, by the same token the extent and nature of that mark depend upon the value placed on the woman. A woman bringing little in the way of value to a marriage does not necessarily experience the same changes to her personal fortune as one who brings a great deal.

Marriage does not straightway remove the dividing line between the respective capital of the married partners: the wife's "savings account" is not immediately absorbed into that of her husband. This division can in fact cause conflicts of interest between the partners since men do not always behave automatically in a way that accepts the right of their wives to own their own capital. Partnership in marriage can create contradictions insofar as it might be necessary, for example, for the couple to have separate bank accounts. For G. S. Becker this is not to be confused with family savings. For these there is no source of conflict within the marriage partnership, since "the function of family savings is closely identified with that of the head of the family, whose job it is to look after the well-being of the others" (1974, 1077; 1981). According to this atruistic hypothesis the head of the family, out of affection for it, "takes sufficient interest in the well-being of the other members of the family to allocate resources voluntarily to them." I do not go along with this theoretical idealism (or paternalism). The refusal *a priori* to amalgamate the two "savings accounts" is easily understood when it comes to conjugal strife. When the family balance sheet is drawn up it is impossible to proceed as if both partners had always been on an equal footing. At that juncture each partner evaluates his or her contribution to their domestic life, as this statement by the wife of the president of France in *Le bon plaisir* clearly indicates:

> In thirty-five years of marriage, to further your career I have attended 3,859 lunches, dinners, or banquets and thirty-five Armistice commemorations... I have accompanied you during the past five years on twenty-seven official visits to countries where all I ever saw were kindergartens and folk dancing, with an opera thrown in each time. I hate opera [and] folk music... I've had enough! (Giroud 1982, 184)

This sort of evaluation of a marriage is a stock feature of certain novels and often takes place after the wife has run off and left her husband. Such an evaluation is precipitated, according to their authors, by a sudden upheaval. Despite their obvious differences in other ways, these novels share quite a number of similar scenarios: a sense of apathy on the part of the wife; her feeling of being bogged down; her sense of alienation and weakness. By giving so much to her husband and children she has neglected her own needs. As T. Leprince-Ringuet writes in *Il faut que je rentre,* "For the past fifteen years . . . she had allowed herself to be overtaken more and more by these intermittent and uncontrolled phases. She was occupied and painstaking in what she did, yet at the same time she was like a sleepwalker" (1985; 88). When she wakes up and looks in horror at herself, she sees the other women who also "live by proxy. They are so-and-so's wife, this or that man's mother. But who are they really? Architects, engineers, chemists, woodworkers, metalworkers? Who knows? They will never know... They simply wait. For what? Their husbands, their children, their grandchildren... death? They do not even know themselves what they are waiting for." (Cardinal 1978, 216)

Even if these evaluations overestimate what married life costs a woman, the very fact that they are made when they are, when the woman demands to know where she stands, indicates a central problem: that of the possible need to equate the direct and the indirect management of a woman's capital resources.

As well as her direct financial value—her paid work, for example—she also has an indirect value related to her husband's worth. This is why the choice of a husband is so important, since it is he who determines to a considerable degree the life style of his wife. As the French diamond advertisement puts it: "Often you just have to look at a woman to see what kind of a husband she's got." Children—and the wealth they gradually acquire—constitute the second element in the indirect value attached to women.

Looking at the topic in this way complicates any assessment of the effects of marriage. The problem resides in comparing the figures in the "direct revenue" column with those in the column headed "revenue from the husband and the child(ren)." A letter published in July 1980 in the "agony column" of a women's magazine by a woman five years into her marriage shows clearly that for her there is no connection between these two types of income—either symbolic or literally financial. Her husband's social success and the advantages that accrue from it do not make up for the fact that she stopped working.

> I'm twenty-five years old. I got married when I was twenty, to a guy whose only future lay in his ambition. He had no qualifications and worked in a plant. I worked in a typing pool, which was really monotonous, so that when my first child was born I quite happily quit working. For five years we had a hard time—poor housing accommodations, a difficult second birth—to the extent that I was worried, really worried. I was totally demoralized... But my husband got on. He had a chance to do a course in draftsmanship and did really well. I admire him for the way he's done so well, and for his courage and intelligence. We have a new life ahead of us because he's got a job as a draftsman with a big company and he'll be earning three times as much as before. We've already moved into a nice neighborhood where we'll have plenty of sun and fresh air and so on. So what's the problem? Well, the problem is that I feel completely useless. I don't know where I am. My husband has a new job, but I have nothing. My place is in the home, looking after the kids and the house. But that's no kind of a life! I'm like a nothing! I feel ugly and stupid. I'm scared I'll lose my husband. I don't know anything anymore! I'm lost! Before, I had a job, I earned money. I bought my own clothes, I used to go out with the people I worked with. Now there's nothing. I'm shut up in the house with the washing and

cleaning; the shopping and the kids. It never stops. Is that living? I know I've got to look after my husband and my kids, but I'm really unhappy now. (*Femmes d'aujourd'hui*, no. 1380, 42).

The capital that the husband brings to a marriage is not always the same as the capital a wife earns and acquires in her own right. The indirect management of capital has a downside, namely dependence. How does the sociologist assess all this? Let us imagine two women with the same academic qualifications. The first has a job that brings in four thousand francs and a husband who earns six thousand. The second, who has no outside job, is married to a man who earns ten thousand. Do we conclude from this that both women have equal earnings from their identical academic qualifications? Should we not take into account in our calculations the way the two women view their marriage and in particular the importance they attach to their independence? All women do not assess their marriage by the same criteria. Short of adopting one particular set of criteria, the sociologist cannot draw up a precise marriage balance sheet without taking into account the way women perceive their own lives. A one-sided assessment of marriage would not give an accurate account of that institution.

LOVE LEFT OUT

The changes in social value of a married woman are not always easily perceived, since they are distorted, masked even, by her being in love. Love expresses itself in the form of generosity towards one's partner and in a lack of self-interest. Not only can the social advantages at play in married life become hidden, but they can also be denied by the actors involved. For example, after an Andrée Michel magazine interview[1] that explained the trend toward unmarried couples living together as evidence of the realization by young women of the unfavorable future reserved for married women, there was a strong reaction from female readers. Typical of them was this one from someone "married for thirty years":

I was astounded by the article, which made out that the majority of young French couples, and especially young women, reduce living together as a couple to a sordid financial arrangement between the partners, without any feelings of warmth or of altruism; in other words, without love, apart from sexual gratification. The arguments put forward by the sociologist remind me of the horse trading at a country fair or business negotiations where the object is to concede nothing and to make sure the other guy doesn't pull a fast one. How can you talk of conjugal union when each partner is doing his or her utmost to defend his or her rights and not concede anything to the other?[2]

Love is blind, which results in those who are hit by it being unaware of the way their capital resources are being managed. It also hinders any attempt to assess the effects of marriage since whenever love is taken into consideration it seems to represent, and be the equivalent of, the sum total of all the individuals' wealth. Consequently a woman who loves her husband and children and who is loved in turn never loses in the marriage game. Any possible losses in her "savings account" are made up for by the happiness and affection she gets from her family. If the love factor is introduced into the analysis the accounts miraculously balance, thanks to this emotional profit. So what does it matter, one might ask, if women suffer such a devaluation in their social worth? Have they not opted for psychological satisfaction and social gratification? Everything is for the best of all possible domestic worlds: the alchemy of love turns desire into capital and transforms a smile into a capital resource.

Let us take two examples of these sorts of exchange, one from literature and the other a popular cartoon. In the novel *Une enfance à l'eau bénite* the heroine is passing through a well-to-do neighborhood with members of her family. Her aunt draws her attention: "'Look at that big place with four stories. The cousin of Mme Bélair's nephew lives there. She won the big prize. She married a lawyer. He's as ugly as sin, but he's absolutely loaded with money.' Later, in the car, the adults were going on about it. 'How did she manage it?' my father asked. 'How d'you think? You know how,' my aunt added with a wink, and everyone burst out laughing. So there was a way of getting rich that squared with the sins of the flesh" (Bombardier 1985, 25). The world does not function entirely according to official moral principles nor according to the rules of sociological statistics. There are other goods circulating on the marriage market besides the social and cultural ones. The second example is taken from an Andy Capp cartoon. The cartoonist, Smythe, destroys the alchemy that puts kisses, sweet words, and money all on the same level by cutting short the dialogue between the husband and wife. When Andy calls out to Flo: "Honey, it's ages since I kissed you. Come here, and let me give you a kiss," she has the good sense to take her purse with her. Even though she knows how much it will cost, Flo still wants the affection. In scenes like this love seems somewhat illusory. Could its function be to charm women so that they forget, as far as possible, the true cost of married life? That is certainly the view of certain detractors, like the woman in *Une vie pour deux:*

> Wife-mother! I can't think of pliers more tightly gripping, nippers more sharply cutting, or shears more mutilating. And what is even more unacceptable is that I must wear them as a decoration. I am to be admired, recognized, respected, and loved because I have been severed from myself by the cold chisel of love, the rasp of kisses . . . and by the piercing drill of motherhood. How absurd! (Cardinal 1978, 223)

There are, nonetheless, those who believe that affection should appear in the credit column. For others it belongs on the debit side of the balance sheet. This ambiguous nature of love means that we cannot mix the flow of love with that of capital. Only if we put love to one side for the moment can we really examine the changes in a woman's social value after marriage. The reader, therefore, will not find here a realistic and complete picture of conjugal life. A fictionalized account of marriage minus the love factor reveals other secrets, especially the effects, for better or worse, of a marriage in which the partners are in love with each other.

Love, the blind spot in my analysis, or the reverse side of the coin, hatred, gradually disappears, since I have tried to bind together the threads of passion with those of social gain. I have been helped in this by literary texts. Into these accounts of people in love suddenly intrude moments where happiness is shattered. Romantic fiction thus sometimes borrows its scenarios from sociological fiction when it wishes to provoke conflict or friction or create barriers between individuals. In *Roman Songe* (Still 1976), for example, social insecurity destroys the chance of love for two young working-class people. One Sunday they meet and feel a mutual attraction. Later a girlfriend tells the girl, Denise, about the young man, Daniel. "'I know him quite well. His father's a foreman at the plant.

His mother runs the company shop. He's got a terrific job... went to college and everything. Fine chance you stand.'" Denise, a line worker in a mill whose late father was a salaried plumber, believes what her friend says. For this reason she cannot understand why the young man should belittle himself by saying that his father is a "first-rate tool maker'" and that his mother "'works at the checkout at the Magic supermarket, but it doesn't pay much.'" In reply to what she believes is Daniel playing down his social background she gives an inflated picture of hers. She says she is the daughter of an engineer and is studying at college. She talks of her privileged existence and describes the big, fancy house she lives in. At first all this makes Daniel feel quite proud. He feels "an extraordinary sense of pride within himself when he heard all this; it was like some wonderful party. And Denise on top of it all... the big garden, her mansion, the father, the mother, the relatives." On more sober reflection, when he envisages the future, and thinks about all the things that Denise would want—houses, cars, jewels, trips—and that he would be unable to give her, he feels inferior. He writes a note—"Goodbye. I love Denise. I'll never be able to make her happy"—and then commits suicide. He kills himself because he is afraid of the risks implied by what he imagines to be the great social gulf between them.

"RICOCHET'S SONG"

Before they set out on a voyage many people like to know not only their destination but also where the stopping-off points and places of special interest lie. With those people in mind I should like to make certain points. A married woman's "account books" reveal a number of contradictions. When she becomes involved in marriage and family life her capital undergoes a devaluation in relation to the labor market, but it also retains its value by being reinvested in the marriage market. A "good" marriage also has its negative. A woman who has married well has less chance of increasing her capital in a professional capacity. However, if she does marry well, the gains can be even greater.

When widowed or divorced, women often experience a gradual loss of social worth that affects neither their cultural capital nor their social relations. Marriage does not have the dire consequences for a woman's capital resources that feminists like to maintain. A married woman is not like the secretary who, according to Honoré de Balzac, "was a perfect partner for the poet... but in the way people are perfect partners for someone, inevitably by sacrificing themselves."[3] The institution of marriage does not, for all that, bring about a magical fusion of both partners' capital resources, nor does it cause a noticeable increase in the value of hers. An inventory of the contents of family bookshelves reveals, for example, that after their marriage each partner's tastes are modified to a certain extent, but with each partner remaining in his or her own "cultural universe" (see chapter 5). A woman's social worth is heterogeneous. Certain elements of a woman's capital resources—for example, those destined for investment in a career—are severely hit. Others, by way of contrast, seem to emerge unscathed from all the effects of family life.

Individuals retain their initial worth after marriage in various ways. They can, to some degree, manage their own capital, with the chance of receiving a bonus in the form of a share of their partner's profits; or they can leave it to their partner to manage their capital, with the possibility of retaining a small personal "savings account." But because of the way work is divided between sexes, both inside and outside the home, a woman never—or at least hardly ever—conducts her affairs in the same way that her husband does. Even if she continues to have a job and to gain some sort of value, it is to some degree with her husband's consent. While a married man sees the return on his personal capital increase by the simple fact of marrying, the same is not true for a woman; she has to draw on other, external, capital (her husband's). Marriage, if not removing it completely, at least severely reduces a woman's independence, offering access to social capital in its place. This is perfectly illustrated by what happens when a woman who has no career is widowed or divorced. Since her capital has been invested entirely on the marriage market she needs to remarry to maintain her previous position. This dependence on marriage and on a husband can vary; it is less when the woman's capital resources are greater than her partner's. A woman in this position is subject to a smaller degree of loss of autonomy than one whose capital is less than her husband's. The particular circumstances of the marriage modify the degree of woman's subordination. When a woman has increased her capital value by making a "good" marriage, she is subsequently less likely to invest her capital on the labor market.

This ambiguous nature of the effects of marriage on women stems from the complexity of conjugal relationships: there is at the same time a partnership and rivalry between a husband and wife. This is why once the reader has put down this book he or she might well hum Ricochet's song by Rabelais. Panurge, undecided whether to marry or not, seeks advice from Pantagruel. In chapter 9 of Book 3 Pantagruel replies with "then for God's sake marry" and "then don't get married" in response to the Panurge's arguments for and against marriage: the advantages of feminine company; being looked after; the need to perpetuate the family name; the inconvenience of being cuckolded or abandoned. Should he go for a worthy lady, knowing that they are "all ugly"? Or should he remain a bachelor, with no one to look after him and "offer me the love that conjugal love is made out to be?"

The work of much research on the family will be used on this voyage through the territory of marriage, along with data on working women, family size, the value of qualifications, the education and scholastic achievements of children, family models, highly qualified single women, and cohabitation.[4] A postscript added to the end of the book since the French edition was published brings the situation on the cost of marriage to women into the 1990s.

Modern Marriage
and
Its Cost to Women

Part 1
Profit and Loss in Marriage

Introduction to Part 1

THE nineteenth-century image of the housewife (Blunden 1982; Knibiehler and Fouquet 1977) is an obligatory reference in any discussion about women and families. By examining marriage and married life from the point of view of the value of women our theoretical case study breaks the rules with regard to this model.

This study concentrates on women's cultural and social capital, whereas the nineteenth-century model of women's triple role as mistress of the house, wife, and mother requires, according to its proponents, that this wealth be used sparingly. A Thomas Hardy short story, "Ollamoor the Fiddler," illustrates the nineteenth-century indifference to women's social value. The hero, Ned, decides to marry Caroline even though she is an unmarried mother and has less value. However, he does not do it without a reason. For Ned, what constitutes a good wife does not depend on social capital alone. For him she is comparable to a cheap teapot that often makes better tea than a much more expensive one. Caroline's social dowry is unimportant in Ned's eyes; what count are her qualities as a wife and mother (Hardy 1981, 228–29).

Our analysis concentrates on the changes that occur in the management of a woman's social capital after marriage, including a consideration of paid work as an example of direct management of her property. However, taking a job makes no sense within the context of the housewife model. As the Vatican has said, work is "a corruption of maternal dignity and everything a woman stands for; it is an upheaval within the family through which a husband is deprived of his wife, the children of their mother, and the whole family of an ever-vigilant guardian."[1]

To understand how a woman's capital increases in value after marriage we have to rid ourselves of the idea that there is only one acceptable way for a woman's capital to be managed: by her husband. The housewife model has so invaded reality, in other words so shaped the relationship between

31

men and women, that it cannot be denied. After all, sociologists use the professional status of the husband as an indicator of the social value of the wife. Giving a wife the same social status as her husband stresses the significance of the indirect management of a woman's capital. It underlines what is at stake in choosing a husband (chapter 1). After her marriage a wife is no longer the same woman. Not only does she increase the social value of her capital through her husband, but she also increases her wealth via her children (chapter 2). This widening of the scope of her investments, together with the division of work between the sexes, in turn creates problems for her on the labor market. A married woman earns much less from her educational dowry than does a married man or a single woman (chaper 3). A woman's domestic responsibilities get in the way of her career opportunities. The reverse situation is not as true as the opponents of working women would have us believe. Thus the children of working mothers are not more culturally handicapped than those of a mother who does not have a paid job (chapter 5).

1

The Husband as Manager of His Wife's Capital

Tarif or Price List for Eligible Parties Wishing to Contract a Marriage without Difficulty

—A young lady with a dowry of from around two thousand livres to six thousand livres

—She can expect to marry a Palace merchant, a government clerk, a sergeant, or a court solicitor.

—One with from six thousand to twelve thousand livres

—A silk merchant, a draper, a wood carver, a court prosecutor, a maître d'hôtel, or the secretary to a great lord.

—One with from twelve thousand to twenty thousand livres

—A Parliamentary procurator, a bailiff, a notary, or a clerk of the court.

—One with from twenty thousand to thirty thousand livres

—A lawyer, a Treasury counselor, a forestry counselor, a magistrate, or a keeper of the mint.

A. Furetière, *Le roman bourgeois,* 1666

WHAT are husbands for? Love, with no strings attached, is so considered to be the official norm that it is only possible to answer this impertinent question by providing a statement of accounts of the movement of capital between a husband and wife. In one respect a woman acquires a substantial part of her monetary and symbolic worth from her marriage partner. A woman's worth, therefore, varies according to the capital resources of her husband. In another respect there is also an exchange of capital, and husband's value is also modified in relation to his wife's capital. In my fictionalized account the husband also has his own "savings account." His wife receives interest from this account, depending on how much she deposited in at the time of their marriage and on how much she continues to deposit during their married life.

THE SHARING OF PROFITS

The whole business starts with marriage. The selection of a husband on the marriage market basically determines the life style of the woman who has made the choice. Given the way domestic life functions, the decision of the couple to live together also significantly modifies the woman's future via the constraints imposed by the division of labor according to sex. Just as in marriage, it is the man who undertakes the rule of principal earner, and the wife's life style depends particularly on the partner she has chosen.

This dependence is quite clear in the different earning capacities (personal income) of men and women and in the differences in their standard of living (total income), as shown by the statistics. A distinct difference exists between men and women on both these counts. As Baudelot and Choquet write, "The relationship between salary and standard of living is inversely proportional for men and women. Men are in a much better position with regard to salary in relation to standard of living; women are better off from the point of view of standard of living in relation to salary" (1981,17). Embarking on marriage, according to this indicator, is much more advantageous for women than for men since the former achieve an improvement in their standard of living.

The family income to which a woman has access is principally made up of the husband's input, even when both sexes work. According to the research into the taxable income of married coupes carried out by the French National Institute of Statistics and Economic Research (INSEE),[1] in the case of senior executives nine-tenths of primary income comes from the husband when the wife has no job, and around two-thirds when she does have one. The contribution of a working woman to family income oscillates an average between one-third for those who have no more than a high-school diploma and two-fifths for those who have had a college education. A woman's academic dowry, when placed on the labor market, in most cases brings in less than half of the family's total income.

This inequality between the respective partners' input into official family income—leaving aside the unofficial contribution in the form of unremunerated housework—does not mean that this income is subsequently redistributed unequally. This is quite evident from the research into household consumption. Those individuals who earn most are not especially favored when it comes to parceling out the income. So-called nonworking wives, with the same standard of living as their husbands, have as great a share of family income as those who have paid work. Even those researchers who believe that women are the losers in marriage do not contest this fact, but they justify this conversion of the husband's income into family income, and the wife's access to it, in two ways. One, a woman's activities and expenditures—hair stylist, looking after her appearance, decorating, and entertaining—are not, despite what they may seem, for her benefit. The main function of these expenditures is to show off the husband's social status. The totality of the family's expenditures and activities, and particularly the wife's, serve as a "manifestation of the social class status of the family, and of the social status of the husband in particular" (F. Bourgeois et al. 1978, 17). The husband is without doubt the single beneficiary in a marriage. The second justification is that the wife's contribution to the family's income is in the raising of the children. A married woman does not have an inferior standard of living simply because it is her role to prepare her sons to have the same life style as their father. She must therefore bring them up in a comparable life style. It is because of this socializing function that a married woman is able to share so advantageously in the family income for someone who is in a subservient position (Sofer 1982). Whatever the theoretical reasons may be—and I point out that I am talking about something that cannot be demonstrated—married women, whether they have a job or not, for the most part share the same standard of living as their husbands.

Are wives a reflection of their husbands?

Does this sharing of the profits between partners imply that a married woman has a social value that is absolutely identical to that of her husband? If we know the social status of the husband can we then automatically deduce the wife's position? Does a woman adopt not only her husband's name but also his social status? Does she become, by marrying, so-and-so's wife?

More often than not sociologists would answer yes to the questions since they assign all members of a family the same socioprofessional status as the head of household—that is, the portion of the man in a family having both a husband and a wife. The presentation of data—interviews or tables— shows how this attribution of the husband's status to the wife is used. In the sociology of the family this is even more evident, since it is almost always the wife who is interviewed. For example, in a book about child-rearing practices (Boltanski 1969, 85) the author follows his extracts from interviews with wives with reference only to the husband's job: "I always boil the bottles before each feeding. You don't ask yourself why. I saw my mother do it, it must be passed on from mother to daughter; there are some things you just accept (Vervins, truck driver, 37, 6 children)." Statistical tables reveal a similar sort of logic. In the tables showing how women spend their day (Huet, Lemel, and Roy 1982) they are classified according to the socioprofessional categories of their husbands, whether they have a job or not. Only single women with a job are categorized according to their individual situation.

Whether they say so explicitly or not, sociologists believe that marriage brings about a change in women but not in men. Men continue to retain their identity, whereas women, even when they have a job, lose theirs. An increase in a woman's value by dint of having a job does not enter into it; she is still inferior or at best no more than equal to the value of her husband. Therefore a man's situation can, to all intents and purposes, be considered as being an indicator of the value of the couple or indeed of the wife.

Since the 1970s American sociologists have tested this hypothesis and have established empirically its validity.[2] According to the research carried out by Mahoney and Richardson (1979), a married woman's profession affects the perception of neither her own status nor that of her husband; the husband's profession, on the other hand, serves as an indicator of the social status of both partners. The perceived status of men is based, as is their wives', on the man's professional situation. The professional value of a wife has little effect on the assessment of her husband's value or on that of her own. The individuals interviewed respond as if, in a marriage, it is enough to know the husband's capital value to know the value of his wife.

By using more complex methodological procedures, the picture obtained of a wife is not a mirror image of that of her husband, even if the view of the wife is primarily based on information related to her husband. In a survey undertaken by Ritter and Hargens (1975),the official identity of the wife is looked at from three different standpoints: the wife's occupation, the husband's occupation, and that of the wife's father. The status of these three elements contributes to a greater or lesser degree to fixing the wife's social position. The influence of the husband's professional status—all other things being equal—is considerably greater than that exercised by the wife's or her father's. When, of the three individuals concerned, only the wife's father is a white-collar worker, the wife sees herself as belonging to the upper-or lower-middle classes in a quarter of the cases. Where she alone is a white-collar worker, she identifies with those social classes in one-third of the cases; and when it is her husband who is in that professional category, one out of two women see themselves as belonging to those social clas es. A wife's objective value helps, to some extent, to determine her own subjective value and the value of the couple (de Singly and Thélot 1986; Vallet 1986).

However, the subordination of a woman's status is sufficiently strong for the attribution, more or less, of the husband's social status to the wife to be acceptable. The social value of the husband often represents a sufficient benchmark of both the couple's and the wife's worth. The use of such an indicator does not imply that we subscribe to the theory outlined by Parsons (1955, 144). Parsons justifies treating the married couple unequally on the basis of normative considerations: "by reducing the number of professional situations conferring status on the partners in a marriage to one only . . . [we] eliminate any competition for that status which might disturb the marriage's solidarity"; thus there is "less room for jealousy or feelings of inferiority to develop."

If the model whereby a married woman borrows her social identity can be criticized, it is less on the grounds of empirical accuracy than for theoretical reasons. The alignment of a woman's value with that of her husband obscures the particular productive contribution that a married woman makes, whether she has a job or not (Delphy 1977, 37; Acker 1973). The wife's marital dependence is hidden by the equivalence between a man's direct relationship with his social milieu and his wife's indirect relationship with it. There is a world of difference between a husband's links with his social milieu through his occupation and his wife's relationship with it through marriage. A married woman is at one and the same time her husband's equal—thanks to the sharing of profits—and his inferior—through her greater dependence. We shall later discover that women attach greater or lesser importance to these two aspects of marriage, as the case may be. Researchers reiterate this duality of position: some believe in conjugal equality, others opt for more inequality and dependence. But this concept of equality is based upon inequality nonetheless. A married man's status is fixed independently of his partner's resources, whereas a married woman's status depends on the social position of her husband. For a woman there are two sides to the marriage coin, and a theoretical choice of heads or tails leads only to a truncated view of the effects of married life. The benefits that accrue from the share in the husband's revenue are only important because of the wife's dependence. The choice of partner is crucial since it predetermines the economic and social standard of living the wife will enjoy.

The Importance of the Choice of Husband

It is perfectly natural that women should dream about making a "good" marriage (and that they do so is well attested in the advice columns of newspapers and magazines—see Cave 1981, 34–35). A woman's aim in marrying is to choose, and to be chosen by, a man with the greatest social value possible. The choice of a husband is not just a question of feelings and sexual gratification; for a woman marriage opens a new portfolio. The value of the man's "savings account" is not independent of the value of the woman's. Indeed, compared with a society in which marriages might be contracted purely on a chance basis, it is quite evident that in modern France they are based on quite different principles. The term used in the sociology of marriage for these principles is *homogamy*. Two people sharing the same social characteristics are much more likely to marry than two quite dissimilar individuals. the daughters of blue-collar workers tend to marry blue-collar workers. Women with higher education qualifications are much more likely to choose men having the same academic level as themselves.

Nonetheless, homogamy does not account for the totality of exchanges that take place on the marriage market. That is clear from two indicators. First, a number of marriages do not correspond to the homogamy schema. Even if it is true that the daughters of manual laborers marry manual laborers to a degree that is not explainable by sheer chance, not all working-class women are handed a ticket labeled "manual laborer" when it comes to the marriage lottery. This is why although 39 percent of the marriages studied in A. Girard's *Le choix du conjoint* involve couples where the wife's father and her husband are from the same socioeconomic group, nearly two-thirds of the women had to marry a man from a different group from their father's (1974, 77). Second, personal classified advertisements show that it is clear that the desire to find a marriage partner from the same social class is not the same for women as it is for men. Women do not present the same sort of picture of themselves that men do. The statistical information relating to the way couples come together too often obscures the question of men's and women's capital on the marriage market. In short, sociologists forget the different characteristics of capital resources based on sex (de Singly 1987).

If we examine in turn these two points we shall see that on one hand a woman tries to find a husband with a social value at least equal to hers in order to protect her interests, and that on the other hand she does so while possessing qualities that are quite distinct from those of her prospective husband.

The academic dowry

Why is it that not all daughters of manual laborers marry manual laborers? Why are there so many marriages in which the partners are apparently so dissimilar? To know the answer we must define more precisely the social value of the wife before her marriage. Initially, her father's social position determines her social value, as does her husband's social position once she is married. The disparity between these two

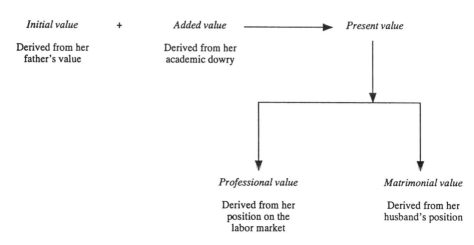

values is linked to yet a third value added by the wife herself. Her social upbringing or her education, by belonging to a particular social milieu, have either increased or decreased the value she has acquired. When she chooses her husband a woman mobilizes not only the social capital she has inherited from her father, but also the capital she has acquired on her own account (added value). It is the combination of initial and added values that the woman, knowingly or not, seeks to have acknowledged on the marriage market (see fig.).

A woman's added value stems particularly from her academic dowry. In contemporary French society, where diplomas play a big role in determining social status, one of the strategies employed to increase a family's wealth is investment in education. The logic underlying the accumulation of academic capital is not the same as the logic of the transmission of economic wealth. As Bourdieu and Saint Martin write (1978, 25), "Unlike the direct transmission of property, where the heir is designated by the immediate holder himself, transmission via the education system" can accept academic failure on the part of individual students from the upper classes[3] or the academic success of those from the middle or working classes. Even if there is a tendency whereby the greater the social value of the father, the greater the cultural value of the daughter, not all daughters of senior executives are bound for a dazzling academic career and not all daughters of manual laborers are destined for a future devoid of culture. The value possessed at the end of adolescence does not necessarily correspond to that possessed at the outset (de Singly 1977).

Table 1.1
The Value of Education in Contracting a "Good" Marriage

Occupation of father (Initial value)	Age at end of schooling (Academic capital)	Value added	Occupation of husband (Matrimonial value)
Manual laborer	17	+2.2	Senior executive
Manual laborer	15.6	+0.8	Junior exectutive
Manual laborer	14.8		Manual laborer

Source: Previously unpublished data from INSEE study, *Emploi féminin*, 1972, for women aged 17–55

The women of a particular social origin who make a "better" marriage than the other women from the same social group owe it to their academic capital. The daughters of manual laborers who marry junior executives have been educated to the age of sixteen, whereas the daughters of manual laborers who themselves marry manual laborers left school at fifteen (see table 1.1).

Upward social mobility through marriage derives from the academic capital accumulated by the wife. The daughters of manual workers who become upwardly mobile socially by marrying can be distinguished from those who are down-wardly mobile by possessing an academic capital greater by nearly three years. A woman's academic capital indeed consti-tutes an added value that plays its role in the acquisition of a man's capital on the marriage market. When a woman has acquired an academic capital superior to that possessed by other women in her social milieu, she finds a different sort of husband. The social heterogamy inherent in such a union reveals the way in which the young woman has sought to obtain through marriage a return on her additional cultural investment. A husband represents her social future to far too great an extent for her to remain indifferent to those men who give off signs that they have significant capital resources. On the other hand, the traditional division of work between the sexes that, as we shall see, stands in the way of a worth-while return from a woman's capital on the labor market con-strains her to try and obtain the best possible return from it on the marriage market. Women students interviewed about their future husbands hope he will have an educational level at least equal to theirs; male students more often claim that this requirement is of little importance or even reply that they would prefer their future wife to be less well endowed than them (Flamenco 1967). Existing marriages confirm women's much greater concern with the wish to win a well-qualified husband. Even if we take into consideration the inequality that exists between the sexes with regard to academic qualifications, the combination of a high-school graduate husband with a university-graduate wife is less frequent than its reverse. This much greater attention paid by women to the cultural or social capital of their husband is easily explained by what happens subsequently within a marriage. For the most part, the exchange on the marriage market is decisive, since after marriage the management of the wife's capital is largely indirect, being associated with the husband's capital. Those men who manage to increase the value of their capital by their own means have other objectives with regard to marriage. They hope to be able to use their economic capital in exchange for aesthetic or relationship capital. From the outset of a marriage the wife's paradoxical position in her relationship with her husband immediately becomes apparent. She has a value equal to her husband's, but it is not the same. A king's daughter will much more easily find herself a prince than will a shepherdess. She will achieve this goal by means of those attributes commonly known as "feminine." The social positions of the couple are comparable, and yet each partner retains his or her role, according to their sex.

Marriage contributes to two types of social reproduction, that of the relationship between the social classes and that between the sexes. This is why, in the negotiations between the prospective partners, two implicit rules are respected: those of social equivalence and sexual differentiation. In the personal columns of the *Chausseur Français*[4] the criteria of value assessment depend on the sex of the individual and the capital resources indicated. The desirable qualities in a partner sought by a rich man are quite different from those sought by a poor man or by a rich woman (see table 1.2).

Beauty

The different matrimonial expectations of women as compared to men can easily be identified. A woman with a large amount of capital wants a man with social qualities (through his profession or his wealth); a man with a large capital pre-

Table 1.2
Desirable Qualities Sought by Those Placing Personal Advertisments

| Self-description | Minimum Qualities Sought in Partner | | |
| | Social | Personal | Aesthetic |
		(in percentages)	
Rich man	28	56	54
Rich woman	54	33	8
Poor man	2	17	12

Source: Previously unpublished data, *Le Chasseur Français*, 1978–79. Cf. de Singly 1984b

fers a woman with aesthetic qualities (in other words, she should be "beautiful" or have an attractive figure). Beauty is a feminine attribute. A man with claims to possessing excellent social qualities dreams of finding a rich wife in 32 percent of the cases and a beautiful wife in 62 percent of the cases. A woman who has excellent social qualities wants a rich man in 76 percent of cases and a handsome one in 7 percent of cases. Matrimonial hopes are colored by the gender of the individual concerned.

Beauty in a woman is not only more sought after than in a man, it has a higher price. Indeed, men who ask for aesthetic qualities in a wife often themselves possess social skills and good looks, whereas women who have the same requirements simply possess capital in terms of their physical attractiveness. Rich and handsome men hope to meet beautiful women more than handsome do. Women who are beautiful hope to marry handsome men more than rich and beautiful women do. The desirability of feminine aesthetic capital is greater than masculine aesthetic capital.

All of this points to what subsequently happens within marriages. The husband's function is primarily to bring in money and to determine the couple's standard of living. The wife has a dual function: on one hand she demonstrates the couple's value aesthetically and on the other she ensures the functioning of the family (by means of her personal qualities). Two-fifths of the women who refer only to their social attributes in their descriptions of themselves require a rich husband; none of them specifies that he should be handsome. Twice as many men with an equivalent capital are looking for a beautiful wife than are looking for a rich one. However, an attractive physical appearance is not a handicap for a woman despite the old saying "beauty is only skin deep" (Shorter 1977, 180). A man benefits from his partner's aesthetic qualities. When he is accompanied by a beautiful wife he is, more often than not, complimented on his intelligence and warmth. The wife's beauty spreads to her companion.

Beauty is more difficult to measure than that of academic or social capital. American studies approach this question either from the point of view of self-evaluation (each individual categorizes him- or herself) or from the basis of independent judgment (a group of assessors classifies photographs of the interviewees). Despite their empirical limitations, these studies are worth reading and interpreting when assessing value. Beauty is a capital resource. Women from a working-class background who have married "well" score higher on the beauty count than women from the same background who have married within their class (Elder 1969; Udry 1977). But even if beauty does increase a woman's matrimonial value, it is not the most important factor in the totality of her capital. Upward social mobility through marriage is more frequent among those women having a good academic capital than among simply beautiful women. With an established initial capital a highly qualified woman has more chance of contracting a "good" marriage than one whose value resides in her beauty alone.

The relative utility of beauty and education

Feminine beauty is not a sufficient quality in itself for working-class women; it only becomes effective when it is combined with academic capital. To make a "good" marriage, working-class women must offer two complementary forms of capital: beauty and education. In the case of women from higher social classes, beauty adds little to their value. Their academic capital, without the additional aesthetic capital, is enough.

When a woman's social origins are considered as an indicator of her initial value,[5] the theory regarding the exchange of men's and women's capital on the marriage market is modified. In this case we see that the woman's academic dowry increases her matrimonial value only if it is associated with another form of capital, either a good initial value, for young women from the higher social classes, or aesthetic capital, in the case of young working- or middle-class women.

Their cultural capital is a great help to the matrimonial prospects of beautiful working-class women and also of women (beautiful or not) from the higher social classes. As it happens, the old instruction "Just shut up and look pretty" fails to correspond to what actually happens in real life. Women from a modest social background need to show evidence, in addition to their beauty, of a certain cultural level, while for women from more favored backgrounds beauty is an optional extra. A woman of low social origins must, to succeed on the marriage market, line up capital of both the academic and cultural kind, while a woman of higher social origins can more easily do without cultural capital and even aesthetic capital. The alliance of beauty and culture can make up for a woman's modest social origins. The novel *Un sot mariage* (with *sot* meaning 'stupid') illustrates this alchemy of matrimonial seduction (La Varende 1959). In it a young man from a family on the way down socially after the death of the father succeeds brilliantly at his studies and intends to become an engineer. The day before the announcement of his admission to the prestigious Ecole des Mines, the family lawyer informs him that he has inherited a title and fortune from a very rich prince who has died leaving no direct heir. The young man is in love with a girl who is also brilliant academically but is from a very modest family background. There is now a conflict between their love and the need for him to contract a marriage befitting his newly acquired status. The previous accommodation between the social value of the young man and the girl respectively now no longer applies, since the young man's value has increased considerably. Their marriage is now out of the question, according to his mother and sister: "The title of Princess of Mauléon is as out of place on her as a ball gown on a flower seller... Could she maintain the necessary rank?... Would she stand up to scrutiny in the light of day?... Some flowers are only made to flourish in the shade" (44). Despite this family pressure the young man prefers to forgo his inheritance (in other words, stay at the same social level) so that he can marry the girl he loves. The story ends up happily with the girl and her beauty being "recognized" by a member of the family, who provides the necessary social capital. The girl can thus legitimately aspire to a marriage that, without the added element of her beauty, seemed "stupid" to the young man's family since her academic achievements were not enough in themselves to provide the necessary "added value."

A HUSBAND WITH BACKING

The resources that a wife acquires from her marriage depend on the type of exchange of capital she has made on the marriage market. If she combines added value with her initial value she acquires a socially more agreeable life style than she experienced during her childhood. She manages to enhance the value of her capital that, from now on, brings in a return on her investment, particularly via her husband's social capital. Although he is the one who brings in the greater part of their symbolic and financial income, the wife's capital does not remain dormant. In particular, it is in the wife's interests, whether she realizes it or not, to keep an eye on the progress of her husband's career. By protecting her husband's value she is protecting herself. A devaluation of her husband's capital would affect her equally.

The concern shown by wives for their husband's professional advancement makes sense when viewed in relation to their dependence: by their wifely devotion they are also maintaining their own value. Seen from this standpoint they might well prefer an increase in their husband's capital to an increase in their own, as this statement by Beatrice, age 36 and a press attaché married to Charles, a career diplomat, shows:

> I chose to be a press attaché not for myself—I have no particular personal ambitions—but for him. Through my work, from time to time I meet people who could be useful to him. One day he told me that the post of embassy attaché, which he's always wanted, had come up. So, for his benefit I arranged through friends to meet the person in charge. It was at a cocktail party. I took his arm, and told him, "I am Charles's wife. My husband is the person you need for that post." And that's how he got it. Deep down, I enjoy doing things like that. I love living vicariously through a man.[6]

The means whereby a wife contributes to the maintenance—and the improvement—of her husband's social value are many and various. The most important, in terms of duration, must be the man's release from domestic duties by his wife's taking them on herself. All the data from the studies confirms this inequality of the sexes with regard to household duties and child rearing. There is also another means: the respect for the principle that the husband must come first. In the event of competition between the partners concerning employment or further studies the husband has priority and his wife will step back. Even those groups most prone to criticize the housewife model do not insist on equality of professional opportunity between partners. Young people, women, and people from upper-class backgrounds rarely consider a woman's job to be as important as her husband's.[7] This support by the wife occurs in a third form, through direct involvement in the husband's business. The wife helps and relieves her partner in the exercise of his profession or keeps herself aware of developments and promotes her partner's image by means of her social skills.

The wife acknowledged

The acknowledgements that appear at the beginning of doctoral theses are evidence of the duly recognized ways by which wives play their part in increasing the value of the partner. The examples below (Gertrude 1979) are taken from theses in African studies from various universities. Wives are praised on three counts:

—"My wife . . . who typed and classified this text with loving patience." (Pierre Bettez-Gravel, "Remera: A Community in Eastern Rwanda," Paris-La Haye, 1968, p. 10)
—"[My wife] whose expert typing relieved me of the burden of doing it myself." (M. G. Marwick, "Sorcery in Its Social Setting," Manchester University, 1965, p. xvii)
—"She also spent hours typing up and sifting through data." (Richard T. Curley, "Elders, Shades, and Women," University of California, Berkeley, 1973, p. ix)

Sometimes wives have the role of research assistant and take part in all the stages of intellectual production—ground research, reading through the thesis, criticizing the work:

—"My wife helped me by reading a mass of general works on ethnology and history." (Max Gluckman, "Politics, Law, and Ritual in Tribal Society," Oxford, 1965, xxvii)

—"I must express my gratitude to my wife who . . . also read through the whole manuscript with me on several occasions." (I. A. Akin-Jogbib, "Dahomey and Its Neighbours, 1708–1818," Cambridge, 1967, p. xi)

—"To my wife, whose work this book is, as much as it is mine." (S. F. Nadel, *A Black Byzantium,* Oxford, 4th ed., 1961, p. 1)

Finally, wives try to lighten the burden of creation by ensuring peaceful family and conjugal relations. The personal quali ties sought by the people putting ads in the *Chasseur Français* are also appreciated by people doing research theses:

—"I would also like to thank my wife whose moral support manifested itself through her infinite patience and indulgence." (W. A. Shack, "The Gurage," Oxford, 1966, p. xii)

—"Barbara, a never-ending source of patience, good humor, and support. . . ." (F. P. Bowser, "The African Slave in Colonial Peru, 1524–1650," Stanford University, 1974, p. x)

—"My wife . . . to whom I am indebted for her untiring support during my daily problems." (D. Zahan, "Société d'initiation bambara," Paris-La Haye, 1960, p. 8)

The generosity of women

University professors and teachers recognize more than anyone the debt they owe to their wives, which is no doubt why they put their wives at the head of the list of reasons for their success, whereas writers—to save face as original creators—stress their own personal qualities (Girard 1962). However, it is not only in prefaces that the wife's role is underlined. The people responsible for training executives also insist on the positive, and sometimes negative, effects of the choice of wife. Note how the following article from a weekly economics news journal stresses the importance of a wife's support of her husband in the context of "the modern marriage, which is an association of two complementary dynamic forces." The author recounts two stories as examples for the reader's edification. One underlines the far-sightedness of the wife of an executive vice president of a large French corporation, as told by the vice president himself:

She realized in time that from then on she had to devote herself to looking after our home and children. And yet she wasn't naturally cut out for that sort of thing. When we first met she had just finished the national fine arts school and had begun a job in an advertising agency. But she very quickly realized that if she wanted to fulfill her own ambitions it could only be done by sacrificing the bringing up of our children and my career. So instead of being bitter about it she changed her interests and took an active part in my career.

Marriage, for a wife, presents a dilemma: either she sacrifices herself or she sacrifices others. According to the author, if a wife chooses the second option she cannot have "a stabilizing influence on the life of her executive husband and make him more human, and thus more effective."

The second story underlines the negative consequences that ensue when a wife fails to sacrifice herself. It concerns an executive who believes he has been successful and yet is "unsettled, on edge. My wife has started up her studies again. At the age of 32 she is doing a degree in sociology; she wants to get a job." Then follows a description of the family's downward spiral. "the children are looked after by a maid. The two eldest start to cause problems and a gulf appears in the relationship between husband and wife. The wife refuses to be neglected any longer; he reproaches her for not carrying out her wifely duties. It is when an executive is most burdened with work that his wife can be his greatest support. She must try and find a way to please him; she must make him rest and boost his morale when he is down."[8]

These descriptions of the ideal wife are often very much the same. They praise the self-effacing wife who is there when her husband needs her. The very fact that men often turn the spotlight on their wives in prefaces to books and theses and talk about their life's companion in magazines is because normally they are out of the limelight. The grayness of these *éminences*, their position offstage in the shadows of the wings, is how men like to perceive women. The following *chiaroscuro* description of the wife of the famous scientist Louis Pasteur, written by her brother-in-law, R. Vallery-Radot, is an example: "She was discretion itself. She never thought about herself; she didn't want anyone to concern themselves about her. The word 'I' was so alien to her character that during the thirty years I had the pleasure of living close to her, loving her, venerating her, I have no recollection of hearing her begin a sentence with that word" (Bensaume-Vincent 1981, 9). This placing of oneself on the periphery seemed necessary to her if she was to support her husband in his research and to carry out all her responsibilities as a wife. "Daughter, wife, sister, mother, Mme Pasteur knew how to live her life to the full; but not in the way that that expression is understood nowadays, with its underlying sense of violence and ruthlessness in the midst of unwavering self-centeredness. For her it meant never thinking about herself, giving total devotion" (10). Her role as a married woman took the form of scrupulously organized domestic activity, a perfect ordering of their physical surroundings to enable her husband to do his research in the best possible conditions. She shared in her husband's research by "finally becoming his secretary, by taking down complicated notes at her husband's dictation. She accepted an existence totally centered around the life of the family and her husband's work" (11). The author asks,

> what would have become of Pasteur's work if he had married a different woman? It does not even bear thinking about. With his obsessive need to work, and at the same time his great need for affection—he had a very loving nature—what might he have sacrificed if he had married a slightly more worldly woman who might well have backed away when faced with the problems of being introduced to laboratory experiments, and who thought that life should have some lighter moments and distractions? (12)

These edifying descriptions draw our attention to the exchanges that take place within a marriage. The wife's taking on of domestic duties enables the husband to carry out his professional duties more effectively. Morally speaking, his wife's devotion enhances the very real benefits for her husband of this assumption of the domestic tasks. But the increase in a man's value, brought about by the fact of being married, sometimes results from a distribution of the wife's capital towards her husband's "savings account." The wife then plays the role of provider of capital, whether it be cultural or personal relations capital.

The wife as provider of capital

The return on a man's professional capital depends on his family and conjugal situation. Moreover, as we shall see, he

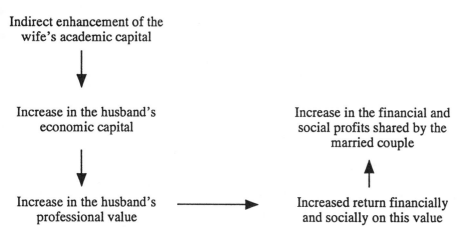

is more successful if married and not single. A married man can also profit professionally from his wife. Upper-class men receive, according to Marceau (1978) and Finch (1983), the dividends that accrue from the social relations capital that women have accumulated during their so-called spare time. The personal relations that women create and cultivate seem to be without any specific instrumental motive since they take place away from the world of work, and yet they represent the husband's own "labor market." By means of these social and family contacts information circulates concerning the possibilities of promotion, availability, and so on. This invisible activity on the part of the wife widens the married couple's social arena and makes the fact of being married more profitable. Cultural cooperation within the marriage team also has positive results. The man sees his capital increase, thanks to a transfer of his wife's capital into his account. He thus increases his professional value. As a consequence the financial and symbolic profits to be shared between the married couple grow and the wife is repaid by this indirect increase in the value of her capital (see fig.).

This roundabout circuit, which initially stems from the wife's academic capital, can be identified through the variations in the professional returns a man obtains from his qualifications as compared to a woman's. The data relating to married couples in France show that there is a transfer of capital from the wife's account toward her partner's. For married men with a given academic level, the greater their wives' academic capital, the greater is the tendency for their socioprofessional category to edge toward the upper end of the social scale. A husband has higher professional value when his wife has a good academic dowry (see appendix 2). Men who finish their studies at age nineteen become executives in 50 percent of the cases where their wives continued in full-time education until that age. Their chances of becoming executives are almost certain when their wives continued their studies beyond age nineteen.[9] A married man's situation is the result of his own academic capital, allied with that of his partner. Whether achieved consciously or not, the sharing of academic wealth between marriage partners does indeed take place since the return on a man's academic capital is directly related to the amount of his wife's academic capital.

Men with substantial academic capital (who ended their studies around age twenty-four) seem to benefit less from their partner's academic "savings account." Their chances of becoming executives do not increase with an increase in the amount of their wife's academic capital. It is as if the transfer of capital mentioned above only operates below a certain threshold. These results confirm the American data from research on married couples where the husband has a Ph.D. (Ferber and Huber 1979). For a man possessing that academic qualification, being married to a woman who also has a Ph.D. brings no advantages to his own professional career, as measured by his salary or the number of his publications. The joining of two substantial academic reserves does not create the conditions necessary for the operation of conjugal osmosis. For such couples the consequences of marriage—according to this indictor—are almost imperceptible. The wife does not indirectly increase the value of her capital in any significant way, while the husband does not feature on the labor market as a member of a team. But for the majority of couples not in this category the husband can draw on his wife's cultural reserves. We must avoid focusing on the individual. Studies into the returns from a particular educational level are too often limited to an examination of the relationship between academic level and remuneration. A husband's value is derived from the conjugal team's shared capital, with "a married man's gains being positively related to his wife's human capital" (Benham 1974, 1975). For a given academic capital and over a given period of professional activity, a man sees his earnings increase by between 3.5 and 4.1 percent for each year that his wife spent in full-time education, while the rate of increase for each year of study he himself undertook is between 6.3 and 7 percent.

Does this variation in a man's earnings in terms of his wife's academic capital really derive from a process of conjugal interaction? To verify this we have to take into account how long the couple has been married. Indeed, if the relationship between a man's return on his qualifications and his wife's were observable right from the beginning of a marriage, we would know that the benefits of the wife's capital are an illusion. The increased return on a man's qualifications would then have to be attributed to some other form of capital or another characteristic of that individual. On the other hand, if the advantages for a married man appear only some years after the marriage took place, then those advantages can be attributable to an exchange between the partners. L. Benaham quite clearly shows that the profits increase as the marriage progresses in time. The rate of increase of a man's earnings with each additional year of study by his wife—all things being equal—is not fixed; it is higher in the case of men who have been married for at least ten years. The hypothesis of a strictly conjugal effect is validated; marriage creates an association within which capital circulates. More precisely, a man who has made a "good" marriage gains professionally from his wife's academic dowry by progressively combining his own capital with his wife's. The family structure has a socializing influence not only for the children but also for the adults. The marriage needs to last a certain period of time for this effect to exercise its influence and for the husband to make up for and erase the cultural gap. This socializing process between husband and wife, like that which takes place between parents and children, occurs at an implicit level and is not done in any explicitly instructional way. The impact of a wife's cultural resources springs more from a logical process of contamination and incubation. The analogy with savings accounts and capital here becomes inadequate. There is not, strictly speaking, a transfer of capital between partners: an increase in the husband's capital resources in no way implies a diminution of the wife's resources. The advantage of forming a marriage team is precisely that it brings about a multiplication of profits.

If an analysis of the social cost of marriage for a woman were to stop there, its effects would seem to be largely positive. By a process of profit sharing, marriage gives a woman access to her husband's social status, albeit a status to which she has made a contribution. However, the magic circle of conjugal cooperation is easily broken, as the previous example of theses acknowledgments shows. The appreciated wife improves her social value—but not her cultural value—if the publication brings about an improvement in her husband's position. Should the marriage break down she will receive no compensation, whereas her husband will retain the benefits of the work undertaken: he remains the owner of the published work. The indirect increase in the value of the wife's capital via her husband carries with it certain risks, particularly that of one day being denied access to the husband's savings account. Officially, since the husband's savings account is in his name only, his wife will have some difficulty in getting back her conjugal investments. A husband is a high-risk investment unless marriage is looked upon socially as a collective enterprise. In the United States, a woman who had subsidized her husband's studies with contributions from her paid work found that the divorce court was prepared to recognize her right to 40 percent of the value of his qualifications. According to the judge, this academic capital had become, momentarily at least, "conjugal property." Unfortunately such judgments are most uncommon.[10]

2

The Creation of a New Capital
Resource—Children

In France the law requires city authorities to open a savings account for each newborn child and to deposit a small sum in the child's name. It then becomes the parents' responsibility to take over the management of this account until their child comes of age. In our hypothetical account, the birth of a child is also accompanied by the opening of a "savings account" into which the parents make educational payments. Marriage for a woman, therefore, almost always means—since few marriages are childless—an extension of her cultural investments in two directions, toward her husband and toward her children.

The sociology of education teaches us little about the indirect increase in a woman's capital value by this new investment since for the most part it has defined the parents by referring only to the father. This empirical approximation is sufficient to show the force of these cultural heritage mechanisms (Bourdieu and Passeron 1964). A child from the so-called upper classes has a greater chance of succeeding academically than one from the so-called lower classes. Nonetheless, the approximation is not enough to enable us to draw up an inventory of the processes whereby a married woman defends her social interests. For that we have to identify precisely the contribution of each individual parent to the building of the child's capital resources. Does the mother, who is involved to a much greater degree in the child-rearing process, have a greater influence than the father? Does the child's cultural capital come more from its mother or from the father? And we must also ascertain whether certain kinds of investment are more productive than others. All things being equal, what system of rules and controls in the child-rearing process produce good academic results? What optimum family conditions are needed for the combined capitals of the father and mother to give a child the best possible start in life, given the fact that schools also play their part in this process?[1]

The mother's recognized altruism

To appreciate how the child becomes the repository of his parents' capital and hopes, recourse to statistical methods is necessary. When asked, both men and women deny that they have children for social and cultural reasons. When parents are interviewed about the "fundamental reasons for having children," far more reply that "children bring parents happiness" than those who say "I hope to be able to fulfill my ambitions through my child" (Kellerhals et al. 1982, 211). This last reply is particularly uncommon with upper-class groups. Altruism is a quality that is particularly found among highly educated women, who are much less likely to see children as a means of "fulfilling oneself." But this by no means indicates that upper-class women are not very interested in their children. This maternal altruism serves to legitimize, through the denial of selfish motives, the cultural value of the child. Denying any investment other than an emotional one and then stating that the child is highly valuable culturally enables the parents to maintain that this cultural value springs not from the way the child has been brought up but is a quality originating in the child itself. An analysis of anti-authoritarian child-rearing practices shows that by denying the effects of parental intervention they focus attention upon the admirable qualities of the child itself. Since children reared in this way are "free," their (high) value comes entirely from within themselves; they succeed on the various markets by means of their own intrinsic qualities, without any artificial additives, as it were.

Children are presented to the world openly, warts and all. Not only does the line between a child's positive attributes and its faults become imprecise, but a child's "negative" characteristics emphasize the quality of the parents' child-rearing techniques and the fact that they were sensible enough to break with the authoritarian tradition and were able to avoid ruining their children by bringing them up "full of moral precepts and bourgeois ideas of good and evil and purity" (Neill

1960, 304). This is aptly illustrated by the following description of her son by Françoise Mallet-Joris:

> We had gone to have tea near St. Severin, in the English café
> where they have such delicious lemon tarts. It wasn't because
> he'd been a good boy... It was simply because he wanted to talk...
> He wanted to talk to me... "Why don't we go to a café and have a
> quiet chat?"... It was one of the high spots of my life, one of those
> moments that... help you to make contact with what your life is
> really about... Vincent was eleven; not doing well at school, rowdy,
> undisciplined, a pain in the neck... and yet affectionate, bursting
> into tears at the slightest reproach; always cutting out and stick-
> ing things together, covered in glue and paint; heavily into nature
> books and detective stories; sometimes a bit of a pedant; as
> grubby as could be, with the most beautiful eyes you ever saw;
> and quite up on theology. (Mallet-Joris 1977, 12–13)

This obfuscation of the child-rearing process in the guise
of parental liberalism is to the advantage of both parents.
They are not "narrow-minded, vindictive and cowardly, unhappy and undeveloped creatures who crudely cloak themselves in authority" (Neill 1970, 48). Nonetheless, their
children do not have any less social value for all that, since
they find themselves endowed with a new sort of capital in
the form of ease in social relationships (Castel 1981). This
apparent denial of the value added to a child by the way it has
been brought up increases that value in the sense that the
upbringing has simply created the right conditions for the
manifestation of the so-called intrinsic qualities of the child.

A Woman's Productive Capital

If we go beyond the consideration of the child as a form of
emotional capital,[2] we must try to find the contribution a
woman makes to the creation of her child's academic capital.[3]
Not all researchers agree about the mother's role in this. For
example, P. Clerc (1964) considers that the mother's academic
capital does not necessarily have an effect on the fixing of the
child's value. In his opinion, what counts is that the married
couple should share a certain total level of capital resources.
The child benefits most, educationally speaking, when the
married couple's combined resources reach an optimal level.
When one of the parents alone does not possess sufficient

Table 2.1
Son's Chances of Graduating from High School
Associated with Mother's Academic Capital
(in percentages)

Father's profession	Higher education	High-school graduate	BEPC[a]	CEP[b]
Teacher	94	83	56	36
Self-employed	79	68	56	53
Senior executive	80	65	65	59

[a] Brevet d'études du premier cycle (certificate obtained at the end of the French equivalent of junior high school)

[b] Certificat d'études primaires (formerly obtained at the end of elementary school and since replaced by the BEPC)

Source: INSEE, FQP study, 1977. Cf. Pohl, Soleilhavoup, and Ben-Rezigue 1983

resources the other partner has to make up the shortfall. When, however, one parent has sufficient academic capital, a contribution from the other partner is unnecessary. A woman's academic capital only has any value in a family situation when the father is relatively academically unqualified.

The data correlating the father's social status, the mother's academic qualification, and the child's academic level (Pohl, Soleilhavoup, and Ben Rezigue 1983) infirm this hypothesis of an optimal level. The child's academic level is increased by the mother's capital resources, whatever the father's capital might be. Even when the husband possesses considerable social and cultural capital, the wife still has an effect on the child. In the case of sons with junior executive fathers who have been educated to the high-school level, 57 percent can themselves expect to graduate from high school if their mother also graduated, but only 25 percent can expect to graduate from high school if their mother did not graduate. The amount deposited in the "savings account" of a woman married to a man from a higher social class and who is at least a high-school graduate influences the amount a son has in his account. He has a greater chance of graduating from high school when his mother has substantial academic capital (see table 2.1).

In every family, the higher the level to which the mother has been educated, the higher the qualifications obtained by her son or daughter. The existence of an upper threshold of parental resources to explain this academic succession from one generation to another is not proven. The wife therefore manages to obtain a return on her capital regardless of any increase in value she may have obtained on the marriage market.

Other studies confirm the role played by both parents in the success (or failure) of their children. In the case of American high-school students whose fathers were successful academically, two-thirds having an academically successful mother and one-third with a mother who was not academically successful are considered to be "very intelligent."[4] In the case of adolescents with a highly academically successful mother, the chances of achieving good results in intelligence tests vary between 45 percent where the father is not academically successful and 63 percent where he is. There is no evidence of a cultural saturation point in a family, which might negate the effect of the mother's (or father's) academic capital in certain capital resource situations. The child inherits both its parents' capital on the academic capital market and then later on the labor and marriage markets. The value of male blue-collar workers between the ages of forty and fifty-nine (in terms of their academic qualifications, their wife's qualifications, their earnings, and their professional qualifications) is related to the social value of their fathers, but also to the academic value of their mothers. For example, blue-collar workers whose fathers were also blue-collar workers and whose mothers obtained the lowest technical training certificate are advantaged in terms of their academic, matrimonial, and professional capital compared with manual workers whose fathers were manual workers but whose mothers had no qualifications at all. It is mothers, more than grandfathers, who determine the son's value (de Singly and Thélot 1986).

The mother's capital is more effective than the father's

It is in no way surprising that a married woman plays a part in fixing the value of her children, given her greater role in the child-rearing process within the home. According to one estimate, out of every one hundred interactions within the family, twenty-nine are between mother and child, twenty-one between both parents and the child, and nineteen between father and child (Paolucci 1978). Studies of family schedules indicate that the time a mother spends with her child is five times greater than that of her husband. The average junior executive spends twenty minutes daily in contact with his children, compared with his wife's 125 minutes if she does not have a paid job (Huet, Lemel, and Roy 1982). If this time is a measure of parental investment, the wife's cultural value must have a greater influence than that of her husband. This in fact is usually the case when we correlate the child's capital and the respective capital resources of the parents. A high-school student whose father is highly qualified and whose mother has few qualifications does less well in intelligence tests than a student whose father has few qualifications but whose mother is academically well qualified. The chances of academic success for children from such families is 33 percent, compared with 50 percent, respectively. The mother's capital obtains a higher return than the father's when there is a marked difference between the capital of each parent. Where the capital input remains constant, it is in families where the wife is better off academically than her husband that the child has a greater academic value.

If we go by school success—graduation from high school—this is certainly true. Women earn a higher return. A child from a family where the mother is more academically qualified than the father has a better chance of graduating than one from a family where the father is more qualified than the mother. For example, in families where the father is a skilled worker and the amount of academic capital is constant, both sons and daughters do better at school when the mother is more highly qualified.[5]

Out of thirty tests of this type, twenty-six show the superiority of families where the wife is more qualified. In terms of the creation of capital for the child, the return on the mother's academic capital is greater than from the father's. The "amalgamation" of both partners' capital does not mean that we still cannot differentiate between the effect of the two distinct sources of capital: the mother's capital earns a higher bonus. The strength of the mother's influence can be observed in other social education areas such as political and religious socialization and the recognition of the child's ambitions (Smith 1981; Acock and Bengtson 1978). In those domains that are socially perceived as being "masculine," the mother is still not without influence: her children take more after her than their father. This close cultural or ideological relationship between a mother and her children creates the right conditions for a close affective relationship. After all, both boys and girls state that they rely more on their mother than their father (Gokalp 1981). The mother's greater involvement in the home results in her greater influence in the child-rearing process, and hence in an increase in the value of her capital via her offspring. A married woman's investment in her children is not entirely devoid of self-interest.

The mother's preferential investment

The parents' participation in the creation of a new cultural product takes different forms. It manifests itself particularly in the extent of their aspirations—that is, in the academic objectives they hope their child will attain. This ambition is very important since the parents' aspirations seem to play as much of a role in the child's academic destiny as its actual intellectual competence (Girard and Bastide 1963). If we look again at the study involving American high-school students we see that parents have greater expectations first for adolescents perceived as being very intelligent than those judged to be not very bright and second for boys more than girls. The degree of parental plans and encouragement depends on the sex of their children and on their academic performance to date. Within the context of this inequality in parental expectations the mother's academic capital plays a very specific role. It manages, in part, to make up for the handicaps relating to the children's sex or intelligence. The disparity between parents' ambitions for boys as compared with girls, for bright children as opposed to less bright ones, diminishes when the mother herself has been educated to a high level. It is precisely those children who are most handicapped in terms of parental investment—girls and the academically less able—who are most supported by their mothers.

The disparity in academic ambition that parents have for their sons as opposed to their daughters is less in families where the mother is well qualified than in other families. There is, one might say, a sort of remedial effect that stems from the wife's academic capital. This effect can be measured by the correlation between the different levels of aspiration for boys compared with girls. In the case of adolescents classified as being of low intelligence the correlation varies from 0.95, where the mother has few academic qualifications, to 1.30, where she is well qualified academically. Thanks to their mother's cultural capital girls are often encouraged to continue with their studies The married woman's capital increases in value to the extent that no particular offspring is given a greater advantage over the others. The main function of this capital is not to add to the children's "savings accounts," which for various reasons can be better increased in other ways, but to offset inequalities. Equal concern for the children, a well-known worry of mothers, does not mean equal treatment—far from it (Gotman 1988, 173–74)! Consciously or not, a kind of support policy is set up within the family. By means of her cultural influence the mother tries to give the lie to the old adage that the rich get richer and the poor get poorer. Consequently she acts as a redistribution agent.

A married woman can manage her cultural capital and identify quite clearly the investments that, through her children, are offered to her. When the mother's capital is considerable—and particularly if it is greater than the father's—conditions are created for a specific investment in a daughter. In a mother's plans for her daughter marriage and children do not take priority. Unlike the father, the mother will want her daughter to do well at school, thereby upgrading the family's social position, and, most important, to escape the domestic role traditionally allotted to women. Women are prompted by their own experience—where studies or careers were interrupted because they are women—to make certain that their daughters do not follow the same path (Battagliola 1984, 106–7). Whether they do it consciously or not, mothers can attenuate, or reinforce, the effects of their offspring's gender. Even if boys and girls finish their schooling having attained the same level, a mother's investments are not the same for her sons as for her daughters. Given the way society differentiates between the sexes, a (relatively) equivalent capital input on the part of a mother vis-à-vis her sons and daughters demands that a woman manage her investments quite differently.

INFLUENCE BY A PROCESS OF CONTAMINATION

Paternal or maternal investments are far from being transparent operations since very little work has been done in this field. The question of the conditions in which a child is formed within the family has only recently become a center of interest. Previous research was only interested in what happened in school. The family was placed on the periphery— a mysterious and magical "black box" from which children emerged, indelibly marked by their social-class destiny. The effects of parental capital resources only seemed mysterious because of the prevailing ignorance about the mechanisms by which they operated. The impression of some magical process is reinforced by the fact that the child-rearing process is an implicit one; that is, it is based upon "the unconscious transmission of principles which only manifest themselves practically when they are being put into practise" (Bourdieu and Passeron 1970).

The "savings account" opened in the child's name only gradually increases in value within the cultural ambience of the family. Indeed, through an overt educational process the child's intellectual level varies only marginally. The intellectual value of children brought up under a regime based on autonomy and that of children brought up with more freedom are comparable (where the mothers have equal qualifications) (Aubret-Benet 1978). The difference between children with a highly academically qualified mother and those whose mother has a low academic level is much greater. It is the size of the mother's academic capital more than the child-rearing style that brings about an increase in the child's value.

The intrinsic effect of child-rearing styles is weaker than that predicted by educational experts. Thus, contrary to psychological theory, a flexible family environment does not enhance a child's intellectual development (Lautrey 1980, 94–96). Children brought up in families of this type (the child "can contribute to the conversation as long as what it has to say is relevant") are no more intelligent than those brought up either in a much more rigid family regime ("children must be seen and not heard") or indeed a more relaxed one ("the child can speak whenever he likes"). Child-rearing methods based explicitly upon a cognitive apprenticeship do not necessarily nurture a child's intellectual development. The greatest variation in intellectual competence within a social group is related to the hierarchy of moral qualities taught by the parents rather than to their child-rearing methods (Lautrey 1980, 94–96). Children of working-class parents who, like parents from upper-class groups, lay greater emphasis on critical thinking skills than on obedience do better in intelligence tests. This hierarchy of qualities, which is untypical of working-class groups, reveals a strategy, conscious or otherwise, of upward social mobility through the child.

The child becomes the depositary of its parents' academic capital and of their ambitions by a process of contamination either, according to P. Bourdieu (1979), in the form of the language and nurturing strategies employed by the mother and father or though the family environment in the form of books, paintings, musical instruments, and so on. The child growing up surrounded by possessions of this kind gradually absorbs this cultural capital. By what means this happens we still do not really know, and indeed, the cultural life style in which the child develops is an insufficient explanation of his academic future, as another American study on school students demonstrates (Sandis 1970). The cultural enrichment provided by the parents is linked to the existence or absence of dance, theater, or art classes attended by the child outside of school or family visits to the theater, concerts, or the opera. The pupil's academic ambition increases in direct relation with his cultural enrichment. However, the investment involved in these activities does not produce a return comparable to that from the mother's academic capital, even when it is not converted into activities directly experienced by the child. Children from those families with a mother possessing a large amount of academic capital but that are low on cultural enrichment are more ambitious academically than those from families with a low maternal academic capital but with a high level of cultural enrichment (Sandis 1970).

THE CHILD'S CULTURAL GIFT

Whether or not it is invested in cultural or educational activities, the mother's academic capital does not remain inactive since it is reincarnated in the child. This transfer can be accompanied by a parallel exchange in the opposite direction, when the child's value contributes in its turn to enriching the cultural value of the mother or father. In the studies on political, ideological, and religious socialization in which the children hold the same views as their parents, the authors almost always conclude that it is the parents who have influenced the children. They thereby exclude the possibility of the children converting their parents to their own view of the world. Even in the domain of cultural socialization such exchanges need to be envisaged. The increase in the value of the woman's capital comes in this case from the cultural interest gained. The child redistributes to his parents some of the capital resources he or she has acquired.

Let us examine the example of individuals enrolled in a university course for the retired (Suaud 1982). More than half of the participants who are married and from the working class have a son or daughter still studying in higher education. This proportion is considerably greater than the chances of the child of a manual laborer or an office clerk attending a university. It stems from two intermingled and inextricable causes: one, the aspirations of the parents that prompted them to orient their children towards lengthy studies and to embark themselves on university courses offered for the retired, and second, the spur provided by the fact of having an adolescent child more culturally endowed than themselves. Intergenerational competition, a desire for some form of dialogue with their children, or a need to get something for themselves are all responses that can prompt parents into the acquisition of cultural property, something they would not normally do. This repayment in kind on the part of the offspring, within the exchange circuit existing between the parents and child, thus enriches the parents.[6]

An example of cultural exchange

This dual aspect of socialization is evident by an inventory of the books owned by one of the families studied. This family is unusual in that it has two book collections—one in the parents' bedroom and the other in the son's—and two readers, the mother and the son (the father not being a reader). The mother has been a janitor since 1971, an occupation she shares with her husband, a former house painter. From a working-class background—her father was a plumber—she has the CEP but her two brothers have postgraduate degrees and are highly qualified teachers. Her twenty-eight-year-old son, after doing a diploma course in technical drawing and then working as a draftsman, took up his studies again to train as a horticulturist. He subsequently obtained a job as a nurseryman and lived at home with his parents.

Of the 265 books listed, 3 percent had not been read, 34 percent had only been read by the mother, 56 by the son only, and 7 by both of them. This literary capital shared by mother and son had been acquired over a fairly short period of time, when the son had returned to his studies. After taking his job in the salt marshes this exchange had ended.

Moreover, at the time of the inventory he was reading considerably less than when he was a student. A comparison of the types of books read by one or the other and those read by both of them show that they fall into very specific types: novels and history books. This shared capital was the result of a compromise between mother and son. Half of the books had been read first by one or the other, with the mother reading the novels first and the son the books on history. The contribution made by the son to his mother's cultural capital was the widening of her choice of books and an abandonment of her exclusive diet of novels. This new historical outlook was readily accepted by the mother since when asked which kinds of books she liked most, she replied "anything historical." Although it did not last long, this exchange of books between the two generations may have had a lasting effect on the mother's cultural capital.

Intergenerational exchanges form part of a cycle in which the child, after receiving part of his parents' cultural capital, puts at their disposal the capital resources he himself has acquired.[7] This process of change on the part of the mother, instigated by her children, is observable in immigrant families. A young Algerian woman living in France recounted to A. Sayad (1979) how there had been a power shift in her parents' relationship by means of an alliance between the mother and her children. One year her mother went camping with her and other brothers and sisters.

Without my father! My father remained at home, and we could tell that by remaining at home he hoped none of us would be able to go—or at least that my mother wouldn't and that she would stay behind with him... We spent three very pleasant weeks together. It was a significant moment in our lives; that vacation was an important event for my mother. From then on she went on vacation without my father; from that time on she gained her independence... It was the first time she had been on vacation, a real vacation; not just going to Algeria. It was then that we realized the limitations of my father's authority. (124)

The children, academically richer than their parents, in choosing to take their mother's side had counterbalanced the father's power. Such a coalition does not happen every time. In other instances the child's cultural capital expresses itself in an emotional distancing from his parents, thus rendering intergenerational exchange impossible.[8]

The second column in the wife's social accounts, then, clearly indicates that after her marriage her cultural capital is enhanced by her children. Just as for the husband, a multiplication factor is present in the woman's capital resources. Moreover, these two areas—marriage and children—are connected. The return that a woman gets from her capital by having children is similar to what she receives from her husband. An academically qualified woman who marries a less well-educated man has children who themselves attain only a modest academic level. When a woman has made a "good" investment on the marriage market she not only receives better interest from her husband's "savings account," but she also increases the value of her own capital by producing valuable resources in the form of children. But this extension of a woman's cultural capital has its limits: it cannot continue to grow by the birth of yet more children. Indeed, in lower-middle-class and working-class families the intellectual level of the children diminishes with the number of children. With more than two children a woman runs the risk of limiting the increase in the value of her capital. Moreover, she has a greater difficulty investing her capital on the labor market, as statistics that correlate the number of children and mother's occupation show. There is a price to be paid for children, and it is not just the time spent rearing them or the reduction in discretionary income (Bloch and Glaude 1983). For a woman, today's family structure means that any child-rearing investment is incompatible with an occupational investment. The effects of marriage and conjugal life have repercussions for a woman that go well beyond the domestic circle; it is in the professional sphere that the price paid for marriage and children makes itself felt.

3

Work as an Uncertain Investment

But let us not speak of the obstacles a wife would entail for
your philosophy studies... What connection can there be between study and domestic activity, between the desk and the
cradle, a book and a distaff, a stylus and a spindle? Is there
a man alive who, if he were meditating on the Scriptures or
philosophy, could stand the crying of a newborn child, the
sound of a nursemaid singing a lullaby, the to-ing and fro-
ing of household activity, and the incessant smells and un-
cleanliness of children?
    —Héloïse, *Letter to Abélard* (translated by Malcolm Bailey)

THANKS to marriage, a woman comes to possess two extra
"savings accounts"—one in her husband's name and the
other in the name of her children. This range of investments
is not, however, to her advantage unless the principal "savings
account"—the one in her own name—remains unchanged.
Marriage therefore offers all the attractions of making social
and cultural gains. But are married women allowed to accumulate capital in this way? The analogy with the writer who
writes under two different names and thereby hopes to gain
from a dual presence on the literary market would seem to
indicate that the answer is by no means positive. Has not the
success of Cécil Saint-Laurent in writing for a wide popular
readership in some way damaged the reputation of Jacques
Laurent, who writes for a much more limited readership (de
Singly 1976)? Does not a married woman's attempt to have a
dual existence undermine the value of her cultural capital,
given the way society operates at present? Are the demands
made by an investment in a husband and child not incompatible with investment in a job?
    Everything we know of society leads us to believe that the

answer has to be yes, they are incompatible. And that answer is further supported when we see the extent of the inconvenience. The price a woman has to pay for marriage is directly related to the difference between the return she gets by the fact of being married and what she would have got had she remained single or been a man. From this standpoint, the professional inequalities existing between men and women are not simply a question of the mechanisms of sexual discrimination; they illustrate the divergent consequences of marriage for women as opposed to men. The smaller returns from a woman's capital resources in terms of salary or professional status stem from the social relationship between the sexes within marriage. A married woman with a job has to take on the burden of both job and family. The conditions in which she can gain a return from her capital resources on the labor market are subsequently less favorable. It is this prospect that leads women to perceive the forgoing of the maternal role as the negative side of a planned career. This is what Marcelle S., a single woman aged forty and head of the maintenance department of an oil company, says:

I'm fortunate, in a sense, to be single, I mean I have no ties ... and in fact I can understand quite well the fears of employers when they say "So-and-so might leave for family reasons," I agree totally with that attitude... I can see why an employer wants to take on a man rather than a woman... No, I don't think I've had to make sacrifices in my personal life, because I don't think you should have any regrets; I think I'm one of those people you can still find who just love their work... We're a dying breed... And if I'd been married, with children? Oh no, I wouldn't have worked! Definitely not! I reckon you have to make a choice; it's not because I was against marriage... but the way I see it a woman has to choose and her first responsibility is bringing up her children, if she has any... I'm dead set against those women who get up in the morning, fling some clothes on the kids, and take them off to the babysitter... Women with children are less motivated, that's evident. A career has to be a vocation, you've got to be dedicated... What strikes me is that you rarely hear a group of women talking about their work—unlike men. Mainly they talk about their domestic problems... which just shows that that's what's most important for them... (Huppert-Laufer 1982, 126)

Not everything is contractual in the marriage contract. The way this woman sees the relationship between the world of work and the world of the family reveals quite clearly, by accentuating the contrasts between the two, marriage's hidden dimension: conjugal commitment demands that a wife renounce thoughts of a career. It is as if the fidelity expected of a wife has a double meaning: she must be faithful not only sexually and emotionally, but she must remain devoted to the family and its requirements. This sense of loyalty on the part of the wife manifests itself by taking her further away from the world of work, which in turn results in a smaller return from her academic capital on the labor market. The bolt from Cupid's bow is frequently followed by yet more arrows.

A Dual Career

(1) Women take precedence over men in the domestic sphere; (2) a woman's domestic life takes precedence over her professional life; and (3) a man's job comes before a woman's: these three rules do not need to be written in some conjugal statute book for women to obey them, as an examination of their relationship in both a temporal and spatial sense clearly demonstrates.

Time

When we read and hear all that has been said in celebration of the sharing of conjugal tasks we could well believe that things have changed. The fact is, however, that no matter how the schedule is constructed, the division of household tasks by sex still appears to very ingrained. The time spent by women doing the dishes is at least four times greater than for men. The time they spend sweeping, vacuuming, and doing laundry is at least eight times greater and at least fifteen times greater when it comes to dusting (Roy and Rousse 1981). These chores, which are the most time-consuming, are undertaken by women in by far the greatest number of cases. The more onerous these tasks become, the more likely they are to be done by women, and the disparity between men and women increases with the number of children.

The so-called upper or middle classes are quick to declare themselves in favor of a revision of the traditional norms, but the truth is that there is always a much greater chance of finding a woman in the kitchen than a man. Male executives spend sixteen minutes on the preparation of meals per day; their wives, if they do not work outside the home, 138 minutes. Male manual laborers spend twenty minutes preparing meals while their wives devote 172 minutes to the task (Huet, Lemel, and Roy 1982). On the basis of these figures male executives are more like manual workers than like their own wives. In all, women do at least three-quarters of the domestic chores.

Variations of this state of affairs can be observed, particularly in couples where both spouses work. When the wife has an outside job, two situations occur:

—A redistribution of household tasks between partners. According to the wives (Glaude and de Singly 1986), the task of preparing meals, cleaning floors, and washing dishes are performed "equally" more often by both partners when the wife also has an outside job. The incidence of equal sharing of floor cleaning swings from 6 percent in couples where only the husband has a job to 15 percent in couples where both partners work outside the home. The husband's greater participation in household tasks is hardly ever enough to counterbalance that of the wife, however. When the wife has an outside job she cleans the floors in 81 percent of cases, while her husband does so 4 percent of the time. The woman's monopoly in the domestic domain is weaker, but it is by no means broken. A working wife also has to arrange her schedule so as to be able to squeeze in her domestic tasks.

—The wife needs to fit domestic tasks into the time she has available. The term *double shift* referred to by wives with outside jobs is at the same time accurate (these women undertake far more of the domestic tasks than their husbands) and inaccurate, since they devote less time to these jobs than do women who do not go out to work. Indeed, when we compare the time each group spends on domestic chores we can see that "working wives" spend a third less time on them. This compression is more important than the ones concerning "spare time," time spent on personal appearance and in sleep. A share of household tasks is sometimes assumed by other women—from the same family in the case of working-class families or by hired help in the case of upper-class groups. Even so, the amount of time spent on domestic chores is also lessened because of the diminished symbolic commitment to the home on the part of wives with outside jobs. They have a more functional relationship with domestic management, and their identity is less dependent on the role of household manager. The dust on the furniture does not have to be dusted, the floors can go unmopped, and meals can remain uncooked; after all, they are now less important as outward signs of personal accomplishment. Working women are less likely to transform "their hidden gestures, their stagnation, their endless patience, their unrewarded tasks" into an emanation of "perfume that vitalizes all those who breathe it."[1] The "smiling cooks" who spend much of their time in the kitchen and who do not mind one bit are often housewives who do not go out to work; the "unhappy cooks" who "claim only to offer very basic fare" and who are not really interested in culinary activities are very often the ones with jobs (Chaudron 1983, 1352–53). This compression of tasks into a limited amount of time, therefore, reflects the constraints of a working woman's schedule and a certain lack of interest as well.

This reduction of household tasks by compression and delegation is not enough to offset the way married women are handicapped in their jobs. The responsibility of looking after a home obliges them to direct a part of their attention to it. The burden of this attention, which does not appear on any schedule, limits the amount of investment possible for a woman in her job and invades her working world. It is no accident that K. Blunden's book *Le travail et la vertu* is dedicated to "all those women who right in the middle of a complicated calculation, of a rushed typing assignment, or of a crucial meeting, suddenly wonder if an omelet will be enough for the evening meal" (Blunden 1982, 9). Trying every day to decide "what to give them to eat" forces the woman who has to make that decision into organizational tasks, even if she does not have to carry them out entirely. This is why even young couples who live together and are more sensitive to the sexual division of work than married couples still rely on the female partner to assume these responsibilities (de Singly 1981b).

The demands of family life prevent women from competing fairly with their male colleagues in the professional domain. Their concentration of domestic tasks into a single day—Saturday—only marginally reduces the problem. Women working outside the home abandon their professional aspirations when confronted with the constant force of the social relationship between the sexes, and young women who had high ambitions for their career before meeting their husbands limit their aspirations once married life is underway (Almquist and Angrist 1970).

This unequal distribution of professional opportunities between men and women is reflected on the one hand in a reduced degree of daily or weekly investment in one's job (as revealed by the demands for "Wednesday off" in French government administration departments) and in the curtailment of their professional activities on the other. The domestic role of women, particularly child-rearing responsibilities, results in periods of inactivity during the course of their professional lives. For any given age group, childless married women have professional lives more closely resembling those of unmarried women than of married women with children (Polachek 1975a). Particularly for women with little in the way of capital resources, motherhood entails underinvestment in the labor market, even when they do have an outside job, and also a tendency on the part of employers to discourage the promotion of married women. This complex game of tendencies and behavior hinders any attempt to unravel the tangled web of reasons for breaks in continuity in a woman's working life. Family constraints on a woman can serve as an excuse for her boss to promote a man instead. At the beginning of their careers in the French Social Security Department, for example, women devote themselves to their work, and it is only when they realize that "only the men succeed" that they lose their positive attitude (Battagliola 1984). Indeed, women in this government department who have the longest service records of any branch tend to extend their maternity leave beyond what is normally legally allowed. The argument used by employers concerning family constraints on a woman can thus reinforce the internal division inherent in a marriage.

Space

Family life results in constraints on a salaried woman in a spatial sense as well. This subjection of women is confirmed in the first place by the distance between the home and the workplace. A married women is limited more than a man by the radius within which she can look for a job. By limiting her travel time she can coordinate her family and work schedules more easily. One-third of mothers with two children and more than half of mothers with four children in the Paris area work less than one kilometer from their home (Fagnani 1986). The job of rearing and nurturing children limits women to a fairly restricted area of the labor market. Women who work outside the area where they live have fewer children than those mothers who are employed near their homes (Lery 1984). It is children who determine where you work. This is confirmed when we measure the time spent in travel between home and work. According to this indicator,[2] here again married women without children resemble more closely unmarried childless women than married women with children. This spatial restriction of their professional horizons affects poorly or modestly qualified women more than well-qualified women having substantial academic capital. The amount of time spent traveling between home and work as a percentage of the total time devoted to work goes from 7 percent for unqualified women through 9 percent for high-school graduates to 13 percent for women with college education.

This state of affairs could lead us to believe that it is the child, not marriage, that places women in a subordinate position. In reality, however, the dependence caused by child-rearing responsibilities comes after that engendered by the priority accorded to the husband's job. Where the family lives is determined by where the husband's work is located. Freedom of movement is much greater for a man than for a woman. An unemployed man, for example, is much more likely to consider moving than a married women who is out of a job (Niemi 1975). Moving is not a viable option for the woman since it would entail her husband having to find a new job, whereas married men move around with an inevitable loss of job by their wives. This geographical mobility might improve a man's management of his professional career but it does not do much for the career of a woman. This can be seen in married women's length of employment in relation to the movement of the family (Mincer 1978). During a five-year period, married women in the United States are employed for a much longer period of time when the married couple have remained in the same area. Moving interrupts a woman's career and shows quite clearly the priority accorded to the respective partners' jobs. Unless they adopt an unconventional solution, such as living apart during the week and reuniting on weekends, a married couple resolve the question of where to live in favor of the husband.

THE COST OF MARRIAGE

Many factors—the husband's job, looking after the children—conspire to devalue a woman's capital on the labor market. A married woman's investments in a career are incontestably less than the investments of other social actors. But we must measure as precisely as possible the consequences of marriage and ask the following questions:

—What is the price a married woman has to pay for family life?
—Does this price vary according to the woman's academic capital?
—Is this price an expression of the fact of being part of a couple or of being a mother?
—Does this price vary according to the husband's academic capital?

The negative side of marriage for a working woman

Marital status has such a marked effect on individuals (and also the image these individuals have on the labor market) that the value of their capital is affected by it. Entering into marriage changes things to the extent where, all things being equal, married men and married women do not have the same professional goals. This general statement, based on the description of women's underinvestment in their careers, consists of four hypotheses:

A: Married men will receive a better return from their qualifications than single men. The professional returns married men receive from their qualifications are greater than those received by single men in that they are absolved to a greater extent from looking after themselves.
B: Single women will have a better return from their qualifications than married women. Married women must

have a smaller return from their academic capital because they assume the housekeeping and child-rearing
tasks and can therefore devote less time and energy to
their careers (Houseknecht, Vaughan, and Statham
1987).

C: Married men will receive a better return from their
qualifications than married women. This third hypothesis is deduced from the first two, marriage having opposite effects on the partners depending on their sex.
Husbands benefit more from being married than their
wives, at least professionally speaking. Moreover, in the
generalized system of exchanges within the "traditional"
marriage partnership, the wife's expectations vis-à-vis
her husband's professional advancement are greater
than the husband's compared to his wife's.

D: Single men will receive a better return from their qualifications than single women. The very fact of being a
woman is in itself a handicap in the world of work, quite
apart from the question of marriage. Sexual discrimination affects the majority of women, whether married or
not (Guillaumin 1978).

From the above we can see that academic capital earns a suc-
cessively decreasing return on the labor market for single men
as compared to married men, and then for married women
compared to single women.

The difficulties created by family life for the smooth progres-
sion of a woman's career have been categorized by socioprofessional group according to sex and marital status
(Mueller and Campbell 1977). This is how P. A. Ross looks at
the access of married and single women to the higher-status
jobs in twelve industrialized countries (1981). In the vast majority of these countries the senior executive category con-
tains more single women than married women. In France this
same relationship can be observed: between the ages of forty
and forty-nine, a quarter of the single women and one-seventh
of the married women in employment are senior executives.
An analysis of those women who are sufficiently well known
to appear in the French Who's Who (1981–82 edition, seven
hundred women out of a total of two thousand entries) confirms the existence of a correlation between single status and
career success (Veron 1984). Regardless of generation, the
proportion of single women in Who's Who is greater than the

proportion of women in the population as a whole. Among those born between 1937 and 1946, more than a quarter of "famous" women and less than one-tenth of "ordinary" women are single.

However, this data does not confirm the previously mentioned hypotheses. Marital selection alone could produce this correlation. All it needs is for the men in the lowest positions and the women in the highest positions not to be chosen, or to prefer not to be chosen, as a marriage partner for this situation to arise. We must also eliminate statistically the effects of this marital selection by introducing academic capital into the analysis. Married women need to be compared with single women and married men having an identical academic level before the differences in professional levels between these groups can be attributed to marriage. More precisely, we need to take as our indicator of the returns on academic qualifications access to senior executive level in terms of three criteria: sex, marital status, and level of qualifications.[3] This evaluation of the price to be paid for family life refers to the 35 to 52 age group, one in which a single person's chances of marrying are very low.

The devaluation of women's qualifications

Married women become senior executives by being more highly qualified than their married male colleagues. One-half of female senior executives have been educated at least three years beyond high school as compared to one-third of the married men who are senior executives. The exchange rate between academic qualifications and a position as senior executive is less advantageous for women than for men. Marriage brings about a devaluation in a women's academic capital as far as her career is concerned.

The chances of a person who is at least a high-school graduate becoming a senior executive and the chances of individuals with lower academic qualifications becoming either a senior or junior executive on the whole confirm our four hypotheses. Indeed, out of our twenty-four predictions (four hypotheses specified in relation to six different academic levels), nineteen are confirmed (see Appendix 1). The statements that are not verified concern hypothesis 4; single men in fact rarely receive a better return than single women. Thus, according

Table 3.1
Social Advantages of Marriage for Men

Level of education	Chances of becoming a senior executive for: (in percentages)			
	Married men	Single men	Single women	Married women
High school graduate	32	17	8	9
High school + 2 years	43	29	21	6
High school + 3 years	90	79	83	79

Source: Previously unpublished data from INSEE, FQP study, 1970, for employed men and women aged 35-52

to the criteria governing access to the position of senior executive, being a woman is not in itself a handicap. The other hypotheses are quite clearly confirmed: married men with equivalent qualifications have a greater chance of becoming senior executives than do single men and married women. Thus, for high-school graduates the chances of becoming a senior executive are on the order of 1 in 12 for married women, 1 in 6 for single men, and 1 in 3 for married men. Married life for men is therefore associated with rapid advancement in their careers and a slowing effect for women. If we evaluate both sexes in terms of the returns to be gained from their qualifications on the labor market, the social advantages for men in marriage are greater than those for women (see table 3.1).

The marriage option tends to result in career success only for men. After all, the average salary level of married working women is below that of childless single women with the same qualifications: for example, for high-school graduates the level is 15 percent less in the case of married women. Women without a partner and with at least one child occupy an intermediate position between these two groups in terms of the career returns on their qualifications.[4] The career success rates of American psychiatrists and clinical psychologists in terms of their marital status also bear out the advantages of marriage to men. An individual is considered to have succeeded professionally when his income is above the average for his profession and when he has published a number of articles (Marx and Spray 1970). Single male psychiatrists and psychologists are less successful than their married colleagues. Beyond the age of forty success levels are heavily weighted in favor of married men, with 28 percent of them being rated as successful, compared with 10 percent for single men.

The cushion of good qualifications

Generally speaking, marriage is costly for women and profitable for men, but the price women have to pay and the profits men gain[5] depend on the amount of academic capital they possess. Married women, as compared with married men, suffer a greater depreciation when they have a low or average academic level (less than a degree for those who are at least high-school graduates; less than a BEPC for non-high-school graduates). Compared to single men, married men receive a better return when they have a low academic capital. Married men who are simply high-school graduates gain more than married men with a college degree. The least qualified men in each of the two groups (at least high-school graduates and non-high-school graduates) benefit more at work by being married.

Marriage is more profitable for men with a smaller academic capital because it comes into play at the point where educational level interacts with job level. The more fixed this interaction, the less positive the effect of being married. The converse applies as well. The chances of becoming a senior executive with a diploma from one of the highly prestigious *grandes écoles* are so great that marital status hardly enters into it. On the other hand, becoming a senior executive simply with a high-school diploma is a rarity: men in this category who reach this position owe it to other factors, particularly to those associated with family connections. It is when a man's career depends less on his academic capital that marriage helps it, whereas it has a negative effect on a woman's career (with the exception of women having only a high-school diploma). The correlation between marriage and work is therefore associated with the correlation between educational level and work, with a high correlation in the first case and a lesser correlation in the second. Good qualifications protect women from the vicissitudes of marriage and guarantee men a higher position without excessive investment. The differences between the careers of married men and single men (or married women) are greater when the certainty of achieving senior executive status is reduced. Marriage is a positive support for a man's career and a liability for a woman's career mainly when the chances of success by academic capital alone are low. Conversely, men with good educations who are senior executives are less affected by being married. Marriage, therefore, is for them, as opposed to their wives, a strictly private business; in other words, it is a purely emotional relationship quite unconnected with the world of work.

The cost of a child

Entering into marriage is not enough in itself to disadvantage women; more than anything it is the fact of having and bringing up children that causes a depreciation in the value of their qualifications. The returns within the world of work from a woman's academic capital follow a continuum: they are excellent for childless married women, average for a woman with one child, and poor for a woman with several children. Thus, for every hundred dollars earned by a childless married woman with a high-school diploma, a mother of two children at a comparable academic level and also working full-time earns only seventy-six dollars (see table 3.2). In eight cases out of ten, a woman with one or several children and having similar academic qualifications earns less than a childless married woman. A professional career and motherhood appear to be incompatible. According to S. Polachek (1975), each child means a 7-percent reduction in the mother's income and an increase of 3 percent in the father's. In fact, a married man registers an increase in the value of his academic capital when he becomes a father. Thus, with a capital at least equal to a high-school diploma, a man earns one hundred dollars when he has no children and 131 dollars with two children (see table 3.3).

A child stimulates its father's career, particularly if the latter has substantial academic capital. This positive effect of paternity demonstrates that the profits a man gains from marriage do not all come from being absolved from domestic chores, since this is guaranteed right from the start of married life. The better returns a man obtains on the labor market also come from the demands made upon him in his function as the main provider of income. Domestic life demands a considerable career investment on the part of a man, matched by

Table 3.2
The Cost of Having Children for Employed Married Women

Married women	Level of Education		
	Low	Average	High
Childless	100*	100*	100*
1 child	88	92	93
2 children	76	83	98
3 children	58	78	113

*Baseline salary. For example:

$$\frac{\text{Salary for married women with 1 child}}{\text{Salary for married, childless women}} \quad X \quad 100 \quad = \quad 88$$

Source: Taxable income study, INSEE, 1975. Cf. Canceill 1984

Table 3.3
The Cost of Having Children for Employed Married Men

Married men	Level of Education		
	Low	Average	High
Childless	100*	100*	100*
1 child	104	98	107
2 children	114	105	131
3 children	105	106	150

*Baseline salary. See Table 3.2 for computation method

Source: Taxable income study, INSEE, 1975

an underinvestment on the part of his wife. Since families are competing socially in order to have the best possible position, the head of the family needs to make the best possible use of his capital. He mobilizes his resources on the labor market, particularly once the couple has become a family, which obviously makes good sense. The paradoxical nature of his situation then becomes evident: because his commitment as a father now demands an increased commitment in his career, a man must spend less time at home to meet his paternal responsibilities. The price that has to be paid in career advancement for having children is therefore much higher for the mother. The social demands associated with motherhood involve a woman's withdrawal, either partial or total, from the labor market. Two studies on specific social groups help us to illustrate some of the mechanisms that bring about this withdrawal.

An anticipated reduction in investment. The depreciation on the labor market of American women who are high-school graduates has more to do with their role as a mother than with their role as a wife (Sewell, Hauser, and Wolf 1980). This effect, however, seems to anticipate the constraints of bringing up children. The difference that can be observed between women with three children and men in midcareer is already apparent to a great extent at the beginning of their entry onto the labor market. It is as if the women had foreseen, consciously or not, their career as mothers and adjusted the level of their investment in a professional career accordingly. Subsequently married women who do not have children right from the beginning have a higher return in their work from their qualifications than those women who go on to have three children.

Excluded from the promotion networks.

This withdrawal from the labor market, whether anticipated or not, does not explain completely why a woman with a family receives a lower return from her capital both financially and symbolically. Women having a doctorate and children are less likely to have a high professional position than those who do not have children (Brochart 1978). And yet they are not identifiable by the smaller number of specialized papers they have published or by a reduction in the number of awards they have received nor by a lack of recognition from their peers: half of them have published articles as opposed to one-third of childless women holding doctorates. Their depreciation is related to interruptions in their careers and to a more frequent change of employers. One-quarter of women with children and one-tenth of those without children suffer a break in their careers. Their investment—as measured by articles published—is not enough to guarantee a good return on a Ph.D. unless it conforms to the dominant male scenario of an uninterrupted career. Childless women are more successful not because of their productivity, but through their continued presence at the workplace. That is where the right connections are made and where opportunities present themselves, opportunities that elude those women who although writing at home are unable to obtain recognition of their work in quite the same way. The depreciation of a woman's value that stems from these interruptions has as much to do with the problems caused by her reentering the professional network as it does with any loss of competence on her part. The rationale behind the functioning of the labor market must not be underestimated; it is regulated by an informal system of relationships, as a study on the comparatively late office hours kept by male executives would seem to show. Women, and more especially women with children, whose job it is to foster the human relationships within a family, ironically are disadvantaged at work by those same human relationships. They are less well integrated into the world of work and thereby suffer the consequences.[6]

Variations in the price paid in terms of the husband

A married woman is handicapped at work by her family life. Does that mean that she gets nothing out of marriage as far as her career is concerned? As we have seen, a woman's academic capital increases the returns her husband gets from his qualifications in his career. Is there a reciprocal transfer then, from the husband's account into the wife's? Do women receive cultural advantages by being married?

In France, at least, one can identify advantages to a woman's career from her husband's academic capital.[7] A woman receives a higher return from her own capital when she is married to a man who possesses a fairly substantial capital himself (see Appendix 2). For example, among those women who have not continued their studies after the age of nineteen, half of those choosing a husband of the same educational level go on to become executives, while three-quarters of the women who marry a man with higher qualifications follow this path. Of those who ended their studies at age sixteen, more than a third married to men without qualifications and a quarter of those married to men with only an average education are factory workers or shop assistants. This second group is twice as likely as the first to be office workers or junior executives. Whatever her capital at the outset, however, a woman is disadvantaged more than her husband by being married, although her partner's academic capital can go some way toward offsetting that fact.

A husband's academic capital can increase the effectiveness of his wife's academic capital. This statement leads us to another observation concerning the effects of marriage: even if it is true to say that a married woman's capital does not increase in value as much as a single woman's on the labor market, her husband's cultural reserves can increase or diminish this depreciation. The price to be paid for family life fluctuates in relation to both the husband's and wife's academic capital. In terms of her academic capital, a married woman more closely resembles a single woman if she has married well. After all, only 4 percent of women who left school at sixteen and married men who left school before the age of fifteen have become junior executives, compared with 17 percent of those married to men who continued their educations after that age.

The costs of marriage are not uniform as far as a job is concerned. They vary according to the choice of partner. The value of a woman's capital on the labor market depends on her family and conjugal status and also on her partner's cultural identity. Marriage can either upset or improve a wife's career. Nevertheless, the price of marriage is never so low that it does not cost women anything at all, as the example of female sociologists clearly shows (Martin, Berry, and Jacobsen 1975). Those married to sociologists achieve higher professional status than those married to men who are not sociologists, but this status is lower than that obtained by their sociologist husbands. Almost all male sociologists, three-quarters of the women married to sociologists, and two-thirds of female sociologists married to nonsociologists have a doctoral degree. It costs the first group of women less to be married than it does the second; they increase their academic capital more easily and thus boost their professional careers. However, female sociologists married to sociologists obtain their doctorates an average of four and a half years after their husbands. Within the family team, the husband's gains do not systematically result in losses for the wife. Marriage is not always a win-lose situation, nor does a marriage partnership exclude the possibility of one of the partners benefiting from their relationship. An increase on the returns from one partner's academic capital through the other partner's capital and the creation of new cultural investments in the form of children show how at times marriage can be a win-win situation.

The advantage that some women receive on the labor market from their husband's cultural capital does not make up for the price that they have to pay for marriage and family life. A married woman's academic capital certainly is undervalued on the labor market, compared with the returns a man obtains. Indeed, the true price of family life is underestimated in the cost calculated here, which has been based only on people who have a job. However, one's presence on the labor market varies by sex and marital status. Single women and men—whether married or not—are more likely to have a job than are married women. The comparisons in returns on academic capital involve men in general, the vast majority of single women, and only a small portion of married women. This distinction is important since the category of women on which the cost of marriage is based excludes those women who have obtained the worst deal from their capital. For example, women with two children who return to work very often find a job at a level comparable to the one they had before.[8] They experience very little or no downward mobility in their work.[9] Married women who would experience too severe a devaluation by returning to work do not attempt to get another job. The working married women who are studied by sociologists are either those who have never stopped working or those who have returned to work without loss. Given that the cost of marriage and family life is calculated by reference to women who have experienced a minimum of devaluation, one may assume that the cost needs to be put at a higher figure. As far as paid work is concerned, marriage is a bad deal for women.

4

Direct and Indirect Investment

My definition of marriage: it resembles a pair of shears, so joined that they cannot be separated, often moving in opposite directions.

—Sydney Smith, *Lady Holland*, 1855

"The value of your capital interests me." Thus does the marriage bank attract its customers by offering them the chance to open one or even several supplementary accounts in addition to their own personal account. However, for women the offer comes with a certain number of restrictions. The returns from their personal account, through investment on the labor market, are less than the remuneration guaranteed to single women or married men. The total amount of interest to be earned is limited for married women, especially for those with children. There can be no doubt that while she gains value from her husband and children, at the same time they cause her to receive lower returns from her own account. But does the reverse also happen? Does the fact of a woman having a job reduce the returns from the accounts opened in the names of her husband and children? If indeed it does, then the husband's professional career and the child's intellectual development should both suffer when a woman goes out to work. Here again a woman would not be able to accumulate all the benefits offered on paper by the marriage bank's financial department.

The answer to these questions should not be found among the arguments advanced by those who oppose women going out to work without thorough examination. These arguments affirm unhesitatingly that husbands and children are handicapped when a wife has a job. They try to convince us with scenarios such as this one:

A mother returns home in the evening after ten hours away (eight hours at the office plus two hours traveling). She feels worn out and returns to a house as untidy as she left it that morning. Dinner is not ready. She needs to wash her hair, which she has not had time to do for the past three days. Her daughter comes into the bathroom asking if she will listen to her recite the poem that she will be tested on the next day at school... Across the hall is her neighbor with a new hairdo. She feels on top of the world. She loves the hustle and bustle in the evenings when everyone returns to the house that has been silent all day. A meat loaf is sizzling in the oven. All that remains to be done is to season the salad. Her son asks her to help him study his history for a test the following day. (Collange 1979, 55)

When Collange asks, "In your opinion, which of these two mothers will be ready to help her children do their homework?", she wants us to answer, "From the children's point of view, the situation is quite clear. They have everything to lose by coming home to an empty house" (55).

These are not new arguments. Half a century ago the same reasoning tried to persuade us that a woman's place is in the home. In homes where the mother has a job, "the children suffer, the mother is worn out, the family breaks up, and the financial situation is shaky" (Baudoin 1931, 28):

Children not only pay physically, and sometimes with their lives, for having a mother at the end of her tether, but they also suffer morally. Where does the child of a working mother get educated? At school and in the street.

[The husband] no longer feels those delicate attractions, both moral and material, that keep a man at home and make him think fondly of home when he is absent, secure in the knowledge that someone has his interests at heart.... [He no longer] has his place in the sun, in other words his share of family love.

A wife and mother who goes out to work invests an abnormal amount of time and effort when she has this double role. Her health is more or less permanently damaged. The hoped-for financial gains do not materialize. Through exhaustion and a lack of personal time when she can think and pray, she is diminished morally. Through fatigue and contact with the wrong kind of people she runs the risk of immorality. (29–37)

In terms of the cost of marriage, these statements contend that having dual investments is a mistake for a woman: by keeping her professional account open, she is not able to enjoy fully the benefits of marriage. The risks associated with paid work endanger not only the future value of the child but also the husband's career, since he loses the support of a secure family environment. As a consequence, work outside the home is definitely a bad transaction for a married woman. On the one hand she apparently does not receive the same return from her capital that a man does from his; on the other hand it would seem that she loses out in the return from her indirect investment because her husband and son are less successful at work and school. For a woman to invest in the labor market would appear to be a waste of time, dangerous even. Academic theories also support such a view. B. Lemennicier, an economist, states that respecting "the division of work within a marriage," with the wife staying at home, "results in extra gains." "A reduced investment in professional skills in favor of domestic skills increases the returns made from marriage" (Lemennicier 1980, 32).

When I subject the case to scrutiny, however, I am struck by the weakness of the empirical arguments—the negative effects of married women going out to work are more often stated than they are demonstrated. I suggest that the case should go to appeal. Do working wives really threaten the social and cultural interests of all the members of a family? In reply, I will examine the correlation between wives who go out to work and the success of their husband or children. Can women get a good return from their academic capital, both directly through their careers and indirectly through their husband and children? To understand fully the consequences of wives going out to work, I need to introduce a new element into our analysis: the interests of the married couple. Once the conjugal unit has been created, various activities by the partners begin to take place and become meaningful by reference to their common interests. A wife's job is one such activity. It is only through this activity that we can begin to make sense of three facts: a lower birth rate among working wives, the comparative lack of career success of men whose wives work, and the increased success of the children of working mothers. It is not easy to trace the ways in which a woman protects her social and cultural capital because she also protects her partner's capital, as well as that of the conjugal unit.

THE CASE GOES TO APPEAL

The appeal is based on the effects of a woman's outside job on the child's academic capital and the returns her husband receives from his professional investment. Does a woman who invests her cultural capital in the labor market receive a smaller return from the account in her partner's name and does she make fewer deposits in the account opened in her child's name?

Work and the creation of a child's capital

Since the value of children is often related to the amount of time their mother can devote to them, a child whose mother has a job should do less well than one whose mother remains at home. Indeed, the latter group undoubtedly receives more attention than the first. Nonsalaried mothers possessing the BEPC claim to spend 131 minutes per day attending to their children, compared with 75 minutes if they have an outside job.[1] Indeed, the reduction in the time devoted to child-rearing activities is even greater than that spent on domestic chores. For women who are high-school graduates, the time spent on housework when they have a job is less than one-third of that used if they do not go out to work; moreover, the time spent on child-rearing activities is less than half.

This limitation of the time a salaried mother spends with her children does not affect their cultural capital. The returns on a woman's academic capital from bringing up children is not proportional to the time she spends on that activity. All available data indicate that children whose mothers go out to work have an intellectual or academic worth at least equal to those whose mothers remain at home. The 1973 INED-INETOP study on one hundred thousand schoolchildren between age six and fourteen observed a higher IQ among the children of working mothers—103.9 and 99.6, respectively. Even when we have eliminated the influence of social structure in each category of the mother's activities, this difference remains. When we apply other indicators—academic qualifications or the child's professional level—"latch-key" children are equal or even superior to the others. The picture painted by Collange turns out not to be so accurate after all; the "harm caused by the stress of the working mother" is not identifiable.

Girls gain more than boys by their mothers going out to work. Research into the social mobility of women demonstrates the importance of this factor (Treiman and Terrell 1975). By adhering more strictly to the traditional norms of femininity, nonsalaried women seem to be unaware of their daughters' cultural educations. Conversely, having a job increases the mother's concern, whether consciously or not, that her daughter should do well academically. It is difficult to distinguish between the amount of capital invested according to the sex of the child since at the end of their school career girls have a comparable level to boys (Hoffman 1974). The relative transformation of sex roles within the conjugal unit can result in a certain "liberation" of girls' intellectual potential. This is why, when students are presented with articles written by both men and women, girls whose mothers go out to work have a higher opinion of the competence of the women writers than do the other girls (Barugh 1972).

One of the fundamental elements of the housewife model turns out to be somewhat fragile. This model was originally constructed to refer explicitly to the supposed needs of the child. In 1855 the *British Mother's Magazine* was claiming that a woman "needs to have time to study the subtle differences of character in her individual children and adapt their upbringing accordingly, just as a gardener matches the seed that he plants to the type of soil in the garden." She needs to remain at home fulltime, since "no-one can understand a child's needs quite like the mother; no-one knows how to respond to a child's needs like its mother, and therefore no-one but the mother should bring up her children" (Blunden 1982, 69). The creation of a child's cultural capital, however, is not harmed if the mother goes out to work. For her, an increase in the direct and indirect value of her capital through her children seems perfectly possible.

The working wife and the husband's career

The studies on the effects of a wife's working outside the home never explicitly contain a section entitled "the impact on the husband's career." Nevertheless, a correlation between the two exists, as research on family migration shows.

When a wife goes out to work the couple experiences a loss of mobility. A wife's work limits the couple geographically. Over a period of five years, more than twice as many couples where the wife has given up working move from one part of the country to another, compared with couples where the wife had continued to work (Long 1974).

The rules governing where couples live vary according to the division of work between the partners. In making this decision, the couple attaches less importance to the husband's job when both partners work. The decision to change jobs becomes more difficult for the husband to make in that his wife's job also has to be taken into account. The relative lack of mobility resulting from a wife having a job is associated in working-class families with the extent to which salaried wives and their mothers help out with each other's housework (Chabaud-Richter, Fougeyrollas-Schwebel, and Sonthonnax 1985) and in higher social classes with the management of the woman's career, as executive recruiters know only too well. The priority given to the man—a wife must follow her husband—is questioned particularly where individuals are in favor of both husband and wife working. In a study on the characteristics of a harmonious family (see chapter 6), the persons questioned had to complete a story in which the husband was out of work and the wife had a job. Some maintained that the husband should accept a job that involved moving and his wife giving up her job, while others would not entertain such a solution. For women between the ages of twenty-five and forty, the most divisive social variable is a married woman's relationship with her work. The married women who are not in favor of a woman committing herself to a career, whether or not they work outside the home, are more ready to give priority to the husband in the decision about where the couple should live. The man's responsibility to provide all the family's income gives him the right to determine where the family should live. When the husband is the only one investing in the labor market, the means of assuring the best return on the investment are decided upon by the couple together. Conversely, those who are in favor of both partners working see this decision as a privilege and not a right. The decision of where the family should live is central to the whole question of investment in the labor market by one or both partners in a marriage.

Is it a handicap for men to have a wife who works?

A married couple's redefinition of the right to work may be accompanied by the lessening of the husband's chances of a successful career. To use an analogy from energy theory, the

Table 4.1
The Impact of a Salaried Wife on a Husband's Career

Age at termination of studies	Percentage of men who are senior executives with:	
	a housewife	a salaried wife
15–19	11	6
20–24	49	32
25–29	89	78
30+	87	83

Source: Previously unpublished data from INSEE, FQP study, 1970, for employed men aged 35–52

existence of two job poles must result in a greater dispersion of conjugal energy. A decline in the husband's monopoly of the work role goes hand in hand with the stagnation of his career prospects. With both members of the conjugal team employed, the success of one particular partner is less necessary. Consequently, in this hypothesis the direct investment of a woman's capital brings about a reduction in the value she receives indirectly from her husband. On one side she loses (indirectly) what she gains (directly) on the other.

This reduction in the importance of the husband's success as associated with both partners working can be demonstrated in table 4.1. When his wife has a job a man receives a lower return from his academic capital. It is less usual for a man whose wife works to become a senior executive than it is for a man whose wife does not go out to work, where their qualifications are the same.

Of the married men who ended their studies between 20 to 24 years of age, half of those whose wives do not work and one-third of those whose wives do become senior executives. More precisely, the advantage to a man married to a wife who does not work outside the home decreases when he has higher qualifications. A working wife affects adversely to a greater degree the career of a man who terminated his studies early. For a man with few qualifications to succeed professionally requires a much greater effort on the part of both partners to achieve that end than is needed by a well-qualified man. This is where the advantages of really substantial capital resources make themselves felt.

For most couples the wife's investment on the labor market correlates with a decreased return from the husband's capital. Here we see, statistically, how incompatible a woman's investment on the labor market is with any indirect increase by her husband. A woman does not seem to be able to amalgamate the gains from her work investment with those that she derives from being married. It is as if, faithful to the principle of interrelated accounts, the wife's investment in her work brings about an investment loss for her partner.

The main argument of those who are against women going out to work is not empirically based. The investment of a woman's academic capital on the labor market does not damage the educational level of her children. But elsewhere a wife's going out to work does have a negative effect—her husband's career seems to suffer from the move away from specific work roles within the marriage.

To sum up, it must be said that the evidence, both for and against, is ambiguous and does not help us to understand clearly the consequences of a married woman taking a job. A study of the effects of a wife going out to work, imposed on us by those opposed to the idea, must be abandoned to enable us to direct our attention to what having a job means for a woman and for her partner.

WHAT HAVING A JOB MEANS FOR A WOMAN

The calls on a woman to remain at home are many. Many women, feeling the pressures, have decided to stay at home permanently. The factor that correlates most highly for a mother thinking about an outside job is the cost in child-rearing terms. The prospect of their child being looked after by someone else makes women more unhappy than the thought of a tiring "double day" or a reduction in their spare time (Thomson 1980). Why is it that despite a generally hostile attitude (Maruani 1985) and a job shortage, women with one or two children increasingly are going out to work? The reasons that lead women to invest their academic capital on the labor market become clear when we note the relationship between the following three facts:

—a working wife is often married to a man whose career is not particularly rewarding;

—she often has fewer children than a woman who does not work;

—she often has children who do better at school than those of a woman who stays at home.

But first, a commonly accepted idea that clouds the issue needs to be seriously examined: do married women work out of necessity or by free choice?

Work by choice, work from necessity

The scenario goes as follows: some women can opt to go out to work while others become employed because they have to. The wives of manual laborers have no choice—they have to work because of their husbands' low incomes—but the wives of executives are free to choose whether to stay at home or to take a job. Some groups suggest that the need to get a job could be removed if women were paid for looking after the home; in that way women would be genuinely free to choose. One family association insists that:

> Any real advancement for women would inevitably mean that the conditions under which a woman went out to work should not force her to deny her real self to the detriment of her family. . . . We need to create a society in which a woman can devote herself to bringing up her children. The fact that a mother should be forced to give up her child-rearing role to go out to work is not just, either from society's point of view or from that of the family, if it denies or hinders the prime objectives of a mother's task. We therefore need to set up the financial structures that would allow a mother to choose quite freely, unhampered by financial constraints, to remain at home should she wish to devote herself to bringing up her children.[2]

If this dichotomy between work out of necessity and work out of choice really exists (and it is frequently mentioned in social science publications), then in working-class families more wives should be employed because the low income of their husbands makes their additional income necessary. By the same token, in the families of senior executives, where financial constraints are fewer, the rate of working wives should not fluctuate in relation to the husband's income. The fact is, however, that the available data contradicts this assumption. It is in working-class families where one finds the lowest incidence of employed wives. In lower- and upper-middle-class families, as the husband's salary increases the wife is less likely to go out to work. Of the senior executive group, when the husband's salary is at the bottom end of the scale, three-fifths of the wives go out to work, whereas only a quarter go out to work if his pay is at the upper end of the scale.[3] In the unskilled blue-collar worker group, the husband's position on the salary scale has little effect on whether his wife goes out to work. The question of a woman's investment of her capital cannot be reduced to a dichotomy between choice and necessity: the higher the social class, the more likely a woman will be influenced by her husband's income when it comes to getting a job.

Conjugal support strategies

The arguments around the question of whether a woman needs to work or not obscure the social advantages of having a job. In the above discussion married women appear to take a job either to guarantee the family a minimum standard of living or for no evident motive. In reality, having both partners working makes possible access to an improved lifestyle and upward movement in a social group. The average annual income of a married couple composed of an unskilled laborer husband and a salaried wife is greater than that of a couple where the husband is a skilled worker and his wife does not go out to work. A clerk has the same standard of living as a junior executive if his wife also has a job. A woman's job is a sure way to maintain or even improve the family's social status. This is the reason why husbands approve of their wives having a job (Spitze and Waite 1981). A married woman's job is one of the strategies employed by couples to preserve their interests as a group.

The part played by both partners in the couple's best interests can be seen in consumer studies. With equal income and family responsibilities, the expenditures of a couple where the wife does not work and one where the wife does work are very similar (Tabard and Clapier 1979). The wife's job provides the necessary financial input for the couple to achieve their reference consumption, which is higher than would be possible with only the husband working. But this function is somewhat obscured in the studies by the need to compare couples at the same income level regardless of whether it is from one salary or two: in reality, the families chosen were different in terms of the husband's social position. For example, in average income families, three-quarters of the men whose wives do not work are junior executives and three-quarters of the men whose wives do work are blue-collar workers. The wife's wages improve the couple's social position in terms of life style and standard of living. The expenditures of a couple living off one salary and those of a couple where both partners work are quite similar and indicate that earnings are put into a "communal pot," where they become jointly owned. The money earned by the wife is not assigned to any particular use; it simply goes to improve the couple's social value.

But what lies behind the pretensions and aspirations of such couples? What motivating factor leads both of them to work? As I see it, wives are more likely to have a job when the husband's investment in the labor market brings in limited returns and when the wife's academic capital is greater than her husband's.

Working women and keeping up with the Joneses

Couples, knowingly or otherwise, hope to attain what they see as being their rightful social position. If there is a discrepancy between the real position and the one aspired to, the wife is more likely to have a job. This is why working wives are more common when the husband receives a low return from his academic capital: the husband's "shortfall" is made up for by the wife's investment of her capital in the job market. This fact leads us to different interpretations of the data correlating the husband's return on his qualifications and the wife's job. The negative correlation previously was interpreted in terms of conjugal rivalry. The wife's professional activity reduced the husband's overinvestment and as a consequence his returns suffered (see figure).

A second interpretation is possible, one that excludes the damage done to the value of the husband's capital by the wife's going out to work. The men who discontinue their studies between the ages of twenty and twenty-four and subsequently become blue-collar workers have a working wife in three-quarters of the cases, whereas men in the same educa-

Scenario No. 1:   Rivalry

Wife's capital investment on the labor market

Reduced investment by the couple
in the husband's career

Poor return on husband's academic capital

tional category who are senior executives are married to a woman who has a job in only one-third of the cases. There is a high correlation between an increase in the returns on a man's academic capital and the chances of his wife not having a job. The better the husband's professional investment, the less frequent is the wife's investment on the labor market.

The negative correlation between the man's return on his investment and the likelihood of his wife going out to work reflects the couple's need to cooperate to attain the life style to which they aspire, given the level of the husband's academic capital. A wife's entry and continued presence on the labor market regulates the inflow of income to the extent that the couple reaches the level they consider to be acceptable. The deficiencies of the husband's investment oblige the partners to work together in a different way and also to adapt their roles accordingly (see figure).

The poor returns from a man's academic capital may be the result of his social-class origins. An engineer who is the son of a manual laborer earns less than an engineer who is the son of a senior executive (Thélot 1982). The former is more likely to be in favor of his wife having a job so that they may attain a standard of living comparable to the latter's and to continue to be upwardly socially mobile. When their educa-

Scenario No. 2: Cooperation

Poor return on husband's   (resulting from social class
academic capital   or devaluation of diploma)

Pooling of capital

Wife's investment on
labor market

tions are the same, a man from a modest social background is more likely to have a working wife than is one from the upper class. A man in this position is more fragile since his whole capital is invested in his academic qualifications, so he protects himself and his family by abandoning the principle of male monopoly in the workplace. A second factor—inflation in the value of education—increases the chances of a discrepancy between the value hoped for on the labor market and the value actually accredited. The devaluation of the value of French diplomas that has hit their holders hard since the 1960s explains in part the increase in the number of married women going out to work. As A. Langevin says, "A double salary becomes an all-risks insurance policy" against the effects of the process of democratization in the educational field and against the employment crisis (1980). A wife's earning a salary reduces disappointment and the impression of losing one's place in the social hierarchy. In short, two are trying to equal one.

The wife's capital, a prerequisite for keeping up with the Joneses

Married couples who pool their resources by both partners having a job usually have a wife possessing a good academic capital. The more substantial the woman's capital, the better are her chances of finding work. An INSEE study on work reports that "No qualifications means a lower probability of finding a job. Among those with a high probability of finding a job are people with university degrees, high-school graduates with a technical diploma, and also holders of a BEPC with a CAP."[4] But what seems to be the deciding factor in the decision whether or not the wife should go out to work is the relationship between both partners' qualifications. Women high-school graduates have a job in three cases out of four when they are married to a man with the CAP and in two cases out of five when they are married to a man with a university degree or its equivalent. In couples where the husband has only the CEP the wife goes out to work in one-third of the cases if she has the CEP, in half of the cases if she has the BAP, and in three-quarters of cases if she is a high-school graduate. The investment of a woman's academic capital obviously depends on the structure of the partner's combined academic capital.

If the wife has a higher educational level than her husband she is also more likely to have a job for two additional reasons. First, in the course of the negotiations between partners over the decision on whether the wife should go out to work, her better educational qualifications enable her to impose the solution that will preserve her autonomy and allow her to manage her own capital more directly. A woman's dependence on her husband is less when the symbolic power balance is in her favor. Second, the better the wife's academic qualifications are in comparison with her husband's, the greater the contribution she makes to the domestic income. The investment of resources by both partners in the labor market is more noticeable in married couples where the wife can play a significant role in establishing the family's standard of living. More women junior executives married to blue-collar workers go out to work than women assembly-line workers, the former contributing almost half of the family income, the latter one-third. A woman's direct management of her capital depends on certain conditions, in particular a considerable weighting in favor of the wife in the structure of the couple's combined capital. This is a situation in which the wife can insist on managing her own capital and at the same time is one in which the partners have most to gain by the wife having a job. Both partners having a job is a maneuver on their part to attain the standard of living to which they aspire; a substantial academic capital from the wife brings that aspiration to the forefront and her going out to work helps in its realization. This process of consolidation of the family's social status is often achieved by a reduction in the size of the family.

Fewer children

In statistics children are referred to as "dependent children." This administrative view of children seems reasonable when we examine family size in relation to the mother's professional activity. Of course, the more children they have, the less married women go out to work. Three-quarters of women in the 30 to 34 age group with one child have a job and one-third with three children go out to work.[5] The wives of manual laborers who have a job, for example, have on average two children, but with three children they stay at home. The interpretation of this data almost always means that the arrival of a third child forces the mother to give up working (Lery 1984). The increase in family responsibility is incompatible with the mother having a job since she cannot cope with both her domestic work and outside employment. Those who subscribe to this point of view stress that women, and especially working-class women, give up their jobs after the birth of a child. According to an INED study, nearly two-thirds of women laborers still at work before the birth of their second child decide to stay home after it is born (Monnier 1977). Two or three children are an obstacle for a wife who wishes to have a job.

Seeing the child solely as an extra responsibility is not the only way to look at the situation. The number of children can be viewed from the perspective of the strategies that couples employ to maintain and, where possible, improve their social status. The consequence of these strategies can be seen in the U-curve in the French birth rate, which is higher in families where the father is a laborer or a senior executive and lower where the father is a junior executive (Bourdieu 1974, 17). For the lower-middle classes a reduction in family size helps their attempts to gain upward social mobility. The cost of this mobility means that efforts need to be concentrated, which means they should have no more than one or two children. This polarization results in a greater endowment of cultural capital on the children through an increased educational, financial, and emotional investment. The working classes (particularly those at the bottom end), too poor to benefit from such strategies, are on average less inclined to limit the size of their family as a consequence. After a period of adherence to Malthusian principles, the upper-middle classes become more prolific since cultural capital is more easily transferred than economic capital.

The vested interests parents have in their children's success in society results in an increased control of the number of births. From this standpoint the correlation between size of family and working mothers becomes clearer. When a married couple hopes to improve their social-class status in the short or medium term, they may have recourse to procedures that increase the family's income and to others that reduce its expenditure. Paid work comes in the first category and birth control falls in the second. Very often these two strategies are employed together since couples in which both partners work have fewer children than other couples.

Planned families

An examination of women's careers as child-rearers and as job-holders bears out the conclusion that having children is a controlled event. It is not the extra work that comes with the birth of a child that induces a mother to give up working. Indeed, the difference in terms of paid work between mothers with two children and mothers with three children already exists before the birth of the second child. As soon as they have children, women's relationship with the world of work changes. Just before the birth of their first child, three-quarters of those women who by the end of the study will have two children have a job; two-thirds of those women who will go on to have three children are in paid work; one-half in the case of those women who will eventually have four children and one-third of the women who ended up having five children by the end of the study are employed when they first became pregnant (Lagarde 1981, 33). Women with two children who go on to have a third are less likely to have had a job when they first became pregnant than women who have no more than two children (see table 4.2).

Table 4.2
The Weak Professional Investment of Future Mothers of Three Children

	Percentage of working mothers (27–31 age group) with two children	
	who have a third	who do not have a third
When they first go out to work	77	98
Before the first child	66	85
Before the second child	51	65

Source: CNAF study, 1970–72. Cf. Lagarde 1981

N.B.   At the birth of the second child, 65 percent of the mothers who will not have another child and 51 percent of the mothers who do go on to have a third child have a salaried job.

All women, including those with low academic capital, control the time they devote to child-bearing and to their working activities, whether they realize it or not. There is a significant disparity among women with the CEP with regard to those who have a job before their first child: two-thirds of them have a job if they subsequently have a second child; half of those who later have three or four children have a job, as do one-third if they eventually have five children.

It is therefore difficult to see the arrival of the second, third, or fourth child as being the determining factor in whether women stop working, even for women who have not completely mastered the so-called scientific methods of contraception, since the differences already exist in women's patterns of employment prior to having children. It is as if the decision is made quite early whether to center their lives almost exclusively around their families or to have a mixed existence in which they invest in both family and work. This decision is identifiable from adolescence. The girls who insist that they intend to work after they have had children see themselves as having fewer children than those who see themselves as stay-at-home housewives (Aneshendel and Rosen 1980).

Besides their personal self-fulfillment, working women reveal through their continued paid employment and by the smaller size of their families a strong wish to maintain or improve their social standing as a married couple. The association of these two strategies is more common among working-class women or women with limited education. The difference between the average number of children of working women and the average family size of non-working women is 1.2 where the husband is a manual worker, 0.8 where he is a junior executive, and 0.7 where he is a senior executive.[6] Having a substantial academic capital makes it easier to combine her maternal and professional careers. Women who are at least high-school graduates and women with the CAP continue to work when they have one child. Once they have three children, half of the first category and only a quarter of the second category are still working.

Restricting family size seems to be more necessary for working- class or lower-middle-class than for upper-middle-class couples, when both partners work. The desire for upward social mobility, whether conscious or not, demands a much greater combined effort on the part of the first two social groups, which involves both the wife going out to work and restricting family size. This is perfectly understandable if we view it in terms of the cost of cultural investment in the child. It costs parents whose economic and academic resources are limited much more to bring up and invest in a child. The creation of the child's capital *ex nihilo* means a tighter restriction on family size is necessary for working-class and lower-middle-class families with upwardly mobile pretensions. Family planning is the first step in indirect capital growth through the child.

The number and "quality" of the children

Birth rates and child-rearing techniques are closely related in working-and lower-middle-class homes; they are expressions of the same productive principle. Families with upwardly mobile aspirations use two complementary strategies: one limits the number of children and the other involves utilizing the family's resources (and moral "energy") to enable the reduced number of children to benefit during their school and "free" time.

The reduction in the number of children and the importance attached to the child's development are inextricably linked. In working- and lower-middle-class families the smaller the size of the family the better the results in subsequent IQ tests and examinations. Family size also influences school achievement except in upper-middle-class families, where the acquisition of a good education depends on the number of siblings (de Singly 1982b). The same is true in the case of the sons of senior executive fathers with a university degree, whose chances of obtaining a degree are not reduced by the number of siblings. On the other hand, the chances of the son of a junior executive earning a degree if his father was not a high-school graduate are doubled if there are no more than two children in the family (Pohl, Soleilhavoup, and Ben-Rezigue 1983). In working- and lower-middle-class families, the contraction of family size comes before educational investment. What psychologists call the "size factor" results from the means employed in certain families to succeed socially through their children. The identification of a correlation between the number and the educational or social "quality" of children is nothing new. Neo-Malthusian propagandists in nineteenth-century France, who tried to influence working-class families, printed wall posters bearing the inscriptions "Fewer children = good quality; a lot of children = bad quality"; "Prosperity with one child, a hard life with two, and poverty with three or more"; and "Large families mean miserable poverty" (Ronsin 1980, 73).

To give her children a capital worth greater than her own or her husband's a woman has to concentrate her efforts. As a result, women married to uneducated workers and having a son who graduated from high school and subsequently became a junior executive are mothers of three children, whereas if they have a son who is a manual laborer they have six children (Tabard et al. 1982). Daughters of blue-collar fathers who subsequently become junior executives have fewer siblings than do the daughters of blue-collar workers who become plant workers themselves. If they are to break out of their social class group it is vital for working-class couples to be able to control the size of their families. Only then can they receive an indirect return from their investment in children. Parents, in their role as entrepreneurs, do not necessarily expect an immediate return on their investments, preferring instead to make a long-term investment in their children. For the couple marriage implies working together to defend their respective interests, which can be accomplished by a process that puts the emphasis on a deferred remuneration of capital,

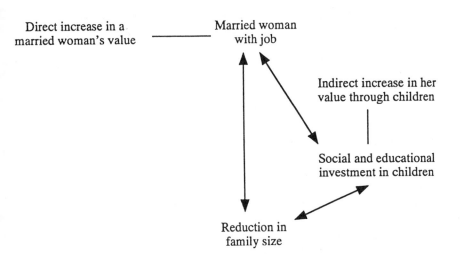

Direct increase in a married woman's value — Married woman with job

Indirect increase in her value through children

Social and educational investment in children

Reduction in family size

or in other words, having the satisfaction of seeing their child move up in the social hierarchy.

The harmonization of professional and educational investments

The circular process by which a woman increases the value of her capital can be traced by studying the correlation between her work and the number of her children, between her work and her children's school achievement, and between the number of children and school achievement (see figure).

Let us take the example of women married to blue-collar workers. Not all of them go out to work or have the same number of children, nor do their children all have identical school records. What criteria can we use to differentiate between women who go out to work and those who do not? How do women who go out to work differ from those who do not? How do mothers of large families differ from those with small families? How do mothers whose children drop out from school differ from those whose children do not? The answer is simple: by the amount of their academic capital.

When the husband is a laborer and the wife has a good academic capital, whether they realize it or not, they employ a number of strategies designed to provide their children with a better future than that available to children of other labor-ers.[7] First, they have fewer children.[8] A laborer whose wife has little education has 2.6 children, while a worker whose wife has a French DEUG diploma has 2.0 children. This re-striction of family size becomes understandable in terms of the couples' educational investments in their children. The salaries of these more highly educated women financially sub-sidize these expenses. A look at the average annual expendi-ture on schooling, private lessons, and artistic and sporting activities clearly indicates the extent of the investment in the child's capital value undertaken by working-class families im-bued with the spirit of Malthusianism. In working-class fami-lies with four children, the amount spent per child is one-fifth that spent per child in an upper-middle-class family. In households with only one child the difference is less: the only child of a blue-collar father receives an investment equal to three-fifths of that received by the child of an executive father. In upper-middle-class families the expenditure increases with the number of children; for every one hundred dollars spent on an only child, four children receive 394 dollars. In working-class families, however, for every one hundred dollars spent on an only child, four children receive only sixty-nine dollars.[9] By limiting family size and pooling their earned incomes, working-class families create better financial educational con-ditions. If she is married to a laborer, a working woman with few children and a greater-than-average academic capital in her group has greater disposable resources to enable her off-spring to have the best possible social and educational capital. Contrary to the critics who see working mothers having a detrimental effect on the interests of the child, it is evident that a direct increase in a woman's capital through employ-ment is not incompatible with the creation of capital in a child's name.

ACCESS TO AUTONOMY

A woman's job supports the married couple's plans to com-pensate for deficiencies in the husband's capital and to in-crease the child's capital value. But if we stopped the film at that particular frame we would have a false picture; the pro-jector needs to keep running since a woman's having a job also reinforces her autonomy. The investment of a woman's

capital on the labor market can be seen as an expression of
the couple's joining of forces and as the claiming of an individual's right.

Those in favor of married women working outside the home
also support a wife's autonomy within the marriage partnership. Twice as many of those in favor of working wives, compared with those who are not, consider it reasonable that a
husband and wife should not always tell each other everything. The first group is happy for partners to take separate
vacations if their schedules do not coincide. They also believe
that personal mail should not be opened by the other partner.
An acceptance of the value of wives having a job goes together
with a demand that both partners should be intellectually and
behaviorally autonomous (see chapter 6). Women who prefer
to have a stay-at-home housewife role reject these marks of
independence much more than do women who go out to work.
One's definition of the mutual dependence of married couples
varies according to one's position on working women: men
and women who proclaim the right to independence are also
the ones who believe in equal access for both sexes in the
workplace and who condemn what they see as the domestic
incarceration of stay-at-home wives.

The reinforcement of a working wife's autonomy can be
seen by the way she takes advantage of the institution of divorce. A working wife is much less hesitant than a non-
working wife about beginning divorce proceedings and breaking away from her husband, as divorce statistics show. On
average, the divorce rate is four times higher in marriages
where the wife has a job, according to J. Commaille (1978).
Marriages in which both partners work are more likely to end
in divorce than those where the wife does not work.

This correlation between divorce and women with jobs is
interpreted by the Becker school (Lemennicier 1980) as a reflection of the reduced profits from marriage caused by the
reduced profits from role specialization. Couples who both
work are instrumental in bringing about their own misfor-
tune. After all, it is these couples who are most dissatisfied
with married life and have the most fights (Michel 1974; Lemennicier 1980). When both partners have had a university
education, the number of fights (according to the wives) is
nearly three times higher among couples where both partners
work than it is in couples where the wife stays at home. A
wife's investment in the labor market could have the effect

of causing couples to fall out of love. Marriage under such conditions could be less attractive and partners could get less out of it, or so the argument goes.

However, this interpretation neglects the absence of economic independence of the stay-at-home wife and its effects on her. A woman who does not increase her capital directly is entirely dependent on the income she receives from the returns on her indirect investments, whereas paid work opens up her possibilities by increasing her "relative autonomy situation" (Commaille 1981; Hannan, Tuma, and Groeneveld 1978). Moreover, working wives are not only likely to divorce more frequently, but they are also more likely to be the ones to institute divorce proceedings. There is undeniably a correlation between divorce and women going out to work, but this does not mean that the wife's working in itself disrupts a marriage. The lessening of a wife's dependence upon her husband through her paid work creates a situation of awareness on her part and a means by which the tensions inherent in a marriage can find expression. The effects of this dependence can be seen in the accounts of married women, like that of Colette Dowling (1981). After having lived alone, she fell in love with a man who seemed to be her ideal companion. Gradually she "dwindles" into the role of wife, to use Jessie Bernard's term (1972, 39):

> I used to spend several hours a day writing. . . . my time seemed to be taken up in homemaking—blissful homemaking. After years of throwing together frozen TV dinners because I'd been too busy to do more, I started cooking again. . . . I was always lingering a bit, tending a flowerpot, building a fire. . . . Feeling safe for the first time for years . . . I made a nest. . . . At night, playing helpmate, I would type Lowell's manuscripts for him. (Dowling 1981, 17–18)

The dependence scenario is all in place, with its costs and secondary benefits—the feeling of security, of protection. A woman's job, whether she has taken it in the name of autonomy or not, changes the rules of the marriage game. It changes the partners' view of family life.[10] It is not the tensions and the dissatisfactions that increase when women go out to work but rather the possibility that a wife now has of giving expression to them by, for example, threatening to walk out. Indeed, divorce implies two conditions: dissatisfaction with one's marriage and the practical possibility of living outside the marriage. These conditions are closely linked since the awareness of unhappiness depends on the real possibilities of breaking away. Discontent and its expression increase when the individual has a real chance to leave her husband. The stay-at-home wife, who is more dependent, is condemned to be content—or at least to pretend that she is. Working wives claim to be less satisfied with their marriages and divorce more frequently; certainly they have a much greater possibility of breaking out of the domestic circle.

It is as if marital disenchantment is resolved in two different ways—for working wives by divorce and by non-working wives by depression. Depression—more frequent in non-working wives (Radloff 1975)—is the language of those women who cannot back out of their marriage vows. In a way, their aggression turns against themselves, which only goes to show how insubstantial interpretations are which state that the divorce rate among working wives proves that these women destroy marriages or that the incidence of depression among non-working wives shows how miserable marriage really is. Each camp chooses the evidence that seems to prove its case. The hell of one side is the propaganda heaven of the other!

A woman's paid work has a dual significance. On one hand it improves the family's social destiny by compensating for the deficiencies in the husband's career and by the creation of capital in the children's name; on the other hand it gives the wife greater autonomy and enables her to directly manage her own academic capital. At the same time her work is one of the supporting factors in the couple's social and financial success and is one of the means by which the wife protects her independence. The investment of a woman's capital on the labor market opens up contradictory ways of viewing the situation:[11] it can either increase the couple's resources or introduce the possibility of the wife opting out of the marriage.

Part 2
The Ambiguous Effects of Marriage

Introduction to Part 2

Two main schools of thought dominate current thinking: one wants women to say at home; the other considers this a mistake. Our theoretical fiction seems to be simply a variation of the second school since in order to draw up the married woman's balance sheet I have had to abandon the model of the stay-at-home housewife, which takes no account of the fluctuations of life that beset women. According to this model a woman should devote herself to her family, and, as they say, give without counting the cost. The crux of the matter resides in the love that a woman gives to her husband and children. My approach—whose aim is to identify the social capital transactions engendered by marriage—does not subscribe to the model of the wife as exploited. In that model the balance sheet's totals are known in advance: marriage is, by definition, a disaster for women. According to F. Engels (1954, 72), "in the family the husband is the bourgeois and the wife plays the part of the proletariat." It would be unproductive to go through this balance sheet item by item; its main feature is a denunciation of love:

> Mutual love is the superstructure that camouflages, and badly at that, the underlying economic basis of human sentiments. There is no way that the terms of this conflict between men and women can be changed, no matter what lengths we my go to in order to try and change them. Monogamous marriage is structurally a means of dominating women and children, and it must be subverted structurally. (Elena et al. 1974, 222)

A literary example of this view of marriage can be found in Guy de Maupassant's "La Dot" (1957, reprint). The heroine, Jeanne Cordier, is a young woman who, although "rather gauche" and "somewhat badly dressed," has a substantial dowry—"three hundred thousand francs in cash and negotiable bonds." After her marriage she is very happy. Jeanne, now Mme Lebrument, adores her husband, who "from the outset treated her in the most delicate and remarkably understanding manner." She cannot bear to be separated from him; she had to have him "by her side every day so that she could kiss and caress him..." Then Lebrument suggests a "romantic trip" to Paris. He also asks Jeanne's father to make her dowry available in cash so that he can buy his own notary's practice. On arriving at St Lazare station they take the omnibus, Jeanne sitting downstairs and her husband going on the upper deck "so that I can have a quick smoke before lunch." When the omnibus arrives at the terminus Jeanne's husband has disappeared. It is only later that Jeanne discovers what has happened when a cousin tells her bluntly that her husband "has made off with all your money, that's what's happened." The whole of her financial capital has gone into her husband's account. The entire operation has been carried out painlessly, thanks to the anesthetizing properties of love.

Unlike Jeanne's case, social accounting, as outlined in part 1, is not only about withdrawals. There is a credit column as well as a debit column. The effects of marriage on a woman cannot be reduced to a single devaluation of her worth on the labor market. Other investments are open to her through her husband and children. I have traced the movements of cultural and social capital, but their consequences have not yet been visible. In the final analysis, does marriage on the whole have a negative or positive effect on a woman's interests? Can scrutinizing the balance sheet help us to take up an unambiguous position and make a final diagnosis? The example of widowed women will show us that the final accounting statement is not definitive. Moreover, an assessment of a married woman's social or cultural value reveals that her capital loses value and yet at the same time it also maintains its value (see chapter 5).

This picture of the ambiguous nature of marriage is reinforced if we examine the way the participants themselves view their situation. Not all women view the guarantee of the advantages that marriage is supposed to give them in the same light. There are many different ways of assessing, counting, and interpreting the management of capital resources within a marriage. For some women there are profits and for others there are losses. There is no consensus of opinion. Women (or men) from working-class backgrounds, women from lower- or upper-middle-class backgrounds, young women, old women, working wives and stay-at-home wives, do not all share the same view of marriage (see chapter 6).

This same ambiguity with regard to the value of marriage can also be identified in comparisons between "good" marriages and "ordinary" marriages. A woman who has married a man with more substantial capital than she has does not necessarily obtain greater profits—comparatively speaking—than one who has married a man with the same capital value as hers. A "good" marriage is not always good business for the long-term protection of a woman's interests (chapter 7).

5
An Initial Balance Sheet of the Effects of Marriage

But may the word "Love" be struck down dead and the cardboard crowns roll; let the waxen sceptres melt, the magnificent palace be rent in two to reveal its woodwork, its tapestries torn down from the walls, its furniture and precious objects tottering on the edge of the abyss.
—N. Sarraute, *L'usage de la parole,* 1980

THE various ways in which a woman's capital is managed after she is married have already been outlined. It only remains, if possible, to close the account. This provisional closing of the account can be accomplished by means of an inventory of the books read by married women—which gives an indication of their cultural level—and by examining the situation of widows.

One of the least arbitrary moments to calculate the final value of the account is when the marriage comes to an end through death. Noting the aftereffects of the involuntary end of a marriage—when the husband dies—is an excellent way to observe the effects of marriage, some of which can only be seen after the event, as it were. This method—tell me how women are affected by widowhood and I will tell you what marriage meant for them—reverses Durkheim's approach (1897). In fact, he believes that the suicide rate among widows and widowers is directly related to the quality of their marriages: "There is nothing particularly different about widows and widowers; they are like married men and women... their state is simply an extension of marriage." He goes on to say: "Tell me how, in a given society, marriage and family life affect men and women, and I will tell you how they feel about widow-

116

and widowerhood" (1969, 206). By focusing on widows and widowers in this study we are able to categorize by a process of induction the modifications in the social and cultural capital of married women.

Three characteristics have been selected to describe widows and to identify the traces left by marriage. The first is directly related to the value a widow receives on the marriage market when she remarries. The second corresponds to the value she is accorded on the labor market, and the third is related to the cultural capital possessed by her male and female friends. The lasting effects of marriage then become evident by these expressions of a widow's social value.

A FIXED MATRIMONIAL VALUE

According to one feminist theory, "marriage results in downward mobility for women and, by contrast, upward mobility for men; this creates a considerable gulf between their respective economic opportunities" (Delphy 1974, 1821). If this assertion is true, a woman should experience an alteration in her social and cultural value during the course of her married life. From this point of view, if a woman remarries, her second husband's social position should be lower than her first husband's. Given that the value of the husband chosen is an indicator of the wife's new value, the difference between the two husbands should thus indicate the downward mobility that every married woman is supposed to experience. Is such a decline in a married woman's capital in fact observable? When she marries again, does a widow choose a husband whose capital is less than her first husband's?[1]

The second choice is similar to the first

A comparison between the social positions of both husbands shows very clearly that marriage is not enough to modify significantly a woman's social value. Widows' second husbands are very much like their first ones. Almost 50 percent of widows choose a second husband whose socioprofessional characteristics are identical to those of their first. Unlike a model in which widows might remarry by taking "pot-luck"—in other words, without any obvious association with their first husbands—in reality they show a marked tendency in their second choice to select one very much like the first. Another indicator—the socioprofessional characteristics of second husbands as compared with those of first husbands—confirms widows' lack of independence in choosing again. Sixty-one percent of widows of manual laborers marry laborers the second time around, but only 1 percent of widows of senior executives do so. A woman's recognized social value during her first marriage often corresponds to her value in the second marriage. This marked matrimonial tendency can also be observed in divorced women. Only farmers' widows buck the trend: far more of them remarry farmers than do divorcees. In this case, not only do they have to find a second husband, but they also need someone capable of running the farm.

Loss and gain in value

The effects of marriage and married life on a woman's social value are not as negative as those visualized by the "marriage-as-takeover" theory. Generally speaking, women retain their value since they are in a position to choose a second husband with an equivalent value to the first.

The refutation of the negative-effects hypothesis is reinforced by a comparison between the upward and downward mobility rates of women who marry a second husband from a different social class group. Similar to the "pot-luck" model for second marriages, there is much greater correlation between empirical and theoretical data with regard to upward mobility than with downward mobility. This means that widows more frequently experience a gain rather than a loss in their value from their first marriage. Reinvestment in the marriage market does them no harm, thereby showing that their first marriage cannot have had too disastrous an effect on their capital resources.

More precisely, the value of a woman's capital is more likely to have been maintained or even improved if her first husband was from a higher social class. The stability index and the gain index (in relation to remarriage by "pot-luck") for a widow whose first husband was a junior executive are better than those of a widow whose first husband was a laborer. Wealth attracts wealth. Marrying a well-off first husband increases the chances of doing so the second time. Conversely, the widows of socially impoverished men are likely to marry down.

Marriage therefore seems to be more costly for women whose value was low at the start.

Is remarriage absolutely necessary?

This unequal cost at the moment that they remarry does not imply that women less well endowed with capital have to pay a higher price for their first marriages. A new element needs to be introduced—the remarriage rate. The widows of senior executives remarry less than the widows of manual laborers. The higher the first husband's social level the less the likelihood of the widow remarrying. If the widows of senior executives seem to protect their capital value better when they remarry compared with the widows of manual laborers, could it not be because the former are economically in a position to put off marrying again until the best opportunity presents itself? Conversely, laborers' wives, who are financially vulnerable, are more likely to have to marry a man with a lower capital value. The social inequality between women when they are faced with the negative effects of remarriage is directly related to their inequality when it comes to the need to remarry. It is in the social classes where widows are less likely to remarry that a loss of value by marrying again is less pronounced. One of the effects of being comfortably off could perhaps be that it gives women the choice of remarrying at all or of choosing a second husband free from the constraints imposed by economic dependence. In the United States, all things being equal, women on welfare with children are less likely to remarry than women who are not on welfare (Bahr 1979). If there has been a traditional division of labor between the sexes in the first marriage, thus increasing the woman's dependence, then remarriage becomes even more necessary. Assuming that they are of the same age, a widow who did not go out to work is more likely to marry a second time than one who did. Remarriage is an option particularly taken by working-class women and by stay-at-home housewives. The considerable stability of their value, borne out by their second investment in marriage, is all the more remarkable.

Fixed cultural capital

As measured by the character of the second marriage, any erosion in a woman's capital value at the end of her married life seems minimal. A second type of measuring technique bears this out. By systematically inventorying the contents of her bookshelves, one can gain some idea of the extent of a woman's cultural capital: that is, her capital in the form of the books she owns and the capital acquired through her reading.[2] A count is made of the books belonging to each marriage partner (material acquisition), the books read by each partner (symbolic acquisition), the date the books were acquired, and when they were read. This inventory makes it possible to calculate the number of books owned and read in a year by each partner and by both partners together, to construct a reading curve, and to identify the development of this cultural capital as the marriage progresses. The inventory is based on an analysis of the titles of books read, as well as their subject matter and level of cultural sophistication. From this measure a woman's cultural capital remains fairly constant after marriage. Married life barely disrupts the previous state of the card game; each partner keeps the hand he or she was dealt at the outset. As the game progresses the trump cards hardly change hands. The "every man for himself" rule prevails. The fifteen inventories carried out do not support the hypothesis of the gradual devaluation of the wife's value.[3] The balance, or lack of balance, between the cultural capital possessed by each partner at the outset of the marriage is maintained. Unlike the ideology where everything is held in common (see chapter 6), in these fifteen cases the partners have separate accounts whether the wife's academic capital is greater or smaller than her husband's. Differences between partners do not lead to one partner trying to emulate the other. It is as if a peace treaty between the partners leads to a mutual recognition of the other's cultural territory, as a description of five typical inventories shows.

Inventory 1

The wife of this couple, married twenty-eight years, has a BEPC and a diploma as a kindergarten assistant, an activity she has only recently begun. The husband, who has attained the same educational level, is employed by the Post and Telecommunications Office. The wife's family background is more cultured than the husband's: her father, who is a high-school graduate, was a commercial manager, while her father-in-law was a tailor and had only a school-leaving certificate. In addition, the wife claims to have had a grandfather who was interested in "holy books" and who visited monasteries to carry out research on this subject.

The household's 272 books are spread throughout the house; some are in an old butter churn on which the television is set, others on a dresser, in the bedrooms, in the cellar. The wife owns more books than her husband and has read more, making her cultural capital much greater than her husband's. Living together has not changed this imbalance, which increased at the beginning of the marriage, declined, and then subsequently grew. Discounting books that have been borrowed from libraries (it is difficult for people to remember what they have read if they have not made a note of it) does not seriously affect the results of the study in this case since the wife has hardly ever used that facility and the husband not at all. The books recognized as being owned in common account for only a very small percentage of the total (about 5 percent), as do those that have been read by both partners (less than 10 percent). The cultural superiority of the wife within this partnership is manifest. The ownership indicator is, in this case, false. The husband owns more books that they have both read, but these were given to him by his wife. She also bought the books recognized as hers, together with those owned in common. The wife is responsible for the books owned jointly, and most of the books the husband claims to have read are in this category. Nearly thirty years of married life have scarcely altered their cultural terrain; each partner is encamped in his or her sector, and the husband, in his weaker position, from time to time simply accepts the odd incursion by his wife.

Inventory 2

In the case of this couple an imbalance exists in their respective academic capitals. The wife, thirty-eight years old and a high-school graduate, is a kindergarten teacher. Her husband, a sheet-metal worker, was a high-school dropout. The fathers of both partners were sheet-metal workers. The couple has been married for seventeen years and has two children. The inequality between their respective academic capitals and their social positions is evident from their reading capital. The 182 books they have in the home were acquired either by the wife or by the children. The husband's lack of interest in reading is recognized by the rest of the family, and so they do not buy him any books. During the interview, however, the husband's negative attitude towards books and reading was at the same time admitted and denied:

—The husband: "She buys them; I've read some of them."
—The wife: "He reads science books. I've bought him one or two."
—The wife: "He's not interested in reading; he's got other interests that he likes—do-it-yourself projects, gardening, and he also plays volleyball. He's the captain and treasurer of the X team."
—The husband: "All that doesn't leave me much time for reading."

This kindergarten teacher, despite her initial intentions, has failed in her pedagogical attempts to convert her husband into a reader. Moreover, he does not like her to go to the library and frequently refers to the high cost of books. She has a struggle maintaining the value of her academic capital; the number of books she reads varies with their family circumstances and they are of a heterogeneous nature (ranging from J. Piaget to G. des Cars). Nevertheless, she has not given up her cultural ambitions, as evidenced by her giving the children a twenty-one-volume encyclopedia set and a six-volume dictionary. So here again we have the continuation of a cultural distance between the partners—no conjugal "togetherness" at all.

Inventory 3

This time the inequality is reversed. The husband's capital—he is a highly educated mathematician—is greater than the wife's, who is a high-school graduate. The husband teaches math, while the wife is an office worker in the marketing department of an oil company. They have been married for twenty-five years and have three children who have all left home, taking most of their books with them.

The parents have 423 books between them, of which 181 have been read solely by the husband and 39 by the wife, leaving 203 that both have read. This last group is made up for the most part of encyclopedias—177 volumes! Nine out of ten of the books they both claim to have read are from this category, which the husband bought. With regard to the other books on their shelves, "each of us buys the ones that interest us." The wife prefers "an easy read," the husband chooses his "depending on the subject matter"; for example, *Differential Anthropology* by G. Mendel or G. Berger's *Analytical Treatise on Character*. He does not like, he says, "bad literature, easy reads," and his tastes are "somewhat classical." His wife admits to having a penchant for "popular novels, easy to read and to get into." Conjugal consensus seems to revolve around the regular acquisition of encyclopedias. Otherwise, there remains a degree of cultural inequality in terms of both quantity and level.

The wife describes her husband as "an avid reader"; he, by way of excuse for his wife, explains that she spends a lot of time in sporting activities and listening to music, which he regrets doing "not often enough." Their separateness with regard to the management of their cultural resources is further underlined by a lack of communication in this domain. In fact, the couple refused to be interviewed together on this subject. They each simply stated that their attitudes were quite different on this matter:

Do you often discuss together what you read?
—The wife: "No, not really. Anyway, my husband reads quite different things than I do."
—The husband: "Rarely. No doubt because we don't read the same sorts of books."
Would you like to talk about them more together?
—The wife: "If we don't discuss them, it's because we prefer not to."
—The husband: "Why not? But it's no problem if we don't talk about what we read."
Do you know what sorts of books your partner has been reading recently?
—The wife: "No. I'm not really interested in what he reads ... Sometimes he mentions a title or says, 'this book's interesting,' but that's all."
—The husband: "Not really. All I know is that my wife reads a lot of novels."

This marriage functions without cultural capital being shared in common because of the wife's disinterest. She has less academic capital than her husband, and they avoid the risks of any explicit discussion of this difference between them. This kind of avoidance, which regulates family interaction, is commonly found within a marriage partnership. Silence keeps the team together, particularly as here, when it is a question of a disagreement not between two legitimate taste preferences, but of a disagreement between a legitimate taste preference and "the other." One of the problems that often arises in questions of autonomy and that is often hidden is visible in this case: the centrifugal forces within a marriage are contained, but at the cost of maintaining inequalities between the partners.

Inventory 4

For some couples, however, reading habits change when they marry and become a shared activity. The creation of a reasonably large common fund, however, does not imply that the wife's capital immediately increases. This occurs from an inventory of the reading preferences of a couple who have been married for ten years. This husband is a building construction supervisor (with a BEI in building construction), while the wife is a junior-high-school teacher (high-school graduate plus teaching CAP). The number of books they possess and have read is far greater than in the previous cases. The wife's library is related mostly to her professional activity (publishers' examination copies, scholarly books, textbooks), but she also has a few novels such as *L'amour en plus* by E. Badinter and *Le lit défait* by Françoise Sagan. The husband owns and reads history books, the complete works of San Antonio, and some paperback novels (particularly J. Lartéguy and P. Benoît). Their common capital comprises books acquired through mail-order book clubs, which they choose together, and also some comic-strip books, which the husband buys. Nearly two-thirds of the books they own and have read together are in this last category. The couple's shared taste for the stories and pictures of writers and illustrators such as Hergé, Franquin, and Morris and Goscinny have made this interaction possible. The husband is in a subordinate cultural position (he was quite uneasy during the interview) and prefers to read material that he can understand.[4] Moreover, the comic-strip genre is not easy to classify, making it more difficult to identify the respective partners' positions in the cultural hierarchy. This compromise between their scholarly and popular reading tastes soothes the husband's sensibilities and at the same time creates an area for conjugal interaction. The wife's capital is therefore modified without its value being significantly reduced. There has been a transfer of capital with neither profit nor loss.

Inventory 5

Sometimes a woman's book capital increases. Two conditions need to be met for this to happen: the woman's initial capital needs to be smaller than her husband's and the couple needs to share a taste in reading matter. This is the case of a couple in which the wife, after graduating from high school and then working as a medical secretary, returned to school to become a social worker. The husband, with a master's degree in philosophy and an engineering diploma, calls himself an "accounting teacher"—in other words, he is a lecturer in economics for a bank. The wife's father worked his way up to executive status in a government-owned company, her father-in-law is a pharmacist, and her mother-in-law is a dental surgeon. They have been married for eight years and have two young children. They have a busy social life and are active members of a political party and a human-rights group.

Of the total number of books in the household (399), 56 percent belong to the husband alone and he has read 46 percent of them; 24 percent are the wife's and she has read 17 percent. The inequality of their academic capitals is reflected in their choice of books, number of books purchased, and symbolic ownership of those books. However, a common fund of books has been created, and the initial differences in reading habits between the partners have been reduced over the years, with the gap between the number of books read by the spouses diminishing during the eight years of their marriage. Before the birth of their first child the husband read twice as many books as his wife if we include books read by one partner only or by both partners and six times as many if we exclude books read by both. After their children were born the wife read as many books as her husband by both indicators. But even though, relatively speaking, the wife increased the value of her cultural resources to a greater degree than did her husband, she still did not reach her husband's initial level. The husband, while passing on to his wife some of the benefits of his own capital, in fact suffered an erosion of it. The compromise reached consisted of a switch from books on political theory (the husband's domain) to books on current affairs and the introduction of a new type of reading matter, that of "leisure reading."[5] The couple came to an arrangement that involved a lowering of their cultural level, as determined by the cultural legitimacy of the books read.

With a few exceptions, the figure at the bottom of the "cultural reading practices" column for all of the above cases involves neither a loss nor a gain for the wife. Each partner remains, for the most part, in control of his or her own cultural universe. Reading habits are not held in common,[6] and this personal autonomy helps preserve both the husband's and the wife's capital resources from any reciprocal contamination. Whereas the child is invested with cultural value through a favorable cultural environment within the family, each partner—being an adult—seems impervious to the surrounding influences. But it is equally true to say that marriage has not brought about a reduction in the value of the wife's cultural portfolio. Neither inventories of the contents of bookshelves nor an assessment of the effects of remarriage on individuals would seem to indicate any serious depreciation in a woman's total value.

A Contradictory Balance Sheet

On the marriage market a widow is considered to have at least a value equal to the one she received in exchange on her first marriage. Overall her marriage has enabled her to preserve her social capital intact. Nonetheless she has not remained completely unaffected. The total size of her capital can stay the same even though its composition may have changed. This is why we can expect a widow's value on the labor market to depreciate, given the conditions under which she is investing. Many women under the age of sixty do not have jobs when their husbands die, unlike those women who have been divorced from their husbands. Social security or welfare payments do not make up for the loss of indirect income. Thus a great many widows find themselves in poverty after losing their husbands (Lopota 1979). They are then forced to take jobs, sometimes for the first time. They do not do this under the most favorable conditions, partly because of the need to earn money quickly and partly because of some women's resistance to the idea of paid work, which contradicts their definition of the feminine role.

Loss of professional value

More than other women, widows tend to hold subordinate positions in the job hierarchy. Among women aged 40 to 50, half of the widows, two-fifths of the divorcees, one-third of those married, and three-tenths of the single women have jobs on assembly lines or as service workers. The inferior professional position of widows comes from two factors:

—Not only are there social risks resulting from the traditional division of labor by sex in the first marriage, but the fact of not having gone out to work before forces widows to accept jobs requiring few qualifications.

—The risk of widowhood is greater in certain marriages—for example, a laborer's wife has a greater chance of being widowed earlier than the wife of an executive (Desplanques 1984).

The effects of marriage that result from the absence of a direct increase in value cannot therefore be singled out from the complex overall picture that emerges from the risk factors listed above. To measure only the loss in professional value caused by widowhood one can compare widows and married women who have assembly line or service jobs while keeping academic qualifications constant. Among women who have a high-school diploma, half of the married women and three-quarters of the widows are employed on an assembly line or as service workers. Regardless of academic qualifications, widows have a subordinate position more often than married women. Unlike married women who have always had salaried jobs or who return to work under relatively favorable conditions, the main objective of widows looking for a job is a steady income. The following interview with a forty-nine-year-old widow who had not gone out to work before the death of her skilled worker husband is evidence of the criteria adopted by job-hunting widows: "I went to the town hall; I went to see the mayor. They found me a job as a cleaner. For example, I work in schools and day nurseries. I've just done a month at the swimming pool." She hopes to have a fixed job at the town hall. "I'm definitely going to have a permanent job—if I can find one. A full-time job, so I can have a regular income. I applied to the town hall to have a job as a home help. That's not a bad job, but you do two hours here, three hours there— when the people get sick you don't go anymore. So I don't think I'm going to do that. I'm going to try and get a job either in an office or as a daily help. The main thing I want is a steady wage" (Lefaucheur 1982).

The cost of marriage—already too high for some women, compared with single women or married men—increases when the husband dies. The returns obtained from their education are fewer for widows than for married women. A more careful scrutiny of the internal structure of categories of female assembly-line and service workers reveals the extent of marriages's negative effects when it is suddenly brought to an end by the death of the husband. One-third of widows who work and have a high-school diploma are assembly-line workers, as compared to just one-twelfth of married salaried women.[7]

Widowhood increases the cost of marriage in that it forces stay-at-home wives to embark on employment, which did not feature in their original plans. The professional recycling of such women is all the more difficult for the fact that women do not easily accept the consequent new vision of themselves. Widows cannot be grouped with divorcees (as they often are with single-parent families) because for divorcees their distant relationships with their former husbands and their removal from the traditional divisions of labor roles are intertwined. This is where the reason one studies widowhood to focus on the effects of marriage becomes clear: marriage remains a handicap for women even when it is over. Indeed, it is then, because of the need to find a job, that its cost becomes most evident.[8] By removing the "academic qualifications" variable one can illustrate the loss of value that widows suffer.

Contradictory effects

The recognition of widows' social value on the labor market is not the same as their recognition in the remarriage market:

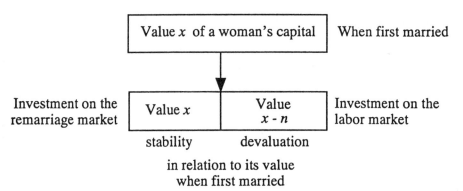

| Value x of a woman's capital | When first married |

	stability	devaluation
Investment on the remarriage market	Value x	Value $x - n$
		Investment on the labor market

in relation to its value
when first married

the first denies the widow's previous value, while the second confirms it. In my view this contradiction is a sign of the ambiguity of marriage when examined from the point of view of its effects. Contemporary marriage usually gives the wife access to the husband's capital at the cost of devaluing her own professional capital. A woman's social and cultural portfolio is not homogeneous. Certain parts of it, particularly those involving work, suffer a loss of value, others do not (see figure). The husband's death and the ending of the marriage partnership make this heterogeneous nature of the effects of marriage and the simultaneous existence of two types of capital with different values all the more transparent. A marriage partnership creates a split in the wife's capital resources that can be detected in the case of widows by the separation between the capital that loses value on the labor market and the capital that retains its value on the marriage market.

All kinds of relationships

Social relations capital is also affected by the ambiguous effects of marriage. This particular capital forms part of a woman's total capital reserves, and its value is directly related to the social and cultural capital of those individuals classified as "friends." A woman who has senior executive friends has a greater social relations capital than one whose friends are humble workers. Theoretically this transfer of value operates the same way that the creation of friendships system resembles the falling-in-love system: mutual feelings are engendered and maintained, usually between individuals with comparable social or cultural capital. The modifications in her social relations capital once a woman is widowed are directly related to the accounts register of her long-standing, recent, or former friends of both sexes. Her social relations portfolio consists of the following:

—Old friends from prewidowhood days who are still friends
—Old friends with whom contact has been lost since widowhood
—New friends, postwidowhood, and still retained.

In the following set of examples, the widow interviewed has provided for each male and female friend a description of the person's professional and academic levels, social origin, age, marital status, sex, and a brief history of the friendship (when they first met, how often they see each other, the depth of the relationship). With this information we can estimate the changes in a widow's social relations capital.[9] Her choice of new friends and her selection of old friends reflect the dual nature of her value.

The traces of marriage after ten years of widowhood

Our first example describes the evolution of the social capital of a sixty-year-old woman who has been widowed for ten years. She has completed only elementary school and was trained as a dressmaker. Her parents were ordinary workers. After her marriage she did not continue to work and followed her husband during the course of his numerous changes of employment. Initially he had trained as a notary's clerk, but during the war he had joined the Resistance and subsequently had a brief military career. For twelve years he was stationed in Africa (Morocco, Senegal, Guinea) but eventually became the manager of a food production plant. On their return to France he held similar positions in four different towns until his death.

After he died this woman's general social relations capital became more mixed. The new friendships that this woman has struck up have a low cultural value since they consist principally of a married couple—a retired laborer aged seventy-five and his wife, eighty, who had kept a shop; both of them had also completed elementary school. The widow visits this couple briefly every day, sometimes staying longer over her knitting. The old friends that she has retained have a greater cultural value in relation to the overall value of her friends before the death of her husband. Among them is a fifty-five-year-old single woman who is highly educated and has a job as a senior executive. What had been originally neighborly contact turned into friendship. The widow goes out in the evenings with this friend and takes vacations with her. The need for new contacts with people resulting from her bereavement has been met by individuals socially quite different from her, almost as if the substitutes for her husband and married life—the functions of a partner and a daily point of reference—do not have the same value; it seems as though this woman, while preserving her previous social capital (in quality if not in quantity, since fourteen people are classified as "old friends no longer seen," twenty are "old friends still in touch," and five are "recent") can no longer strike up friendships with individuals possessing a fairly high value. Here a decline in value coexists with the retention of value.

The second example concerns a widow of fifty-eight, at the time of the interview working as a service worker in a high school. She has a school-leaving certificate and her father was an immigrant laborer from Spain. Her husband, who was a high-school graduate, had his own fishing vessel. Their three children are a skilled technician, a social worker, and a forest ranger. Since the death of her husband this woman has maintained and even increased the value of her social relations capital. The capital, in terms of new friends acquired since her husband's death, is greater than the capital of old friends retained, which in turn is greater than that of old friends lost. To be more precise, the level of value varies according to the sex of the friends: her female friends have a lower cultural value than her male friends. The husband's position in the partnership is reflected by the dominant position held by men in her social relations. This dominance persists with new friends as well as old friends. She insists on having male friends with a reasonably substantial academic capital, as if in some way they are a substitute for her late husband. In contrast, she pays less heed to the cultural quality of her women friends, and one wonders why such an imbalance exists in the composition of her cultural relations capital.

Duality of networks and ambiguity

The third case sheds light on these contradictory developments. It concerns a forty-year-old woman who has been a widow for two years. Her late husband had worked his way up with the minimum qualifications to the position of assistant principal of a junior-high school. His death was apparently related to depression brought on by overwork and problems associated with his job. He had studied at a university for a time and his wife has the elementary certificate of the BEPC. She had not worked throughout their married life, part of which had been spent in Algeria, and since the death of her husband she has found employment as an office worker.

This widow's present social capital exists on two levels. The first, which dates from before the death of her husband, comprises five couples; one of the men is a teacher like her husband. The second level, which postdates her husband's death, is very heterogeneous, consisting of on one hand a married man who is a well-qualified literature teacher and on the other two unmarried female clerks. This woman has selected as her "special friend" a man who outwardly seems to resemble her late husband (with perhaps a slightly larger capital) and as her confidante a woman whose cultural and professional interests compare with her own. This woman, for whom widowhood has meant social relegation,[10] has chosen as a female friend a person who reflects her present situation and as a male friend someone who represents her desire, conscious or otherwise,[11] to begin a relationship with a man whose social capital is at least the same as her first husband's.

This woman regards her widowhood with feelings of regret, and yet she also experiences a sense of freedom. She hesitates and cannot choose—"I was happy in my marriage and I'm happy now"—between the two contradictory feelings: the satisfaction obtained through her husband's social status ("What is at stake for a wife who does not go out to work is social status; I was in a prosperous social environment, so I gained as an individual... My husband's job enabled me to improve myself"), and the welcome discovery of independence through having a job. Being on her own "has enriched me in a way, forced me to look outwards, has opened up new horizons... My husband was stifling me... being a stay-at-home housewife somehow seems much more timid than being a working woman."

The composition of her social relations capital reflects this ambivalence. Her desire for contacts with married couples and her relationship with a new companion who resembles her first husband do not exclude the need for friendship and solidarity with single women from a social level inferior to the one she shared with her husband. The duality of this woman's situation as the former wife of a senior executive who has become a working woman and the duality in the network of friends correspond to each other. Downward mobility— through a late entry into the labor market—coexists with her attempts to resist that trend.

Capital conversion

To some degree marriage alters a woman's "portrait." Certain colors lose their intensity while others retain their original freshness. The first effect leads us to denounce the corrosive feature of the institution of marriage; the second prompts us to be thankful for the preserving side of family life. But both of these effects fail to take into account one very important element, namely the dual and contradictory nature of marriage and married life.

The above examination of the social value of widows should lead one to realize that women are not generally impoverished by marriage. Otherwise, how could a woman whose first husband was a senior executive possibly marry, on becoming a widow or a divorcee, a second husband with a social value equal to the first? This retention of value shows that, from this particular market's point of view, a woman does not lose her initial capital value. Nevertheless, it would be unrealistic to forget the cost of marriage in terms of job prospects. A stay-at-home housewife married to a senior executive cannot by dint of her husband's position consider herself to have equal standing with him, whereas a woman senior executive could be considered to have every right to demand a senior-executive husband on the marriage market. Indirect gain in value via a husband is less easily converted into another form of capital than direct value obtained through a job. For a woman the path leading from the social recognition of capital worth through paid work to recognition via the choice of husband seems more easy to tread than the one that goes in the opposite direction. Direct gain in value through work and indirect gain in value through a husband can be related by a criterion of transferability. The capital invested in the first of these two markets can also be invested in the second with the same returns. The reverse is not true, however. This is why social success achieved solely through marriage can only be guaranteed to continue, should the marriage end, by a further investment in the marriage market. Marriage implies remarriage for women whose social value depended entirely on the value of their husband.

The cost of the marriage balance sheet puts the capital invested in the marriage market in the safe sector, while the capital invested in the labor market is at higher risk. The protection of a woman's capital is only partially guaranteed during and after marriage, and then only on condition that women possessing it continue to invest in shares on the marriage market. Investment in marriage—particularly if it is a woman's sole investment—makes her dependent on being married (Zick and Smith 1988). The highest cost of marriage lies in this difficult switching of capital. In its most dominating form, marriage functions like a banking system that gives a reasonable return on the deposits that women make, but one which demands in return that its clients remain totally faithful to it. They can change from one bank to another, as is shown by the possibility of remarriage, but they must stay within the matrimonial banking system, otherwise they run the risk of losing their initial investment. Marriage only pays out to those women who continue to believe in it—or at least pretend to believe in it—as an institution.

6

Two Models: Conjugal Collectivity and Female Autonomy

Each year I expect fifty-two delights and fifty-two sorrows—about one of each a week. I keep careful count. If I receive a nice letter, a visit from a close friend, if my husband is particularly affectionate towards me, I note down these moments of happiness; I also note down any act of injustice that does me wrong, any hurtful calumny, etc. These two accounts exist more or less in parallel; sometimes one is in front, but the other soon catches up, and from one year to the next, my accounts always balance.
—Readers' letters, *Le Petit Echo de la Mode*, 1907

THE conjugal family, which came into general existence at the end of the eighteenth century, is based upon two principles: the primacy of affection in both the conjugal and child-rearing relationships, and task specialization on the part of the husband and wife. It might seem that these statements are mutually reinforcing. After all, the stay-at-home housewife model is justified in the name of love. From the point of view of a woman's social relations, however, the two principles directly oppose each other. A woman's advantageous investment in her husband's and children's accounts demands stability within the marriage. If the division of labor between the married couple is not to prove dangerous for the maintenance of the woman's capital value, the couple must remain together. However, love accentuates the fragile nature of marriage; changes in one partner's feelings towards the other do not guarantee solidity within marriage, particularly now that French law no longer prevents divorce.[1] The breakup of a marriage partnership clearly shows the cost of marriage, particularly for a stay-at-home housewife. When divorce occurs, the closing of the husband's account threatens the growth of a woman's capital resources and starts the vicious cycle that marriage represents for women: love calls for a woman to manage her capital independently, whereas the fact that a housewife works at home means that this management is being handed over to someone else.

So what do women do when confronted with this inherent contradiction in marriage? They resolve it by choosing one of the options available to them. There are two types of marriage that exist side by side and that reflect two different ways that a married woman (or cohabitant) can handle her accounts. In the first, the fickleness of human feelings and the basic instability of marriage demand that she should put greater emphasis on her professional investments. How could anyone invest all of her capital in one husband if she was not, from the outset, sure of the solidity of a matrimonial investment? A diversification of investments would make individual autonomy within the marriage more likely. In the second kind of marriage, confidence in her partner and in the permanence of the relationship must be a *sine qua non* if reliance on her husband as her agent is to be possible and even desired by a wife. The scenarios that the interviewees of our study completed show us that these two marriage types are not only in opposition with regard to the value accorded to a married woman going out to work, but also with regard to the nature of the exchanges of capital between the partners. The ways in which financial, social, and cultural resources are distributed within a marriage partnership are inseparable, at least theoretically, from the ways in which they are accumulated.

Two Conceptions of Marriage

In order to describe the way in which individuals perceive marriage and the defense of a woman's interests, I have borrowed Goffmann's concept of territories (1973). All individuals possess a certain number of territories—both symbolic and material—that they watch over and whose borders they defend. Among these, for example, are the contents of their pockets, bodies, and thoughts. When interacting with others, they have to relinquish, at least temporarily, one of these territories in order to make interaction possible. This relinquishing of territory is, as Goffman says, "the symbol and the very substance of the relationship" (1973, 69). On the other hand, a rebuffed advance (in the form of an inappropriate question, for example, or an aggressive gesture) is immediately construed as an attack and must be met with a similar response.

How is a marriage, then, perceived by the proponents of these differing world views? Which territories must a partner "relinquish" and share with the other? Which ones can be protected without seeming to be a bad husband or a miserable wife? Which are the resources—income, authority—that need to be held in common? Which ones can remain (or become) the exclusive property of one partner? Can what many people consider normal behavior be offensive to others? Is having a job a woman's right, an inalienable part of her capital, or is it an encroachment on a masculine prerogative, made even worse by her desertion of a woman's "natural" territory?

Social and sexual differences

The removal of barriers between marriage partners is sought more by men than by women (aged 25 to 40). In general men claim to be more in favor of the sharing of capital and personal property. They cannot conceive of vacations without their wives, and they are more ready to compromise about where they should be spent. They also indicate clearly that the financial resources they provide for the family also belong to their wives. Their conception of conjugal communication is more dogmatic, however, and they are less reticent about the principle that "married couples should tell each other everything."

However, this tendency to share is not as uniform as these indicators might seem to suggest. Thus, when it comes to sharing domestic decision making, women are more egalitarian than men. But it is particularly with regard to women going out to work that men are more jealous of their prerogatives: women should give up their jobs if it interferes with the husbands' careers or they should not necessarily take full-time jobs.

While males can share, particularly when it comes to the distribution of financial resources, they also claim supremacy in two masculine territories, authority and salaried work. This dichotomy is also reflected in their replies to the reduction in inequalities between partners. Men approve of such reductions when they are in their favor—deciding which partner should be able to attend evening classes, for example—and oppose them when they are not, as when they further the career interests of the wife over the husband's. Men and women do not see marriage in quite the same way and define their respective roles differently. Men strongly emphasize the partners being together outside of working hours and on the maintenance of sex-specific tasks (specific to each partner) Women value personal autonomy, even if it means that the traditional distribution of tasks is disturbed to some degree.

Even though marriage creates a common legal framework for each partner, the relationship that individuals have with their domestic universe depends on their social class. Working-class couples have a larger area of shared participation and therefore less individual autonomy. They reject the right to separate use of leisure time and the freedom to keep private thoughts from their partners. For these couples only one domain falls outside the principle of shared activity—that of the responsibility for the family's income. Faced with a choice between the wife working full time and the husband having to work longer hours, they opt for the second solution.

The sharing of conjugal responsibilities that working-class couples clearly favor does not mean that there is an equal distribution of resources nor that there is any confusion about sex roles. They accept the fact that married women receive an unequal share of family savings (which might go towards the acquisition of a motorcycle, for instance) and leisure time (housework must be undertaken by the wife, even if she works parttime). Moreover, these couples greatly stress the differences between the sexes; paid work is the man's domain. This respect for "traditional" sex roles does not indicate resistance to change; rather it reflects the role played by sexual identity in the definition of a positive social identity (self-esteem) (Mauger and Fossé-Poliak 1983, 1986; Schwartz 1990). A survey of the sex-specific territories of middle- and upper-middle-class couples reveals another type of conjugal organization: "pockets," areas that are vigorously defended by each partner and yet at the same time an area—such as the world of salaried work—that is no longer exclusively a man's domain.[2]

According to the psychologists (Moscovici 1972) social actors do not like to live in the middle of contradiction; they also resolve in their own fashion the ambiguities of married life. Some opt for stability in their marriage and a strict division of labor between the partners; others, aware of the fragile nature of the marriage partnership, look for a redefinition of that division. The first group is predominantly working class; the second, middle and upper class. Twice as many working-class wives as those with university degrees claim to have married "for life" and have considerable difficulty envisaging divorce. At the same time they agree with the unwritten law of marriage that says it is the husband's responsibility to provide for his wife and family (Kellerhals et al. 1982). The paean to marriage without end has a verse that refers to the housewife and the song of love has a line or two about working women. These familiar refrains praise two different ways in which a woman's capital can increase in value. In the indirect way the wife shares in the resources her husband brings from the labor market; in the direct way each partner contributes to the acquisition of the resources. Behind these songs are two secondary themes. The first song promotes marriages where everything is held in common except the two masculine domains of authority and providing for the family, while the second song values autonomy except in the work domain, where sharing is absolutely essential. If we had to title these songs we would probably call the first "The Hymn to Domestic Communism" since it corresponds to what Max Weber (1971) described in the following fashion: each partner makes the contribution of which he or she is capable according to one's talents and gains pleasure from seeing his or her needs fulfilled without calculating how things are shared. The second song, in contrast, could be titled "The Hymn to Anti-Communism." The demand that each partner should have a great deal of autonomy implies a blurring of masculine and feminine characteristics, whereas the insistence on the primacy of conjugal fusion depends on very differentiated sex roles.[3]

For Goffman, voluntary renunciation of material or symbolic territory forms the basis of the relationship. It is the sign by which interaction takes place or continues. If we were to continue to examine superficially the claims we have just been looking at, we might well believe that for certain social actors being in a marriage partnership should in no way modify the definition of personal territories. For the partisans of autonomy marriage should not change their lives; they refuse vehemently any annexation of personal territory in the name of love and marriage.

The theme of autonomy—with its dogmatic insistence—must not be allowed, nonetheless, to drown out the lyrics of other songs. These are the songs that propose the principle of conjugal parity instead of the union of two egocentric individuals, with each partner holding back from a total embrace. The desire for autonomy does not negate the sharing principle, but moves it into other areas and disguises it. This becomes evident when we examine the arguments of the proponents of intellectual and behavioral autonomy and those of the "pro-fusionists" (the "tell-each-other-everything" and "do-everything-together" camp). The autonomists prefer to choose solutions that maintain equilibrium between husband and wife with regard to power, cultural resources, the undertaking of domestic tasks, and access to paid work.

These two polar opposites—autonomy and fusion—cannot describe accurately the different perceptions of marriage, even if the words themselves (as "in preserving one's autonomy," for example) are useful as explicit reference points for the social actors. When questioned about less-familiar themes the autonomists reveal their interest in the marital sharing of financial or cultural resources, domestic tasks, and decision making. Conversely, the degree of conjugal fusion insisted on by the other camp does not go quite to the limit since they are in favor of the husband working fewer hours overall, having a greater say in decision making, and having priority in the choice of cultural opportunities. These two groups—the fusionists and the autonomists—have a point in common, despite their divergences. Their perceptions are constructed in the same way: the insistence on the abolition of certain barriers and certain personal property is directly linked to the possession of other territories or other personal domains. Neither conjugal program is characterized by the simultaneous desire to offer the sharing of leisure activities, an acceptance that one does not have to tell a spouse everything, and the function of family provider.

THE ROLE OF WORK

The fundamental essence of the doctrine of marriages where everything is held in common revolves around the

question of working women. No sooner has a newspaper published an article either for or against stay-at-home housewives
than a battle is engaged through letters to the editor. For
example, when Jacques Roudy announces that "stay-at-home
wives are vegetables," women immediately rush to defend
themselves: "I am not a vegetable when my children get home
from school and call out 'Mom, where are you?'; I'm not a
vegetable when I make the house cozy and welcoming for the
whole family, when it's pretty, a place where they feel at home
and that they want to come back to. I'm not a vegetable, or if
I am it's one you put in a soup, one that blends in with all
the others and smells good and warms and nourishes you,
and that everyone loves whatever their station in life."[4] These
arguments around a woman's "vocation" to keep house are
heated because at stake is the entire conception of married
life and the defense of the wife's interests. This much is clear
from the arguments and counterarguments of the supporters
and opponents of working women.

Belief

A belief in the right of women to go out to work can be
identified through the following question: "In your opinion,
in a family where the children are of school age, does the fact
that the mother goes out to work offer more advantages or
disadvantages?" I call those who reply that it offers more disadvantages the "nonbelievers" and those who see more advantages the "believers."

To declare that you are in favor of women being able to go
out to work does not necessarily imply that you are in favor
of both partners having equal opportunity to work. In the
scenario where the wife's choice of a full-time job brings her
into conflict with her husband's choice of work, only one-
third of the believers back the wife against the husband. The
two-thirds of the believers who hesitate to back the wife seek
a middle way out of the dilemma that is not spelled out in the
scenario. In the example of the unemployed husband being
offered "a good job some distance away," one that involves the
family moving and means that the wife will have to give up
her present job, almost a quarter of the believers want the
husband to take the job but the wife to keep hers as well. The
increase in value of a woman's capital through work seems

not to be as essential as the corresponding increase for a man. In the event of conflict between the increase in value of the two capitals, even those in favor of women being able to go out to work often support the man. Equal opportunity in the work sphere cannot be assumed even though both partners share the function of provider.

Autonomy, whether behavioral, intellectual, or financial, is an essential element in the conjugal ideology of those backing working wives. Twice as many believers as nonbelievers approve of partners not telling each other everything. A preference for a clear division in the types of tasks undertaken by marriage partners joins a preference for nonspecialization in leisure activities. Conversely there is less criticism of specialization in professional activities according to sex where there is less criticism of conjugal "togetherness." When one partner prefers the beach and swimming and the other enjoys mountains and hiking, the nonbelievers consider that the couple should compromise: the partners should alternate the type of vacation from year to year or spend half the vacation by the sea and the other half in the mountains; come to an agreement about where to spend the vacation; or opt for a completely different type of vacation. Failing that, they prefer the problem to be solved to the husband's advantage. This rejection of separation during vacation or leisure periods implies a decision accepted by both partners. Moreover, this situation is frequently used in game theory (Luce and Raiffa, 1957). For example, a married couple decide to spend an evening out. The husband wants to see the big fight, the wife wants to go to the ballet. But most important they want to go somewhere together. This game, called "the battle of the sexes," revolves entirely around the principle of "togetherness" and the compromise that necessarily must ensue. Indeed, if neither of the partners is ready to concede, they are both losers. When confronted with this situation, the nonbelievers are characterized by their refusal to allow the partners to act autonomously and by the decision-making powers that they attribute to the husband. Six times as many nonbelievers as believers say that as a last resort the husband should decide. The need for decision making inherent in conjugal togetherness demands particularly that the husband should exercise authority within the marriage partnership.

Believers and nonbelievers cannot agree about the delimitation of common territories; the former in regard to the work domain and the latter with regard to confiding in their partner and leisure activities. Those in favor of women going out to work consider the type of partnership propounded by their opponents as a barrier to one's personality development. Retaining the right to keep something from their partner and being able to use their financial resources (by having separate accounts) without the expenditure having to be approved by the partner seem to them to be inalienable rights. Nonbelievers, on the other hand, view any sharing of the role of provider as a feminine encroachment on a masculine prerogative. Not everyone defines what constitutes a good marriage in the same way. This is why the life style of those who are against women working is perceived negatively by those who approve of women having a job. The convictions of the former are in direct opposition to the beliefs of the latter.

The everything-held-in-common theory advanced by the nonbelievers is sometimes put out of joint. When a married couple in which only the husband goes out to work has an argument about how to spend their money—the wife wants to take a cruise, for example, something they have both dreamed of doing, whereas the husband wants to buy a motorcycle—those not in favor of wives going out to work back the husband and see no reason why the money should be spent on both partners. If this choice seems to contradict their fusionist position, it is nonetheless in perfect accord with their ideas on how resources and responsibilities should be allocated. The decision to give the role of provider to the husband is closely linked to an inegalitarian conception of the marital relationship. Husbands have certain advantages: they do not have to do housework and consequently work fewer hours overall (professionally and domestically) than their wives; they can improve their qualifications even when they are married to someone less well educated than they. For those who favor a strict division of labor between partners, marriage does not result in husbands and wives being affected in exactly the same way. In a marriage where the husband is the dominant partner culturally, the wife has to step aside and allow her husband to further his education. The husband is singled out for preferential treatment. It is he who assumes the responsibility of going out to work, and it is he who in return is given the opportunity to increase his value on the labor market. In "sharing" marriages between nonbelievers the husband's value is heavily protected. The "separatism" in marriages between believers implies that there will be a redistribution of opportunities between the partners so that neither suffers to the advantage of the other. A married woman's social and cultural value is not protected in the same way by believers and nonbelievers. Among the latter, the husband is given an advantage because he has the job of accumulating the profits in which his wife will share. It is only logical that the husband should be given all the means to do that. Among the former group, neither partner is denied access to the working world, and as a consequence there is no reason for the husband to be favored since he is only one half of an equal partnership.

In practice

There is, in general, very little change from the declared views (for or against wives going out to work) to what happens in practice (do both you and your spouse go out to work?). The differences between those couples where the wife goes out to work (practicing), and those where she does not (nonpracticing) closely resemble those between couples who declare themselves either for or against wives going out to work.

It is not the fact of wives going out to work that divides couples into different camps. For example, one-third of the husbands with working wives put it on the debit side of the balance sheet ("wives going out to work results in more disadvantages"); as many also put it on the credit side. The question of autonomy separates the two groups far more, with working-wife couples rejecting the "togetherness" model of marriage. On one point—the question of children—working wives can be distinguished from nonworking wives far more clearly than their husbands, however. Two-thirds of working wives and only one-third of nonworking wives (under age forty) consider that a marriage can still be successful without children. This success—perhaps synonymous with happiness—is possible, as far as working wives are concerned, without the marriage partners becoming parents. Is this evidence of a substitution effect between direct and indirect enhancement of value, or is it more a matter of recognizing the constraints that children place upon a woman's professional career?

Practicing couples see marriage as a negotiation between

two autonomous partners that is based on relative equality. The decision to have an equal say in financial matters and in access to cultural opportunities is evidence of less importance being attached to one's gender. The husband is no longer seen as the "head of the family," having a monopoly of the right to have a job and priority when it comes to the creation of cultural capital. Nevertheless, this shakeup of the conjugal regime is not a complete one. In the event of marital conflict about work, couples where both partners go out to work take the husband's side or refuse somehow to cast their vote. They are no more likely than nonpracticing couples to preach the principle of genuine equality between husbands and wives when it comes to access to career opportunities. The sharing of the role of income provider does not mean that the cards are redistributed between the two partners. A wife never has as good a hand as her husband; she always needs to be his partner and to share in the points he wins. A wife's management of her own capital resources is still deeply rooted in dependence on her husband.[5]

Codes of good conduct

The domestic world is haunted by the specter of ambiguity. A marriage partnership presents the contradictory demands of love on the one hand and specialization according to sex on the other. It also has contradictory effects on a wife's capital: marriage helps maintain her matrimonial value, but at the same time it causes a decline in her value on the labor market. The individuals involved, however, do not simply accept this dichotomy passively. Depending on their academic capital, social position, religious beliefs, or political persuasions[6] they create various forms of regulation of their marital relationship that emphasize certain ways the family is organized.

In particular, couples devise different forms of exchange within the marriage partnership. For some, the husband—who is seen as the main income provider—needs to have as much capital as can be mustered to be able to guarantee as far as possible the family's social and economic status. For others, a concentration of means in this way is less necessary since both partners can lay claim not only to having a job but also to improving their personal capital. The scenario involving a couple in which the partners are competing to be able to continue with further studies shows how each of these two conceptions advocates an entirely opposite means of resolving the conflict. When couples favor conjugal collectivity the husband has to provide all or almost all of their financial resources. Consequently he has priority in the acquisition of cultural resources. When couples favor autonomy both partners have to contribute to the household's income and the husband's priority for cultural acquisition is no longer guaranteed.

This rejection of masculine priority is only an infringement of the rules for those men or women who recognize their validity in the first place. For the others, nothing untoward has taken place since such a rejection is contrary to the laws of conjugal equality. It is as if the marriage highway were filled with individuals using the highway signs of different countries. The result can be accidents and symbolic battles between sexes, generations, and social classes; it also complicates the work of the researchers who are trying to monitor marital behavior. Thus, by which sociological code should researchers assess the conduct of the social actors and the cost of marriage? Whichever code they operate by, whether inadvertently or not, they favor the individuals closest to their own value systems and discredit the others. Is that really the function of researchers? Shouldn't they point out the ambiguous nature of marriage, even if it involves having the accounts audited? Indeed, to do just that, one would have to point out the degree of importance attached to each section of the accounts to decide if the wife's indirect gain in value via her husband is equivalent to her capital gain from her job. When confronted with two women who initially had identical capital resources (one, married to a junior executive, is herself a junior executive; the other, wife of a senior executive, does not go out to work), should the researcher say which of the two has made the best investment of her academic capital? Not making a definitive judgment does not mean that the sociologist considers them to be equal. They are clearly different, as we have already seen, in the different ways they reconvert their capital value should the marriage come to an end. The first woman is less dependent than the second on her value being recognized a second time on the marriage market. The effects of their respective marriages are not the same, nor are their value systems. The first woman, with a job, has a much greater chance of achieving personal autonomy and management of her own capital resources; the second, not having a job, will prefer a "sharing" domestic relationship. If these contradictions do not cause chaos within a marriage partnership it is because to a certain extent people end up having the kind of marriage that they wished to have. Two elements, however, threaten to disturb these arrangements. For the partisans of domestic togetherness the devaluation of qualifications and severe unemployment make it more and more necessary, if only for a while, for married women to go out to work (Barrère-Maurisson 1982). For partisans of self-management, the almost nonexistent move towards a fair division of labor between the sexes (as evident, for example, in the low level of sharing of domestic tasks) prevents equality on the labor market. Neither of the two main strategies employed to resolve the ambiguities present in marriage is completely successful: they both continue to survive, however, and are the source of the dynamics of the different domestic arrangements.

7
The Benefits of a "Good" Marriage

As soon as it is a question of marriage men hide their true colors, replied Mme Latournelle, and women do likewise. For as long as I can remember I have heard people say: "Mister or Miss So-and-So has married well." Does that mean that the other person has married badly?

—Honoré de Balzac, *Modeste Mignon*, 1884

JUDGING by what has been written about so-called good marriages,[1] people might be forgiven for assuming that sociologists are spoilsports. Instead of rejoicing, the experts predict the separation of such couples. Marrying well from a woman's point of view means living with a man who has greater capital resources than she does and entering a heterogeneous union. Marriage counselors, however, assume that a heterogeneous marriage is fundamentally fragile. Cultural and social similarities encourage consensus and mutual agreement, whereas basic differences between partners cause dysfunction. This assumption is often found in sociology manuals on the family, perhaps to demonstrate the validity of social norms. Homogamy, which occurs most frequently, is perhaps a guarantee of a lasting marriage, and woe betide anyone who strays away from the diagonal matrices of marriage!

In *La maison du chat-qui-pelote* (1829) Balzac gives us an example of a union between two quite different individuals. Augustine Guillaume, the daughter of a cloth merchant, has married a painter, Théodore Sommevieux, who has a much greater cultural capital than she. After an initial period of happiness Théodore grows tired of his wife's errors of taste. She offended "her husband's vanity, when, despite her efforts, she allowed her ignorance to show through, revealing her de-

148

ficiencies of language and the narrowness of her intellect...
His wife did not respond to poetry; she did not live in the
same world; she was unable to follow in his steps ... she in-
habited the real world with her feet firmly on the ground,
while he had his head in the clouds... and so he began to feel
a certain coldness towards her which could only grow more
intense. . . . With every day that passed the veil between them
grew thicker and thicker." Augustine, forever conscious of her
cultural shortcomings, tried to "change her character, her
manners, and her way of doing things," but despite reading
book after book she could not reach a state of "complete union
of her soul with Théodore's." Is this story typical? The fact
is that the fragility of marriages between partners who are
culturally and socially heterogeneous has by no means been
proved. The assumption is based upon rather weak empirical
evidence (Glenn, Hoppe, and Weiner 1974). Some American
authors rather ironically have pointed out the example of male
sociologists. Those married to a woman from a different social
background are no more likely to get divorced than anyone
else would be. In fact, the lowest recorded divorce rate is
among men from a low social group who are married to
women from a high social group. For them, marrying well
does not turn out as badly as sociological theory would have
us believe.

What are the consequences, then, of marrying well when
viewed from the standpoint of the defense of a married
woman's interests? Compared to other wives, does a woman
who is involved in such a marriage gain or lose from it? Do
the excellent returns that seem to accrue at the outset of the
marriage continue to be maintained? Does the social success
of landing a husband with considerably greater capital mean
that marriage is therefore less costly for the wife? Or, on the
other hand, is it simply that the higher cost of such a marriage does not become apparent until later? The answers to
these questions are not clear: the effects of marriage on a
woman's capital are ambiguous and so is a good marriage.
The giving up of their personal accounts is more frequent for
women who have married well, but when they retain their
personal accounts marriage pays them extra dividends. The
price to be paid for marrying well, in terms of a career, is
sometimes higher or lower than the price paid for an ordinary
marriage. Over a period of time an excellent matrimonial

investment can sometimes turn out to be either a good or bad deal.

THE MANAGEMENT OF A "GOOD" MARRIAGE

A good marriage amplifies the normal effects of marriage. By marrying well a woman is more likely to lose some of her independence. For a married woman, having a job depends on the returns she gets from her academic capital on the labor market. Three-fifths of women with substantial academic capital who have married an executive and three-quarters of women with the same academic capital who have married manual laborers or clerks go out to work.[2] Women who have made a good investment of their academic capital on the marriage market are subsequently less likely to invest that capital on the labor market.

A good marriage means early retirement. Women who have married up are more likely to be stay-at-home housewives. Do women who have married someone on their own level therefore try to make up for having acquired, by comparison, an "inferior" husband by going out to work? Does the evident shortfall in their choice of husband lead them to prolong their involvement on the labor market? Or are these women concentrating on the acquisition of status through their work, in contrast to women who have married well and who are seeking status through their marriages?

Quite different from the compensation and specialization hypotheses, a third theory can be advanced. A woman who has married well is living with a man having greater capital resources than she possesses. In her subordinate position she is unable to insist on keeping her personal account open. In contrast, a woman who has married down has more substantial capital resources than does her partner. Because of this inequality in her favor she retains direct control on her own capital, all the more so for making a significant contribution to domestic income and thereby compensating for her husband. Therein lies the negative side of a woman's of marrying well: the higher the returns from her matrimonial investment, the fewer her chances of being able to go out to work and the greater her dependence on her husband. This reveals the limitations of those studies that only identify women's social mobility at the moment of marriage. Should a woman who marries an executive and gives up working be considered to have made a better investment of her capital than one who, with the same amount of academic capital, marries a clerk and continues to work? Which one has gained the most? Once again we are faced with the ambiguities of the effects of marriage. It almost seems as if, to make a good investment in the marriage market, a woman subsequently has to forgo any direct management of her capital. Women who reveal themselves by their marriage to be strategically very shrewd are, paradoxically, the ones who then give up the management of their professional affairs, preferring to rely on their partner. The women who seem to be less clever at choosing a marriage partner are the ones who insist on continuing to manage their own capital. But this insistence is necessary if these women are not to be handicapped all their lives by an inferior investment in the marriage market. By continuing to go out to work they are able to have a life style comparable to that of women who have made a better "catch." Having accounts in their own names makes up for the income deficiencies from their husband's account, whereas women who have married well are encouraged by the interest earned from their husbands' accounts to close their own.

Women in subordinate positions

An individual who has married well is more dependent on his or her partner. When applied to the different marital situations, resource theory (Blood and Wolfe 1960) says that the partner having fewer capital resources (the one who has married well) is less likely to be the decision maker and therefore the dominant partner. This is what seems to happen to Georges Dandin, a peasant who has made a lot of money and who marries a "lady." He later regrets his choice:

"My marriage is indeed a salutary lesson to all those peasants who want to rise above their station, and like me, marry into a family of gentlefolk! There is nothing wrong with nobility in itself ... but it carries with it so many problems that you are better off having nothing to do with it. I am now a wise man, but at a price! I would have been better advised, as rich as I am, to have married someone of good peasant stock, rather than to take a wife who feels superior, cannot stand to bear my name, and who believes that for all my wealth I have not bought the right to be her husband. Georges Dandin! Georges Dandin! What a fool you have been! No bigger fool exists! I find my own house unbearable now, and every time I walk through the door some misery or other greets me."[3]

Is domination the price to be paid for marrying well? If so, the tangled web of attempts to have control within a marriage partnership must result in the partner with the greatest capital emerging as the winner. In order to show how married couples themselves perceive the outcome of these power struggles I used the classic questions on the sharing of tasks and decision making. The wife was to answer two series of questions. The first set involved household chores such as "Which one cleans the floors, does the dishes," and so on. The second group of questions dealt with decision making: "In every partnership, decisions affecting family life have to be taken. Quite often husbands and wives discuss things together, but very often one of them makes the final decision. Can you tell me who makes the final decision about where you will spend your vacation, about improvements and changes to the house or apartment?"

Replies to the twenty-four questions put to the couples make it possible to construct different types of domestic organization.[4] Interestingly enough, couples in which the woman does most of the household or associated tasks do not all operate in the same way. We can distinguish particularly between "senior executive or manager wives" and "small business-type wives" on one hand and "housewives" and "subordinate wives" on the other hand. In the first group women have the power: the important decisions—about raising the children, the choice of apartment, of friends, of where to spend vacations— and the lesser ones about equipment—changes and improvements to the home, which household appliances to buy— come within their sphere of influence. The territory of "housewives" and "subordinate wives" is limited to the everyday housekeeping and shopping decisions, while the big decisions are taken after discussion between the partners. One of the most influential factors explaining this duality lies in the relative size of each partner's capital resources. A wife who has a more substantial cultural capital than her husband makes more decisions than one having a lower academic capital than her husband.

A good marriage gives a woman, whatever capital resources

she may possess, the impression of being excluded from the decision making. Twice as many women who are high-school graduates and who have married a university graduate end up being "housewives" and "subordinate" wives, compared to those at the same academic level who have married non-high-school graduates. The form that the marriage relationship takes stems from a symbolic power relationship between the partners, which is in turn determined by the type of marriage contracted. The larger cultural resources that a woman may have at her disposal enable her to take a dominant position, or more precisely, to extend her sphere of influence beyond that traditionally considered to be a woman's domain. By contrast, possessing a smaller cultural capital than her partner keeps her enclosed within traditional spheres and reduces her influence in other areas related to family matters. Marrying well, according to the accepted social criteria, condemns a woman to conform subsequently to her husband's wishes. Her failure to acquire power is ambiguous, however, since it usually means the woman has been successful in terms of upward social mobility. By leaving the decision making to her husband, a woman who has married well finds herself conforming to the norms of an individual who is her cultural superior. Her family circumstances have improved, compared to her reference (or original) family. In terms of the defense of her social interests this loss of power on the part of a woman who marries up does not necessarily constitute a defeat: is it better to have power or to be subservient to a partner better endowed with resources? Are the gains to be made in power capital equal to those to be made from an excellent but indirect source of capital? Studies in domestic power (McDonald 1980) often forget to inquire into the way marriage partners perceive conjugal rivalry. There is no point in designating winners and losers unless what is at stake socially in this battle of the sexes is clearly defined. Women who have married well and who admit to not having very much say in important decisions affecting the family are not only the victims of an unfavorable power relationship. They are also "dominated" because it is in their interests for the conjugal program not to be drawn up by them alone. An excellent indirect gain in value via their husband requires a sacrifice. Conversely, women who have married down are in a position, thanks to their superior capital, to construct their families as they see fit and thus do not suffer any losses. The

154   THE AMBIGUOUS EFFECTS OF MARRIAGE

way in which capital is exchanged on the marriage market is important because it determines to some degree the couple's objectives and the ammunition available to each partner in this battle of the sexes.

Higher interest

Women who have married well are more likely than other women to assume the role of a stay-at-home, subordinate housewife, but not all of them fit this mold. Some women who have pulled off a good deal on the marriage market nonetheless continue to go out to work. They are characterized by the higher returns they receive on the job market from their academic capital. Their marriage to a man with greater capital resources than their own seems to create the right conditions to encourage emulation and socialization on their part, with a resulting increase in their chances of obtaining job promotion. Among the working wives who continued their studies until the age of twenty-four, two-thirds of the ones who married well and one-sixth of those who contracted an ordinary marriage have jobs as senior executives.[5]

Men have an identical correlation between the type of marriage contracted and returns on job investment. Among employed married men who have continued their studies to the age of twenty-four, 80 percent of those who have married well become senior executives, compared with 50 percent among those who have married a partner of similar status.

An excellent indirect increase in value via one's partner and a similar one in direct value through one's work are largely compatible for employed men and women. Among government employees, more than one-third of the women who are daughters of junior executives and who have married senior executives have "category A" status (senior executive level), compared to only one-tenth of those who married a junior executive.[6] For those women (and men) who have retained their personal accounts, marrying well does not rule out the possibility of a good deal on the job market. It is possible to do both. However, the strong correlation between the type of marriage and the returns on job investment cannot always be ascribed to marrying up. A woman who has chosen (and been chosen by) a partner who is academically richer than she is no doubt has other resources that are not so easily discernible in the context of a study (such as aesthetic and social relations capital), the positive effects of which become apparent only later in the marriage. Nonetheless, there is no doubt that a wife who goes out to work is not deprived because of her choice of husband. At the same time, marrying well does not remove all hope of a woman having a successful professional career.

The cost of marrying well

Earlier I defined one of the prices that women pay for marriage in terms of the return on her academic capital on the labor market compared with the return earned by a married man. This cost varies according to the type of marriage partnership involved. When measured by the relationship between the probability of a man and a woman becoming a senior executive, the cost is reduced when an individual marries well. The women who convert more advantageously their academic capital into matrimonial capital more closely resemble men than other women in terms of their professional careers.[7]

When women have pulled off a good deal on the marriage market they lose less on the labor market if they continue to invest their academic capital there. Marrying well reduces the disadvantages created by the fact of being married. There is less difference between men and women who have married well than there is between men and women who have entered into an ordinary marriage. Which sex gains more by marrying well? It is difficult to say for certain because self-selection by women who have married well is greater than among other women, since the former are less likely to have a job. Women who have married well continue to work, particularly if they obtain a good return from their academic capital. When there is a clash between their good marriage and their investment in the labor market, they prefer to stop working. Their higher expectations, as evidenced by their choice of partner, extends also into their professional activities. By contrast, women who have married less well continue to go out to work, even if it is less profitable.

Self-assured women

Women who have married well are different from other women in that they manage their capital resources differently long after the moment when they chose their partners. What explains this difference? Is it that the former concentrate more on the indirect improvement of the value of their capital, which requires the best possible return from their matrimonial investment? Women who have married well and who continue with their careers nonetheless also get higher returns on the labor market. Is it perhaps more a question of specific competence, not possessed by all women, such as a greater skill in social negotiation? Nevertheless, all things being equal, some women manage to promote themselves better, personally and socially, and to induce a readier acceptance of their value on both the matrimonial and labor markets. There are more women who have married well among this group. The fact that they do not have the final say at home does not invalidate this interpretation. They are subordinate to their husbands because they are the main prop to their ambition. Paradoxically they give way to protect their social advancement. On the other hand, such acquiescence on the part of a woman in the working world would stand in the way of her ambitions. If this hypothesis is valid, then women who have married well should make better use on the labor market of their talents for skillful negotiation to promote their interests. This particular talent of self-projection is linked to another indicator—insistence on one's rights. Mueller, Parcel, and Pampel (1979) measure this degree of self-assurance by a woman's "support for equal rights," determined by her replies to four questions:

—Should a woman have exactly the same career opportunities as a man?
—At work, should a man refuse to work under a woman?
—Should men and women receive equal pay for equal work?
—Should women and men be considered equally for positions of responsibility that are usually considered to be in the male domain?

This self-assertion, which is linked to a refusal to accept male domination in the professional domain, varies according to the type of marriage. The highest scores for insistence on rights are registered among those women who have succeeded in maintaining their matrimonial value.[8] The women who get the best rate of exchange for their capital on the marriage market demand to be treated equally with men. They insist more forcibly on their rights than other married women. For them, marrying well is not an end in itself; it is no more than a stage in the process of improving their social status. A significant enhancement in their value via their choice of husband is not enough, it is simply the springboard towards another domain to be conquered—the world of work. During their lives these women, to defend their interests, adopt apparently contradictory attitudes: they are submissive at home and dominating at the office. For them the marriage balance sheet is in the black, thanks to the addition of the interest from their professional activity to the interest acquired from the account in their husband's name. By contrast, the balance sheet is more ambiguous for those women who do not work and who represent a significant proportion of the women who have married well. Their success in their choice of husband leads them to give up working; having a job seems, in their eyes and the eyes of their husband, to be demeaning and devaluing. They concentrate on the domestic domain, but even then they cannot genuinely claim to be "mistress of the house" without endangering the indirect enhancement of their value.

Is a "Good" Marriage Really Good?

Marrying well is a form of insurance against the risk of disappointment with married life. This type of marriage is in fact more satisfactory than other types. Marital strife, as assessed by questions put to individuals concerning their feelings about their married life (Pearlin 1975), varies on the type of marriage. There is less strife for those who have married well. Women who have married up are more satisfied with their married lives than are those who have married down. In addition, the former are happier in their relationships than are their partners. Similarly men who have married well are less conscious of marital strife than are their wives. The individual who marries someone with more substantial social capital has a more positive attitude towards his or her marriage, whereas the spouse who has married down admits to being more disappointed.

Marrying well does not seem to exclude the possibility of having a good marriage. Partners whose marriages have resulted in upward social mobility are the most contented with their domestic lot. When marriage enables one of the partners to improve his or her social position in relation to family background, the result is a greater attachment to the other partner, who has been instrumental in bringing this about. Conversely, a partner who in marrying was not able to sufficiently protect his or her capital value views this as a relative failure and describes the other partner and their life together in negative terms.

The alchemy of love

Marrying well does not, however, automatically mean that one's marriage and partner can be seen through rose-tinted glasses. Only those people who are most preoccupied with social success have a rosy view of things. The correlation between the type of marriage contracted and satisfaction with one's marriage only makes sense by reference to the importance the social actors attach to their upward social mobility (what Perlin calls "social striving"). Good marriages only bring increased satisfaction when the individuals concerned have a positive impression of upward social mobility. The most flattering description of one's partner is given by those people for whom social success is most important.

The individuals who admit to attaching a great deal of importance to their social status and who have demonstrated it by their choice of partner describe their partner as being an attentive listener, someone in whom they can confide, having "therapeutic" qualities, and extremely supportive.

There is one area, however, in which the descriptions are not necessarily glowing—that of sexual relations. People with greater social aspirations and who have married well do not obtain greater sexual satisfaction from their partners than do others. Does this mean, perhaps, that sexuality enjoys greater independence within the conjugal exchange system, or is it that partners concerned about upward social mobility are less interested in sex?

With the exception of sexual relations those individuals who have been instrumental in helping their partner improve their social status are deemed to have the necessary qualities that make a good husband or wife. Conversely, those who are not interested in social advancement have a lower opinion of a partner owning more capital than they do, generally preferring someone who resembles them more in terms of social value. Indulgence towards one's partner depends, therefore, on two factors: the individual's relative position within the marriage relationship and the importance attached to social success. Those who, intent on improving their social status, succeed in that aim by contracting a good marriage will credit their partners with a range of positive attributes. In such cases the partner's superior social value is magically transformed into personal qualities. An individual who has married badly will have been successful in personal relations, but not socially or culturally. Their unfavorable matrimonial exchange becomes positive when viewed from a different angle. For the persons who have married well the reverse is true; they live with someone with whom they are highly satisfied but who, in return, views them critically.

Sensitive women

By a process of social alchemy the persons who have enabled their partner to realize their dreams of upward social mobility are guaranteed to be accredited with wonderful personal attributes. Is this rose-tinted view more likely to be found in women or in men? We need to be aware of the sex of the individuals concerned since marriage is viewed differently by men and women. Both sexes do not attach the same importance to marriage as a means of acquiring social status. While for women, even if they have careers, marriage constitutes one of the principal pillars of social identity, for men it plays a more modest role in determining social status. A man who values his status is in a position to invest less in his relationship with his higher-status partner since he does not consider it to be the best way of bringing about his upward social mobility. Women, on the other hand, feel more indebted towards their partners and consequently feel more affection towards them.

Even though the incidence of a relationship between partners turning sour and antagonistic is less common among individuals who have married well, women experience such deterioration more than men. In terms of the frequency of marital conflicts, the difference between women who have married well and those who have not is greater than between men in the same situation (in the subgroup of individuals concerned about upward social mobility) (Jorgensen 1977).

Women experience a conversion of their social gains into emotional benefits more often than men do. For them in particular, perceiving married life to be a source of conflict would be incompatible with marrying well. The women who are dissatisfied with married life because of discord are found more among those who, although they had high aspirations, contracted an ordinary marriage (three-quarters admit to frequent disputes) and those who, despite having low aspirations, nonetheless married well (two-thirds). By contrast, the unhappy are less frequent among those who had high aspirations and married well (one-quarter) and those who had low aspirations and contracted an ordinary marriage (one-third).

The mismatch between social aspiration and its realization can produce profound dissatisfaction and dysfunction. For example, women who are fairly unconcerned about improving their social status but who have nonetheless married a man of higher status than their fathers admit to experiencing a great deal of marital conflict. Unconcerned with the process of social differentiation, they are no doubt more oriented towards family life and perhaps disappointed by the attitude of their husbands for whom work plays a central role in life. Their definition of a "good husband" is different from that of their partners, whom they think put too much emphasis on their role of financial and symbolic providers.

In marrying well the spouse is more likely to consider the marriage good when the choice of partner is the most important factor in the value enhancement of his or her personal capital. Since an indirect increase in value through a husband is greater than that through a wife, women feel more reason to be grateful than men do, and their gratitude is expressed in their indulgence towards the provider of their enhanced social capital. Ambitious women who make good catches are considerably less aggressive towards their partners. The following account by Nadine de Rothschild (who came from a much lower social-class background than her husband, Edmond) illustrates this process: "I have been a part of Edmond's life now for twenty-four years... I make the very most of the incredible luck that life has dealt me. But I have never lost sight of one thing: I do not see myself as a rich woman; I am the wife of a rich man. I take nothing for granted. You have to take great care of the things you hold dear, lest one day you find your treasures broken." She also tries to go along with whatever her husband wishes: "Horse-riding is a perfect example: he likes it, so you like it. Like sleeping with the window wide open even when the snow is drifting in... I go along with whatever he wants; I never nag him. I just soldier on and do whatever he wants." Sometimes his friends, who have a higher social background than she does, express surprise: "How do you put up with it?" She does not complain: "I am housed, fed, cared for, and I'm very grateful to him." She accepts that her husband is the master of her fate. Without him she goes back, as she puts it, "to square one." She puts up with her husband's need to "surround his expressions of tenderness and concern with numerous barbs, like roses among thorns" (de Rothschild 1984; 221, 208–9).

For a man, even though the difference is less evident, a good marriage has its enchantment. The fact that his identity as "head of the family" might be undermined by the social gap between the partners does not seem to bother him in the marriage: a husband's dissatisfaction with marriage does not increase when his wife is from a superior social background (Richardson 1979). Tolerance of one's partner is a characteristic of husbands and wives who have made the kind of marriage that matches their aspirations. This indulgence on the part of those who marry up makes sense in that it is extremely difficult for them to opt out of the marriage. The social success represented by their marriage encourages their tolerance. They wish to avoid the possibility of separation and have difficulty even considering it, since there is no guarantee of being able to pull off such a good match a second time.

The balance sheet of a good marriage is ambivalent, as is marriage itself. A woman who has married a man with a value greater than hers protects her interests both better and worse than does a woman who has married a man of equal or lower value. Even if a good marriage does not preclude the possibility of a woman obtaining an excellent return from the labor market, it certainly limits the possibilities. Fewer women who have married well go out to work, and as a consequence their objective dependence on their husband increases. Moreover, even if a good marriage results in an excellent indirect profit via the husband, the price to be paid for this upward social move is greater subservience since women who have married up feel that they have less power within the marriage partnership.

For a woman the price paid for a good marriage is not automatically higher than that for an ordinary marriage. As always, everything depends on the "direct outcome" column on the balance sheet and the way it is expressed symbolically within the marriage partnership in terms of personal autonomy and dependence.

Part 3
Love and Capital

Introduction to Part 3

THE reader will remember that love has been eliminated in order not to falsify the accounts. Assuming that love (or hatred) is a capital resource meant that I could not attempt to discover if a woman's social value was maintained by marriage. I did not wish to define pleasure, joy, or an affectionate exchange of looks between a married couple as momentary illusions that hid the price women had to pay for marriage, nor did I wish to assume *a priori* that a cultural gain was the same as a moment of happiness or that a social investment equaled an emotional one. Ignoring love in marriage does not mean that emotions do not have their effect on the management of the partners' social resources.

In reality, the two areas are definitely connected, as Monsieur Le Trouhadec, the hero of one of Jules Romains's novels, learned to his cost. Le Trouhadec, a lifelong bachelor and geography teacher at the prestigious Collège de France, falls in love with a young actress, Rolande. Rolande treats him with disdain until she learns that he has won a fortune at the tables. She tells him, "I love you too... It's not just affection I feel for you; I know myself well. You do believe me don't you? Anyway, a woman can offer proof of her feelings, thank God! Proof that could not leave a man unconvinced." Le Trouhadec realizes that Rolande's love is linked directly to his wallet and does not respond to these belated advances. Rolande becomes worried, fearing that she has rivals:

> "You must be careful. Around here there's a whole host of very dangerous women who are now going to throw themselves at you. They'll tell you absolutely anything. But don't for one minute imagine they are motivated by affection for you! They're just after your hundred thousand francs. Oh! You would be blind, you would be stupid not to see through their little game, and (here she sobbed violently) if you were to sacrifice someone who had loved you long before." (Romains 1924, 98–100)

165

Rolande is not the only one seduced by capital. Our analysis of so-called good marriages has revealed other cases of the alchemy love is capable of creating. If the relationship between value and love always took this simple form, those individuals who find themselves excluded from the marriage market should be the ones with the least capital. In fact, however, single women are the ones who possess the most substantial academic and social dowry. What explains the existence of this particular group of unmarried women? Are they rich women who refuse to pay the price other women have had to pay for marriage? Or does it have something to do with the damaging side effects of the acquisition of academic capital (discussed in chapter 8)?

The amassing of social capital and its subsequent management are not always compatible, from the owner's point of view, with one's feelings. In *Love and Mr Lewisham*, H. G. Wells offers a similar scenario (Wells 1983). The novel's hero, a young man from a modest background, wishes to succeed in life by obtaining a Bachelor of Arts degree. He has his future all planned and follows a strict timetable. He rises every day at five o'clock to study and takes pleasure in knowing that he is three hours ahead of everyone else in his studies. One day he meets Ethel and falls in love. He is convinced that this young woman will be his inspiration and that he will be able to work much harder as a result. In fact, love proves to be a distraction and he has to revise his plans. The university place he had desired for so long has to be postponed. Love, marriage, and career are not all automatically in harmony: the defense of one's social capital makes demands and so does the defense of love. Living together outside of marriage could be viewed as a means, for certain social actors, of reconciling these dual constraints (chapter 9).

8

Celibacy: The Harmful Effects of Substantial Academic Capital

> ... *why* am I a girl? ... here I am with the brains to do
> everything, yet tied to the sinking ship of future matrimony.
> If I were born a hundred years from now, well and good, but
> now what's in store for me—I have to marry, that goes with-
> out saying.
> —F. Scott Fitzgerald, *This Side of Paradise*, 1920

UNMARRIED women do exist. Before the increase in the number of couples living together in the 1970s (see chapter 9),
about 10 percent of all women had not married by the time
they were thirty-five. The celibacy produced by our love-ori-
ented society would *a priori* have the same characteristics as
that produced when marriages were arranged. Love has not
actually abolished the social inequalities inherent in a so-
called good marriage. A senior-executive husband is not
within the price range of every young woman. Marriage is a
"product" that must be also accessible to women endowed
with a minimum of capital. This is what feasibility theory
predicts (Dixon 1971): individuals remain single by being excluded from the marriage market through lack of social capital. Only those with sufficient resources can marry. This is
what happened, of course, when marriages were arranged to
suit the interests of the two families. For example, on a little
Greek island at the end of the nineteenth century, the daughters of Canacares (who owned a large portion of the valley's
agricultural land) were more likely to find a husband than
were the daughters of poor peasants or shepherds (Vernier
1977).

Nowadays the correlation between a woman's value and

167

marriage is becoming an inverse one: the women with the most social or cultural capital find it more difficult to find a husband than do other women. It is as if they try to avoid marriage in the same way that in the past rich men avoided the draft by paying others to take their places. Has marriage somehow lost its attraction for women, despite romance? A woman with substantial capital can escape being trapped into dependence on a husband. This hypothesis does not, however, take into account the fact that unmarried women do try to find husbands, whether through personal classified ads, matrimonial agencies, or singles clubs and vacations. Not all unmarried women are turned off by the idea of love and marriage. Why then are so many rich women unmarried? Why is it, paradoxically, that so many women with substantial academic capital seem to be unable or do not want to invest in the marriage market?

Are Educated Women Dangerous?

Studies on the unmarried often concentrate on men. Being married is usually considered an indicator of a man's social worth since it is the latter that makes it easier for him to marry. The inability to find a marriage partner is one of the most revealing indices of the numerous forms of inadequacy that beset certain social groups, according to Brangeon and Jegouzo (1974, 1978). Poverty encloses the poor in a vicious cycle that deprives them of a particular capital resource, namely matrimonial capital. Matrimonial capital is closely linked to the positive identity that married couples, or couples living together, possess, compared with unattached people. For example, in the opinion of psychology students, the characteristics of sociability and seduction are more often attributed to people who are married (Etaugh and Malstrom 1981).

It is the men with the most substantial capital who get married. Among the 40 to 49 age group (considered to be the group where celibacy is definitive), 34 percent of married men are junior and senior executives when only 17 percent of single men belong to the same social group.[1]

Two factors have a bearing on making men unlikely to marry: working in agriculture and having a very low income. This greater exclusion of agricultural workers from the possibility of marriage is due to the fact that women shy away from the difficulties associated with that kind of work. However, it is the owner-farmers who are the major factor in this, since the likelihood of them remaining permanently unmarried varies according to the amount of land they own. One-third of owner-farmers with fewer than twelve acres are unmarried, compared with 5 percent of those with more than 120 acres. The probability gap, with regard to their chances of marriage, between a rich farmer and a poor farmer is greater than that between a senior executive and a skilled worker (between 40 to 49 years of age).[2]

It is white-collar workers with the highest positions and the richest farmers who are the least likely to be unmarried. A man's social status and the likelihood of marrying are thus directly linked. The reasons for a reduction of marriage chances identified in other cultures and in other times remain unchanged even today, when love is deemed to be an obligatory element in marriage. A man's capacity to choose a partner, and be chosen, seems clearly to be based on the extent of his wealth. The recognition of a man's value through marriage depends on the level of that wealth: the lower it is, the less his chance of investing in the marriage market. Today marriage is a privilege as far as men are concerned. Compared with the average figures related to unmarried men (with a base of 100), the index for senior executives is 32, for skilled workers 79; for semiskilled workers it is 99, and for unskilled workers 200.[3] For men, remaining unmarried is a sort of matrimonial state of unemployment. The marriage market is like the labor market in that the chances of being taken on depend on one's social and academic capital. Just like employers, women seem not to appreciate the charms of men lacking this capital.

Unmarried women and social capital

The correlation between unmarried women and work is different from that of men. Compared with married women, there are more unmarried women in posts at the senior-executive level: 39 percent as opposed to 22 percent.[4]

The nonsalaried professions, on the other hand, seem inaccessible to unmarried women. In the salaried professions, one can find more unmarried women at the higher levels. Compared with the average figures relating to unmarried women (with a base of 100), the single-women index ranges from 92 for plant workers through 173 for junior executives to 231 for senior executives.[5] While, on the labor market, academic capital makes investment easier, on the marriage market the opposite is true. By age thirty-five a woman with a basic school-leaving certificate has a 5 percent chance of being unmarried; for a woman with at least a university degree it is 18 percent.[6]

Women's social inequality in comparison with men when it comes to marriage does not reflect their inequality in the working world. Unlike men, women with very substantial capital find it more difficult to find a husband. Men's and women's matrimonial and professional chances are in direct opposition to each other. The fact that among executive and highly intellectual jobs there are more married men and unmarried women than unmarried men and married women is not only because of the effects of marriage. The matrimonial selection processes are not the same for men and women. The "stocks" offered on the marriage market reveal this quite clearly: the men and women available vary widely with regard to their capital resources. Dating agencies conceal this imbalance to attract qualified women as clients. Their window displays—in the form of advertising—promise men who are also executives or highly qualified. But the window display is deceptive and is not a true reflection of the goods on sale inside. To tell the truth would discourage potential customers. This is why one woman with a university education who enrolled with such an agency received details of only five prospective partners in four months, whereas a man with comparable qualifications received 150 in the same period (Duteil 1979).

Marriage seems to be a capital resource of a rather ambiguous kind, and most accessible to the richest men and the poorest women (see table 8.1). Male executives find it easier to find a marriage partner than male laborers; in contrast, women executives are more likely to be single than women manual workers. The principle of the "matrimonial minimum" does not apply in the case of women; it is rather more a question of the "matrimonial maximum," beyond which marriage chances grow rarer. Unlike the highest academic credentials, which are sought by men and women with the greatest social capital, marriage is sought by women who are the most impoverished socially and culturally. Our analogy of

Table 8.1
Percentage of Married Men and Women, by Profession

Profession	Married men	Married women
Manual laborer	88	92
Middle-level professional	95	85
Executive	96	82

Source: INSEE population census, 1982, for ages 40–49

marriage as a financial investment is less appropriate for women than it is for men.

Why is it, however, that the correlation between capital possessed and conjugal investment is inverted according to the sex of the individual concerned? Why are women who possess considerable capital less likely to enter into marriage? Three contradictory answers to these questions can be suggested. Women with considerable capital resources are more likely to remain unmarried either (1) because they are less able to make a good investment on the marriage market than other women; (2) because they refuse to invest in a market they consider to be too risky; and (3) because their offer of marriage is likely to be rejected by men, who see them as too dangerous.

The impossibility of upward social mobility via marriage

Some sociologists (Rubin 1968; Glenn, Ross, and Tuly 1974) believe that for women marriage operates "from the bottom towards the top"—in other words, it involves upward social mobility. Women try to find a husband who can guarantee them upward mobility because they are less likely to achieve that aim through their own work, given the fact of sexual discrimination in the workplace. Social mobility takes different forms for men and women. The former achieve it through the labor market and the latter through the marriage market.

The extrapolation of such a hypothesis enables us to understand why men with poor social value remain unmarried. The choice of a husband from this group prevents a woman from realizing any upward mobility, real or imagined. George Orwell points out that a tramp "is condemned to perpetual celibacy. For of course it goes without saying that if a tramp finds no women at his own level, those above—even a very little above—are as far out of his reach as the moon. The reasons are not worth discussing, but there is no doubt that women never, or hardly ever, condescend to men who are much poorer than themselves" (Orwell 1933, 204). This question of social mobility through marriage throws a great deal of light onto the handicap experienced by men with few capital resources, but it does not explain why women with considerable capital resources are similarly handicapped. Why do these women who can make a success of a career attach so much more importance than other women to upward mobility through marriage? On the marriage market, since they are competing with women with fewer capital resources, they should be able to be chosen by (and choose) the wealthiest men. The reason why women remain unmarried therefore remains a mystery.

A woman's lack of interest in marriage

The feminist theory of C. Delphy (1974) helps to explain why women with substantial capital remain unmarried. Delphy believes that men grab the benefits of marriage for themselves and leave women to foot the bill. This is why women avoid marriage when they are in a position to do so. A realization of the negative effects of marriage leads women with substantial capital in particular to reject it. Conversely, men with few capital resources find it difficult to find a wife since they have little to offer in exchange for the services that a wife can offer.

Women do not remain unmarried for the same reason as men. By not marrying a woman frees herself of the domestic responsibilities entailed in looking after a man. For a man, on the other hand, marriage frees him from these same responsibilities. Selection on the marriage market (Mueller and Campbell 1977) reflects these opposing interests. The wealthiest women can opt out of paying the price of marriage, while the poorest man cannot take advantage of the benefits it has to offer. If this theory of marriage as a form of exploitation enables us to explain why marriage chances are unequally distributed, the theory of marriage as a form of domination also leads us to make similar predictions.

A man has nothing to gain in marrying a highly qualified woman

As perceived by feminists, female celibacy is self-exclusion; it is an expression of their rejection of marriage. But from a functionalist point of view, which considers the husband as the authority figure in a marriage (Parsons and Bales 1955), highly educated women who remain unmarried are seen as having been excluded. They are less frequently chosen as partners by men on the marriage market; they are a threat to domestic harmony. They usually have a career and are opposed to the necessary division of labor between a married couple, and their resources provide ammunition for them to "stand up" to the head of the household.

Men do not appreciate highly educated women; from their point of view they disrupt harmonious relations between husband and wife and thereafter the husband's authority. Some of the data on choice of marriage partners reveal the existence of these masculine fears. For example, some students hope to have a wife whose educational level is beneath theirs (Flamenco 1967). The actual differences in academic capital between partners shows that men have a marked preference for women who are culturally inferior. The prospect of a more highly educated wife leads men to feel that she will take charge in the marriage partnership (Segalen 1980), an arrangement they find intimidating and an affront to their masculinity. Ms. Duteil, unmarried and highly qualified, noticed this aversion when she was looking for a potential partner: men were frightened of her reputation as an "intellectual." She interprets this description, when used by men, as meaning "difficult to dominate."[7] One man with a professional career, when invited to her home, asked if she was really a woman: "I see you surrounded by so many books that I begin to wonder whether you are truly feminine, if you are interested in other things." On another occasion she had invited a divorced senior executive to her home, and he too expressed similar unease, as their dialogue shows:

"I'm afraid of not being up to your level from a literary point of view. For example, I've never read Pascal's *Pensées*, which I can see on this bookshelf, nor most of the books next to it, and I honestly don't feel like starting now. Could you live with a man who has not read the same books as you? I never forgave my wife, for instance, for not sharing my enthusiasm for art. But I don't think I could stand one who was more knowledgeable than me in certain fields. In fact, in my opinion the man should be the dominant figure in a marriage partnership. How do you feel?"

"I don't expect a man to be a walking encyclopedia. Indeed, I think a relationship is successful when a couple can replace domination by dialogue and exchange; the aim of a relationship should be the mutual development of both individuals, not the subjugation of one by the other."

"You're putting words in my mouth: domination is not the same thing as subjugation; it means that an individual imposes himself naturally through his authority and influence. A man who can do that earns the respect and admiration of his wife because she is happy to follow his guidance and example."

"It seems to me that your wife didn't particularly appreciate being dominated by you!"

"It's because I didn't really manage to that our marriage failed. But from the way you're talking and from the way you want to prove me wrong, it's quite clear to me that we could not get on together."

A woman's academic capital can be an asset in the marriage stakes insofar as it is appreciated by certain men. A woman with substantial academic capital, knowingly or not, presents a certain image of herself that means she is less likely to be considered "a real woman." According to F. Dorin (1984), "This category is made up of women who are 'feminine'; these can be subdivided into hookers, wives, and mothers. They want to be dependent on men; they have not responded to changes in social attitudes; they gain certain advantages from this male domination and accept its drawbacks." To be identified as likely to want to "wear the pants" increases a woman's chances of not attracting the attention or the affection of the opposite sex. According to this view, highly educated women are a dangerous group that men, even when highly educated themselves, try to avoid.

Do women with substantial capital choose to take themselves off the marriage market or are they excluded from it? The special case of female celibacy can be explained either by the feminist theory of "domestic means of production" or by the theory of male domination. In both cases the failure of "superior" women to marry is explained by the differences in what the two sexes have to gain from marriage. Not marrying, according to the first theory, protects women from the risks that marriage entails, whereas the second theory states that it is single men who are protected from the risks of marriage. These two interpretations have a second factor in common: they explain the inequalities between the sexes with regard to marriage and life as a single person exclusively by what is at stake strategically. Some men reject marriage with highly educated women to protect their sexual identity; some women, if they have sufficient means, turn down offers of marriage to maintain their independence.

These strategic analyses, however, forget the specific constraints of the marriage market. If some people do not marry it is not necessarily because they refuse what is on offer (the "means of production" version) or because of the lack of success of certain products (the "male domination" version); rather, it can also be the result of a malfunctioning of the matrimonial distribution circuits. The fact that many highly educated women remain unmarried is also related to the mismatch between the time needed to produce the goods (the acquisition of degrees) and the most opportune period to enter the market. Certain stages of an individual's life are more conducive to romance and marriage. Timing has its part to play in matrimonial affairs.

THE UNSYNCHRONIZED CALENDARS

Women remaining unmarried is not something that began with universal education in France. More than a quarter of the women with at least a university degree and born between 1920 and 1924 were still unmarried at age thirty-five—three times more than the women who had left school at fourteen. When talking about their pasts these women, many of them high-school teachers, indicate the mechanisms in operation that gradually led to their single state. Often they maintain that they did not remain unmarried by choice—"celibacy is never a vocation," according to one teacher—but that the realization that they would never marry crept up on them gradually (Cacouault 1984). Having completed their studies and found their first jobs they discovered that marriage was not that easily accomplished since the men they might well have married were already spoken for. They found themselves in a matrimonial desert, having passed the normal marriageable age (at least in the eyes of society). In my opinion, highly educated women remain unmarried as a result of a mismatch between the time it takes to obtain their education and the most advantageous time to be on the marriage market. The demands made of an individual in acquiring a higher education and the norms associated with the marriage market are incompatible: the former require individuals to put off marriage while the latter urge them to find a partner before it is too late. Women with substantial capital remain single because they try to invest in the marriage market too late, given the requirements of the marketplace. There are three elements that support this interpretation of why women do not marry:

—the average age at which people marry, and what happens if they do not respect the norm;
—the difference between the age at which men and women marry;
—the difference between the average age at which women with little capital marry, compared with the age at which women with substantial capital marry.

Unmarriageable age

Not every period in an individual's life is an opportune moment to find a marriage partner. Marriage takes place within certain limited periods. In the past in France, any young woman who went over the "normal" age limit was publicly singled out at the feast of Saint Catherine. Young women in this situation saw themselves as unable to find husbands and excluded from the possibility of marriage, so they would pray to Saint Catherine (Segalen 1981):

> You are our last hope
> You are our patron saint
> On our knees we beg you
> Help us to marry
> For pity's sake, find us a husband
> For we burn with love.

Even if this tradition is rarely followed nowadays, it still matters at what age women marry. Even if women officially can marry at any age, in reality the age at which they do marry is within a very limited period. A television commercial for one beauty product shows that when people meet a woman they give her a certain age and by implication assume whether she is married or not:

"Do people still address you as 'Miss?'"
"To tell you the truth, it's very nice to be still called 'Miss' when you've got two children."
"Admit that it doesn't surprise you. In fact, you've got the secret of how to remain fresh and young-looking... O.. of O.. If *you* want people to go on calling you 'Miss,' use O.. of O.. every day!"

The pleasure felt at being called "Miss" comes not from the fact of having avoided marriage but from having avoided the ravages of time. It is the married woman who is happy to be called "Miss"—"still young for her age"—whereas the same form of address for an older unmarried woman can mean "still single at her age." The commercial expresses both the value accorded to the woman's youthfulness and the existence of a "normal" age for marriage.[8]

The period of time during which a woman needs to find a husband is limited, as is shown by the figures relating to marriage age in any given year. One-third of the women who marry are under the age of twenty-one,[9] half are under twenty-three, and three-quarters under twenty-six. The marriage ages of men also fall into a short period. They are, on average, two years later than women. One-third of the men who marry in any given year are under twenty-three, half are under twenty-five, and three-quarters under twenty-eight. This relatively short time period considerably reduces the marriage chances of anyone advancing beyond what is considered a marriageable age. Only one-third of single women aged 28 to 29 will be married before the age at which demographers consider them to be "permanently single" (forty years). Marriage opportunities are directly related to the period when a woman is a candidate for the marriage market; for those who invest heavily in a career or in the acquisition of academic capital, the risk of missing the boat (if marriage can be seen as an opportunity) is great.

Those women not respecting the marriage age norms end

up paying a price that can be roughly calculated in terms of their chances of marrying once the "maximum age" has been passed. These individuals, as a result of being older, will find it more difficult to find a partner. The marriage chances of a single woman diminish very rapidly the older she gets. Once past the "unmarriageable age"[10] the single person is in danger of remaining permanently single. Whatever their age, divorcees have a greater chance of remarrying than do other single people (Glick and Norton 1971). At a given age, one is better off already having been married if he or she wants to find a marriage partner.

Delaying marriage—defined as going beyond the "normal" marriageable age—gradually turns into the impossibility of marriage, whatever the reasons for the delay. For those individuals in this situation, there remains the possibility of transforming this exclusion from marriage by some form of religious vocation or by a last-ditch effort to marry "at all costs." Before the decrease in the number of women joining holy orders in the 1960s, the female religious orders in the Vendée recruited heavily from women who had followed a career in social work and who had gone past the marriageable age (Suaud 1978; Knibiehler 1984). The religious communities were populated by women who wished to avoid the common matrimonial fate of others with a similar academic background—marriage to a peasant farmer—and by women who, by the nature of their jobs, were "expected" to remain single. Today, single women are more likely to have recourse to marriage agencies or to place an advertisement in a newspaper. In the words of one marriage agency director: "After the age of thirty, a lot of women come to see me because they no longer wish to remain single—and 90 percent of them have a job. Seeing their youth disappearing, they are afraid they will no longer be attractive in a few years' time. It is the age when single women experience a crisis that can be summed up in the phrase: 'Not a moment to lose!'" (Leroy 1977, 65).

Despite the poor public image of such agencies—which somehow seem incompatible with a "real" love match—men and women invest in this parallel marriage market in the knowledge that their provisional single status is in the process of becoming a permanent one. This internalization of the functioning of marriage market norms can be seen in the age range of the individuals who place ads in the *Chasseur Français:* one-fifth of French women over the age of twenty are between thirty and forty-nine years old; in the *Chasseur Français* two-thirds of the ads are placed by women in that age group.[11]

After age thirty, single men and women realize the difficulty of finding a partner through the accepted social relations channels (Bozon and Heran 1987, 1988). That does not mean they have given up hope of ever marrying. Once past fifty, they seem to accept the fact of their exclusion from marriage since they publish fewer appeals for a partner. Knowing and feeling that marriage is possible, then knowing it is possible but feeling that it is almost impossible, and finally realizing that marriage is impossible are the three stages in the attitude of single men and women towards marriage. The first stage is accompanied by a random and *laissez-faire* investment strategy; the second by an explicit strategy involving intermediaries; and the third is characterized by the abandonment of all strategies.

Delayed marriage and women's acquisition of wealth

The requirement to marry is more explicit in those cultures and those times where marriage is an indication of the value placed upon women by society. Early marriage has come to be viewed differently as cultural capital as increased. An increase in academic capital delays marriage for both men and women. Women with university degrees marry an average of two or three years later than women who left school at the earliest opportunity. Men and women executives enter marriage later than manual workers. Unlike other markets where the financially richest women marry youngest, academically rich women marry later because the accumulation of cultural capital takes a certain time. A cultural inheritance would, at the very least, have to be recognized by schools before it could officially be considered as cultural capital. It is impossible to acquire academic capital without passing through the different stages of study. Obtaining worthwhile degrees takes time; inheriting land does not.

The acquisition of academic capital is only associated with delayed marriage because of the implicit time period by which marriage has to come after an individual has embarked on a career. For men an old rule that could require them to put off marrying was the need to wait for promotion (Burguière

1972). Sometimes, as in Foucry's 1806 study of the teaching profession, the chronological order in which things had to be done was specifically noted: "A teacher could not marry until he had moved up several grades; marriage for him was, as it was for all men, a prospect for the future that he could only contemplate once he had established himself and his financial future by having a position with an income sufficient to maintain a family" (Julia 1981, 86).

As higher education and paid work became more and more accessible to women, they too were subject to this norm. Marriage was only possible once they had acquired their academic capital. Marriage could only be consecrated when their value had been recognized by the educational institutions and they had begun to work. The end of academic studies and entry into marriage are closely linked. Among the women who married between 1970 and 1974 (for the first time and under age thirty-five), one-sixth of those with the minimum school-leaving certificate married after twenty-three, compared with half of those with a university degree.[12]

Delayed marriage among more educated women is a reflection not only of the normal course of events, but also of their greater investment in the labor market. Conversely, women who wish to be stay-at-home housewives marry younger, since the return on their capital depends principally on their choice of husband, as is noted in a long-term study of single women (Cherlin 1980). The replies to the questionnaire that reveal most clearly, two years later, the difference between the married women and those who are still single, concern the following questions: "What are your future career projects? What job do you see yourself doing when you are 35?" Those women who at twenty-two see themselves as housewives subsequently married much earlier than their colleagues who envisaged following a career. All things being equal, the young women who plan their futures exclusively in terms of marriage and family marry earlier than other women. The women with career plans put off marriage until they finished their studies and found a job (Allen and Kalish 1984).

Women and early marriage

Delaying marriage to acquire academic capital is common to both sexes, but it does not mean that these men and women marry at the same age. Among married executives, six women out of ten married before age twenty-five, compared with four out of ten male executives. On average, there is a three- to three-and-a-half-year difference with regard to the age at which men and women marry. This difference leads to an age gap between partners. In seven couples out of ten the husband is older; in one in ten it is the wife who is older; and only in two in ten are they of the same age.[13] Quite obviously, from the point of view of both behavior and attitudes, the early marriage norm persists among women more than with men. A male laborer marries at age 25.5, his wife at 22.5.

The fly in the ointment

The reasons why women with substantial capital do not marry are more easily understood when the previously noted three factors are taken together. Exclusion from the marriage market results from a lack of synchronization between a woman's academic and matrimonial timetables. In the 1990s the academic and career schedules of both men and women coincide, whereas in the matrimonial world considerable gender differences still exist. Women who start their first jobs under the normal age for marriage have few problems. On the other hand, women who undertake prolonged studies and who attach great importance to a career find that this double investment diminishes their marriage chances: they finish their studies just as the opportune period for finding a partner is coming to an end. The fact that most women continue to marry early means that those who have undertaken lengthy studies are more likely to remain single. Men who have gone the same route do not run a similar risk; their exit from the academic system coincides with, for them, the most propitious time for finding a marriage partner.

Academic capital can turn out to be a burden for a woman by consequently denying her the opportunity of marrying (if she in fact wishes to marry). Because her academic and marital schedules are not synchronized, unlike a man's, a woman who invests the most to obtain academic capital will have the most difficulty achieving any returns on the marriage market. This factor, then, is the most important reason why women executives with university degrees remain single. Once they have finished their studies and started working, their network of social relationships does not include many available men. They are not necessarily without friends, contrary to the dating agencies' insistence on "the loneliness of the modern world," but for the most part they socialize with married couples or other women.

Unlike men, women can acquire considerable cultural capital without being able to invest it on the marriage market. Good academic capital provides added value and increases a woman's chances of exchanging it for a husband who himself has considerable capital, but all this takes place at a bad time for women as far as marriage is concerned. The ideal time to find a husband is during the period when marriage does not stand in the way of the accumulation of academic capital (a risk associated with early marriage) and when the accumulation of academic capital does not rule marriage out of the question (a risk associated with putting off marriage). The exclusion of highly educated women from the opportunity to marry because of conflicting timetables is, moreover, reinforced by an institution that functions with a sexual division of labor and also by the prejudice men have against "intellectual" women. Everything, therefore, conspires to create a paradoxical situation for the choosing of women: it is for the possession of their academic capital that they risk never being chosen nor eligible as a marriage partner. (See the theoretical graph explaining the number of highly educated single women).

Love possible; love impossible

In the twelfth century "true love" was impossible between married couples since they had married for a very different reason, namely self-interest. The following statement by the Countess of Champagne in 1174 describes why such a union was impossible:

> We state and maintain quite firmly that there can be no love between husband and wife since those who are in love are bound to each other quite gratuitously and without any necessity; husband and wife are obliged to respect each others' wishes... their honor would gain nothing if they took pleasure in their union like lovers; and in no way can the probity of either be increased since the way they behave towards each other is no more than

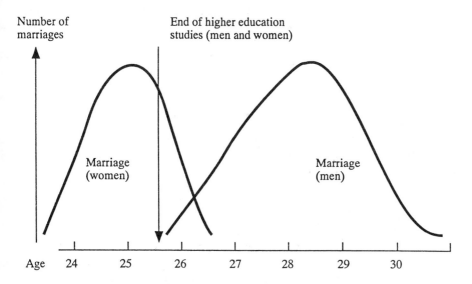

they have engaged to do before the law. This is why, according to this reasoning, we do no more than the precept of love teaches us—namely that no marriage can be crowned with love. (Lafitte-Houssat 1979, 68)

Very gradually throughout the Western world, beginning half-way through the eighteenth century, love and marriage came together (Flandrin 1975; Pillorget 1979; Solé 1984). Too often this fusion is presented as a sign of a change in the function of marriage. Marriages are no longer arranged since what is at stake is no longer the continuation of the family line but the emotional development of husband and wife (Shorter 1977). The history of marriage could be viewed as a rebellion against the yoke of family inheritance and interests and consequently the beginning of a long march toward happiness.

This view is mistaken, however, since it fails to take into account the parallel change that has taken place in the process of social reproduction, together with the growing importance of academic capital (Bourdieu and Saint-Martin 1978). Indeed, it is this change from a system emphasizing economic capital to one stressing academic capital that has made love matches possible. In fact, unlike economic capital, cultural capital is an integral part of the individual; it is invisible and cannot be removed. The conditions required for a love that is both passionate and reasonable are there. A man and a woman can "fall in love" and marry without any social risk. Without them knowing it, their feelings for each other are based on similar cultural values. There is no need for an outside agency since the emotions are usually enough to guarantee a balance between their capital resources. The love process does not contradict the social process; the former backs up the latter in a social system in which cultural capital dominates.

Academic capital, more than economic capital, has been the foundation of what we know as married love. Nevertheless, the harmony between love and capital is by no means perfect. Cultural capital takes a long time to acquire and has to be recognized by the educational establishment. As mentioned above, the time spent in collecting this capital is out of step with the social timetable that love imposes. Cultural capital thus becomes a handicap when it comes to love and marriage. Some women pay a high price for their degrees and their careers, as this letter to a women's magazine column entitled "Heart and Mind" testifies:

> I am 28, with a job—I'm a personal secretary—that I find satisfying. Throughout the period of my studies I had only one thing in mind: to get them finished and then be free. When finally that moment came I quickly thought about marriage... But that's the problem: I have the feeling I'll never find the right man, one who'll suit me morally and intellectually... I am perfectly "normal," well-balanced, and sociable. But there are no single men where I work... I can't accept the idea of remaining single.

The response to this letter indicates that only women who have something wrong with them make love impossible:

> Pretty, intelligent, thirty-year-old women can't find husbands because they have "relationship problems." What is it that makes it so difficult for some people to find someone to love? Unfortunately, it is something that cannot be controlled consciously... Love is a person-to-person relationship, and sometimes there are deficiencies or difficulties that prevent people from forming interpersonal relationships, particularly where sexual relations are concerned... This is why many girls who want to marry find it difficult to establish a relationship that could lead to marriage.[14]

It is not the well-filled heads of highly educated women that stand in the way of their hearts, despite this psychological explanation. These women remain single, more than for any other reason, because of the condition under which they embarked on their academic venture. The gradual erosion of the inequality of the sexes in education has had its negative effects (Boudon 1977) since it has reinforced the inequality between the sexes with regard to marriage chances.

9
Living Together: A Less Costly Marriage

The president, delighted, thanked Blouson-Bleu:

"I give you the hand of my daughter."

"Her hand?" cried Blouson-Bleu. "How horrible! I beg you not to cut it off."

"No, I mean I give Eglantine to you in marriage," said the president.

"In marriage?... I've read too many stories in my own country that ended like that: they got married, were very unhappy, and had no children."

"He's right," said Eglantine. "People no longer live happily ever after."

"Very well, we'll say no more about it. But I made you a promise, Blouson-Bleu. What do you want?" asked the president.

"What do I want? Why, I want your daughter to be happy!" answered Blouson-Bleu.

—J. Joubert, *Blouson-Bleu*, 1980

MARRIAGE introduces important modifications into the management of individuals' capital, particularly by authorizing and even recommending transfer and investment of capital into the accounts held in the partner's or the child's name. For a wife, conforming to the housewife model results in her indirect increase in value being more than the direct increase of her social and cultural capital. Indirect value enhancement takes precedence over direct value enhancement. According to the arguments in favor of this model, for a woman to give up her career can be explained not because she calculates that it will be to her advantage, but because of the demands of love. The principles of self-denial and of putting the other person first lie behind such an action. A stay-at-home housewife, married to an engineer, when asked if she could envisage life without children, protested that such an existence would not be worth living and that life is about more than living for oneself. In her 1982 novel Delly considers that only a selfish woman refuses to live for others. To convince us she paints a portrait of the superior, intelligent woman, a woman who, while retaining "her complete freedom of action," shows herself to be incapable of being a proper wife and mother. Through her ignorance of the devotion required by these two roles she "wishes to remain herself and herself alone." When her son is very ill she does not remain by his bedside because it would interfere with her intellectual work. By way of contrast, Delly gives an example of a self-effacing woman, "an elite soul whose virtues and nobility made her genuinely superior." It is as if the act ending one's career ideally coincides with the end of a woman's personal happiness. To "provide the sacred joys of the hearth," a woman needs to know how to "devote herself and forget herself entirely"; she must not always be "the person who knows it all, but often must know how to pass unnoticed" (Delly 1982, 34, 187).

This exemplary life can have rather paradoxical consequences, according to other female novelists. The individuals to whom a woman devotes her life can gradually end up not seeing her at all. The stay-at-home housewife can, thanks to her own self-denial, become invisible. Throughout her novels, and in her short story "Room 19" in particular, Doris Lessing describes this self-effacement on the part of some women and their desperate attempts to recover their own identities (Lessing 1983). Susan, a designer in an advertising agency, marries Matthew, an editor at a newspaper. When she becomes pregnant, she gives up working and family life establishes its pattern: Matthew worked for Susan, the children, the house, the garden; he had to earn a great deal of money to keep this tribe. Susan devoted her intelligence and her practical sense to Matthew, the children, the house, the garden—otherwise the whole lot would have collapsed inside a week. Everything is fine until the day the children start school. Susan now feels ill at ease and wishes to learn how to be herself once more. After numerous attempts, she decides finally to rent a room in a hotel several days a week. "What did she do in the room? Why, nothing at all. . . . She was no longer Susan Rawlings,

188 LOVE AND CAPITAL

mother of four, wife of Matthew, employer of Mrs. Parkes and of Sophie Traub, with these and those relations with friends, schoolteachers, tradesmen. She no longer was mistress of the big white house and garden. . . . She was Mrs. Jones, and she was alone, and she had no past and no future" (Lessing 1963, 280, 304–5). Sitting in the armchair or leaning out of the window, she thinks to herself: "Here I am . . . after all these years of being married and having children and playing those roles of responsibility—and I'm just the same. Yet there have been times I thought that nothing existed of me except the roles that went with being Mrs. Matthew Rawlings" (305). In reality, however, Susan has been so affected by her family life that her attempts to rediscover herself come to nothing and end with her committing suicide. Lying on the bed in room 19 with the gas turned on, she finally feels at ease. She has not rediscovered herself because too many years of devotion to others had accustomed her to denying herself completely.

The devaluation of a woman's professional capital is not the only consequence of a management of her capital where the emphasis is on the acquisition of indirect value; other consequences can be either delight or disenchantment. These novels present the two sides and reveal the fragile nature of the division between the world of work and the world of the emotions. Investments in social or cultural capital and investments in affection do not appear in the same account books, and yet they cannot be managed independently.

The Loss of Love

Even though many women "earn their living from marriage," as Harriet Taylor puts it,[1] they need this income to be backed up and reinforced by an element of love. A married woman's lack of professional career prospects and the taking on of the running of a household demand in return that the husband should remain loving and faithful. Happiness wipes away all the shadows. That is the moral behind Arthur Laurents' story *Le tournant de la vie* (1978, 183). Twenty years into her marriage, Deede, "who has sacrificed her career and her dreams for love, marriage, and children," meets an old friend, Emma, "a leading dancer who had chosen to climb the steep slope to stardom." Initially Deede feels regret at having missed similar career success but she ends up with a different view: "You get what you are looking for. She had certainly wanted other things, but had finally preferred a husband, married life, and children. When she looked at him, when she saw how he loved her, and how she could make him happy, she was delighted with her choice. What she now had, she had wanted, and had obtained it."

When the love relationship goes wrong, however, this upsets the tacit contract giving the husband's career precedence. We see this in C. Crozet's *Marianne ou les autres* (1972). Marianne, who has a university degree, marries Charles and identifies completely with him, "marrying his ambitions and abandoning her own with dangerous willingness." Charles wishes to become a great virtuoso and is "ready to sacrifice everything to his career," a statement that Marianne repeats "with open pride, ecstasy even." While she supports them with the money she earns as a secretary, he plays his music and tries to realize his professional ambitions. A few years later, the situation remains much the same but Marianne discovers that Charles has been having an affair. When she demands an explanation, he replies "that he surely had the right to enjoy himself from time to time; after all, music was not the only thing in life." Deeply hurt, Marianne obtains a divorce; she cannot forgive him "for having demanded so many sacrifices from her and the children, in the name of an artistic ideal that she had fully embraced." She refuses to be the only one to pay for her husband's possible future success; her contribution has now become meaningless. Her husband's infidelity is, for her, incompatible with her own self-denial. Marianne discovers that her hopes of her husband's success have led her to neglect her own career: how could she have been so passive, been satisfied all those years with a job so low in status, and which provided neither a decent salary nor any satisfaction? In her case the type of marital cooperation chosen presupposes the permanence of the relationship and the fidelity of the partners. However, the gains made by the husband from the professional point of view do not mean that he is in complete control of his sexual and emotional investments. Because of his affairs, the wife is no longer able to identify with her husband and can no longer accept him as the representative of the family unit.

The loss of love ruins future hopes and invalidates the past. At the moment when a couple separates, at which time they

draw up their accounts, the wife does not get back her investment, even if she has had access to her husband's financial
and symbolic gains during her married life. The increases in
his capital that a man receives after marriage continue to be
his exclusive property. A wife's indirect enhancement of her
capital, through her husband, depends on the continued stability of the marriage. Stay-at-home housewives believe, more
than other women, in everlasting love and are less likely to
seek divorce. Unfortunately, there is no way to insure that a
love relationship will not end, even if a policy is bought from
a marriage counselor. That being so, thousands of women
protect themselves by continuing to have a job.

Infidelity by the child

Capital invested in a husband or child runs a double risk:

—a woman cannot be certain of a return on her investment,
   since not all husbands and not all children behave as
   women hope they will;
—when these investments seem to be turning out to be
   profitable, another danger can crop up in the form of emotional distancing. A man who, by a major effort by himself
   and his wife manages to achieve upward social mobility,
   might then feel that his wife is no longer at his level and
   begin to look for a woman he considers superior to her.

The sociology of education and of social mobility suggests
that the first of these two risks is more likely to occur in
working-class and lower-middle-class families, where the children have higher social status than their parents. According
to this sociology, the families having children with higher social status than their parents have controlled their family size
and thus should be pleased by their children's success. On
the other hand, children's achievements can lead to parents
and children having different values, which then in turn
bring about a deterioration in their emotional relationship
and reduce the child's feelings that he should somehow repay
his parents. A mother can be proud of her son's or daughter's
academic or social success while at the same time failing to
recognize fully the repercussions of that success. On the other
hand, to achieve upward mobility and success, the child can

be led to betray, in a sense, his family culture and become alienated from his own people.

The works of Annie Ernaux refer to this ambiguity associated with successful parental investment. A married couple who keep a café-cum-grocery store want their only child, a daughter, to do well academically. To this end they enroll her in an expensive private school. The daughter rewards them with her brilliant progress. However, she gradually assimilates the values of her teachers and her classmates. At school she rejects her background—"already dirty and ridiculous into the bargain"—and invents a new one—"pretty and clean, a proper one." She accepts this other world's norms to such an extent that she sometimes wishes she were an orphan. At the university she is horrified at the thought of going to see her parents. Particular words comes to mind when she thinks about them: "dirty, grubby, ugly." She realizes how she has changed: "I was a little monster, a vicious little girl; I hated both of them. I wished they were different—presentable, people I could show to my friends in the real world." She longs to change them: "They would be my parents, looking the same, built the same, but different... I would be able to love them completely, not hate the life they lead, their manners their tastes... Not being able to love your parents is unbearable" (Ernaux 1974, 1984).

The daughter's success—in her studies, as a teacher, in her "good" marriage—is paid for at the cost of her relationship with her parents. Parents who cannot bequeath cultural capital directly to their child have to buy it in installments, paying for it with emotional capital. For mothers, who have made greater investments in their children, these payments are even more painful. The social and cultural gains made from indirect sources—which come when people marry and have children—must not obscure the negative cost in the form of lost affection.[2]

The Miracle of Cohabitation

The returns on investments in a husband or a child are uncertain since they depend on the maintenance of the emotional links between the members of the family. The triumph of love in marriage increases the risk of instability and as a consequence the drawbacks of indirect value enhancement.

This dual increase of risk is evident not only in the increase in the number of women who go out to work, who divorce, and who live with men, but also in the reduction in the number of marriages, and of births. Herein lies the success of the new matrimonial doctrine that resolves (or attempts to resolve) the historical contradictions of married life by placing the emphasis on love, unstable though it may be, and by rejecting the strict division of work between the sexes. The matrimonial bank's female customers are changing their habits; they are less inclined to open accounts in their partner's or their children's names and to close their own career account.

Couples living together without marrying are the best illustration of the changes that are taking place since it is mostly younger people who are involved and since they are the most enthusiastic proponents of the new matrimonial doctrine. Age-group differences are much more significant than differences between social class or gender groups. Cohabitation is perceived by those who practice it as a more flexible way of life than marriage in that it makes possible a much greater range of feelings and sex roles (Béjin 1982). It provides, for women in particular, a management of capital that takes into account the uncertain future of love between two individuals.

Compromise between the sexes

Cohabitation is not the same as a trial marriage. A long-term study of a large number of marriages shows that one of the variables that distinguishes couples who have divorced from couples who are still together after ten years of marriage is cohabitation before marriage (Kellerhals et al. 1985). Interestingly enough, having lived together before marriage is no guarantee of lasting marriage: in fact, it is quite the contrary. Cohabitation seems to contribute to the break-up of the couple. From the outset cohabitants do not have the same perception of married life as other people do. When they marry they do not automatically rule out the possibility of divorce nor of entering into another relationship (Roussel and Bourguignon 1979). Remaining with the same partner is equated with routine and habit. Marriage, whether a civil or church ceremony, is not entered into with the intention of making the partnership more enduring by means of a legal commitment; rather, it is the result of family or social pressures. Whether they eventually marry or not, cohabitants are likely to see their future together as being short-term. Nevertheless, while they do not fix the length of the lease in advance, they do have doubts about the survival of true love. They do not attach less importance to their emotional relationship; it is the importance they attach to their individuality, and to the other person, that changes (de Singly 1981a).

The value system of couples who live together is a part of the contemporary narcissism in which all institutions are felt to be traps that stifle genuine feelings (Sennett 1979). Marriage has lost its attraction because, according to cohabitants, it forces individuals to play roles, to become "actors," to present themselves first and foremost as "husbands" and "wives." Cohabitants long for a world free of theater in which role-playing would be forbidden; individuals would have to be "real," come what may. Doing what your partner does just because you are married runs contrary to the ingrained desire to be true to yourself. Couples who live together are more hostile than married couples of the same age to any move that in their view would stifle their individuality.

Not everyone is critical of conjugal fusion. When it comes to work, whether professional or domestic, cohabitants are wholeheartedly in favor of tasks being shared. Housework, cooking, and dishwashing are more often done by both partners in cohabiting couples than in married couples (Stafford, Backman, and Dibona 1977). For cohabitants, genders must not determine who undertakes particular tasks or responsibilities. Individuals are not to be identified in this way, and therefore there is no reason why domestic tasks should not be shared. The same logic applies to paid work. The man's right to take priority is condemned and the right of both partners to have a job is maintained. In the 35 to 39 age group, three-fifths of married women and three-quarters of women cohabitants have jobs. Both partners going out to work and cohabitation are directly linked.[3]

A woman cohabitant's professional account remains open, since for her it has a different significance than it has for a married woman. For the former, paid work is directly related to strategies aimed at improving the couple's social value and is more an affirmation of self and of independence. A married woman who has made a good investment on the marriage market by finding a husband with a higher value than her own is more likely to give up working immediately than is a woman having the same value but who has contracted an "ordinary" marriage. She makes up for her relative loss of value and improves the couple's standard of living by continuing to work. This is why a greater number of female junior executives married to blue-collar workers have a higher employment rate than female junior executives married to senior executives have. This distinction disappears in the case of cohabitants.[4]

Paid work, for a female cohabitant, takes on a higher profile and is less open to question. Since she does not believe that love can last forever and therefore assumes that her relationship will probably be of short duration, she protects her interests, whether consciously or not, by avoiding a situation where she is dependent on her partner. Cohabitation does not induce her to give up the direct returns she can obtain directly from her academic capital.

Cohabitation is a way of life that is defended more by women than by men when partners are negotiating about what form their life together should take. Among the middle and upper classes, the former are more skeptical than the latter about the respect accorded to traditions governing marriage. This greater belief in the new matrimonial doctrine on the part of women leads them to prefer, and to persuade their partners to prefer, living together. For those women it is a means of avoiding the strait-jacket of gender roles that society automatically imposes. Seen from this perspective, cohabitation results primarily from the strategies women employ to "defer, displace, indeed put off indefinitely the place in the family structure that marriage and motherhood impose on them" (Battagliola 1988). Having children is not an immediate prospect since paid work provides the basis of social status. Besides, children threaten the gains achieved in the slow progress towards sexual equality and are indeed perceived as a convenient alibi for those who wish to see women return to their traditional roles. It is certainly true that children, especially where there are more than one, are linked with family structures where greater emphasis is put on differentiating sex roles. Couples who share tasks and responsibilities are more likely to be childless. In the case of male executives under the age of thirty-five, there is twice the likelihood of them having a marriage relationship based on equality if they are childless than if they have children (Glaude and de Singly 1986). Conversely, a job enables a woman to step outside the domestic domain. Her involvement in domestic tasks and in decision making diminishes while that of her partner increases. The capital a woman has at her disposal as a result of paid work does not serve to give her greater power in her relationship but allows her to opt out as much as possible from household duties. She is not attracted by the acquisition of this power: the management of her own capital forms part of the shared management of the household.

It is younger women who are more in favor of this program, which associates autonomy with the sharing of work; they are also less formalistic than young men with regard to marriage. Young women are not concerned whether they and their partner get married or cohabit, whereas young men prefer to live in an officially recognized relationship. When they are presented with three types of partnerships, male high-school students show a preference for marriage and a strict division of labor between partners. The following scenario—"Isabelle and Frédéric have been married for eight years and have three children. Frédéric works hard and earns a good salary, while Isabelle, who had to give up working when the first child was born, has preferred not to go back to work and concentrates on looking after her children, her husband, and her house"—received the approval of two-fifths of the male students and one-quarter of the female students.[5]

Being a husband's "better half" no longer forms part of a young woman's balance sheet, particularly if she is educated. Young women try to gain an increase in capital by selecting a man who will accept her terms, as this statement from an interview with a twenty-six-year-old kindergarten teacher shows, when she explains why she has taken up with a twenty-year-old carpenter: "Dominique is a fine person. He respects women. Which is perhaps what makes him different from the other men I've had relationships with. He's the only guy with whom I've felt I'm treated as a real equal."[6] For these women, cohabitation seems to be the relationship in which they have the best chance to feel like "real equals." The open nature of this structure offers them the opportunity of redefining the relations between the sexes, and by extension, the chance to increase their security—not in terms of the security offered by marriage, but rather in terms of the defense of their interests. The way they protect themselves within the family structure is by the greater presence of their partner within the home—particularly in the kitchen!

The preference of women for cohabitation does not derive principally from their desire to escape paying taxes; rather, it springs from their refusal to depend on a husband's benevolence and to pay him too heavy a tribute in the form of housework. These women want the exchange between the (man's) job and the (wife's) domestic work to be reduced, leaving just the emotional and sexual exchanges between the couple. With each partner managing his or her own account, the couple becomes what Sennett describes as an exchange market of intimate relations (1979).

The generations compromise

When couples live together without marrying, a woman hands over less of her capital to her companion and invests less in the production of children. This practical consequence of the new matrimonial doctrine does not trigger a hostile reaction on the part of the parents of cohabitants, whose disapproval is more discreet. This seeming parental tolerance can be explained by the fact that cohabitation is a compromise between the demands of the two generations. Young people want to live together without waiting too long and their parents do not want them to get married too early. Once again, the timetable problem intervenes in the life of a family: marriage needs to be put off, given the length of time spent in study and the time it takes to get established professionally. At the same time, marriage should happen earlier, given the ever-earlier arrival of sexual maturity and the difficulty of repressing the sexual urge. Cohabitation makes it possible to reconcile sexual precocity, late entry into the world of work, and the need to put off marrying (de Singly 1982c).

Even though in Western societies the function of marriage is to regulate sexual relations, it is not entered into at the moment when young people become sexually active. Marriage has other functions, particularly that of ensuring social continuity from one generation to another. The defense of family interests requires that marriage be contracted relatively late so that the new couple can be sure, through income and position, that the household will possess a social status at least equal to that of the parents. A successful passing from one generation to the next, which is directly related to the respective positions they each have in society, requires that events like marriage take place after education has ended and after entry into the labor market. Respecting this chronology pays dividends, as is shown by a comparison of the earnings of people who married before they had finished their studies and those who married after (Hogan 1980). The "deviants"—that is, those who did things in the wrong order—have lower salaries than the "conformists," given the same academic level. A substantial academic capital invested on the marriage market first nets a lower return on the job market than an equivalent capital invested on those two markets in reverse order.

Since marriage is entered into, perhaps unconsciously, by those who have completed the accumulation of their capital resources and have begun working, cohabitation is an option chosen by those who in a sense do not have the right to enter into an official union. Students and the unemployed between the ages of twenty and twenty-four[7] are more likely to choose cohabitation than marriage. Living together is also a more favored option among people (within the same age group) working part-time or on short-term contracts.[8] It attracts in particular two types of individuals: people whose professional investment is unstable and who are discouraged from starting a family and students (who later will not suffer the same uncertainty) who have not yet completed the accumulation of their academic capital. When these two groups enter into a relationship it is in the form of cohabitation and not marriage. In spite of their heterogeneity, these two groups do have something in common—they have not yet become fully established professionally. The continuation of studies and unemployment both contribute to increasing dependence upon parents, to delaying marriage, and to encouraging cohabitation. Late entry into the job market results in late entry into the marriage market, even though the conjugal socialization process is over. Young people therefore can choose between getting married earlier, and not respecting the normal order of events, or putting off marriage and living together instead.

Although previously, roughly from 1955 to 1970, the average age at which people married decreased, more recently cohabitation has changed the form that relationships take. In this way, with the ever-present respect for the correct order of things, academic and professional investments are protected without thwarting a couple's desire to live together. For young people, conformity to the requirements of accumulation of academic and professional capital is achieved by matrimonial deviancy. In addition, relations between cohabitants and their parents would appear not to be compromised—living together being the lesser of two evils. Three-quarters of the parents of cohabitants regularly allow both partners to visit them, and more than half provide material help. The parents accept the situation since they think (although they do not always voice it) that cohabitation—which in their view involves a lesser degree of commitment than marriage—is preferable while careers are not established. On the other hand, these same parents become more critical when cohabitation is extended and appears to have taken the place of marriage. Cohabitation is "perfectly acceptable" in eight out of ten cases when it involves a young couple with no children but only in three out of ten when it involves an older couple with children who have no plans to marry (Roussel and Bourguignon 1979; Chalvon-Demersay 1983).

This parental indulgence with regard to young cohabitants reveals their implicit value hierarchy, in which the accumulation of academic capital takes first place. The serious business of investment on the job market comes before "real" marriage. Parents turn a blind eye to the life styles of their postadolescent offspring as long as they do not endanger previously acquired cultural capital and respect the principle of heterosexuality. This broadminded attitude is helped by the fact that the parents of cohabitants are often from the middle and upper classes, where the living together concept has spread more widely. These children are also twice as likely to have divorced or separated parents.[9] In both the older and the younger generations, conjugal love is no respecter of the frontiers of the institution of marriage.

If the decision to cohabit were taken only because it helps to fill the vacuum of postadolescence, living together would be exclusively a prenuptial phenomenon that would eventually lead to marriage. Cohabitation would simply be a temporary stage within a sexual and emotional relationship. But other factors intervene to have a certain stabilizing effect this new institution, particularly the emphasis given to love and to insistence on autonomy. A live-in relationship has a greater chance of remaining a "free" relationship if the participants are also believers in cohabitation. This is why living together is more frequent among people possessing substantial academic capital who are even beyond the age of thirty, when studies usually have ended.[10] Two to three times as many women with good academic qualifications than with poor qualifications are living with their partners.[11] The former have practical reasons to choose this option because of the size of their academic capital and ideological ones since they are loath to take on the roles of wife and mother. As one female student puts it, "I have no desire to be only that... a mother, a wife; that's something you can do when you're still quite young; but you, your own life, that's not something that's so easy to create... I have no wish to spend my life dishing up meal after meal, emptying potties, waiting for hubby to come home, and putting his slippers by his favorite armchair" (Battagliola 1988). These women wish to be addressed by their own names (Valetas 1982) and to keep their professional account open in that name. However, the increase in the number of these new couples is such that each one adopts its own form of relationship (Léridon and Villeneuve-Gokalp 1988). Both cohabitation and marriage have open borders, and those involved are less different from each other than they were in the 1970s.[12]

LOVE WITHOUT COST—AN ILLUSION

Life as a couple should be pleasant and easygoing. The ultimate aim is an ambitious one, indeed—that marriage should be invisible. The proponents of living together want the couple to be as unaffected as possible by married life. They insist on individual autonomy and respect for each partner's territory and possessions. The membership fee to join the matrimonial club must be as low as possible.

John Stuart Mill also wished to achieve this aim as far back as the middle of the nineteenth century. He wanted to marry Harriet Taylor without disadvantaging her and without their marriage taking its usual form—that is, with strictly traditional sex roles. To that end he drew up what he considered to be his contractual obligations. In a letter to his future wife he expressed his intention that their marriage should not give him legal control over her and his refusal to take advantage of the powers over her that marriage gave him. He wanted his wife to retain, in every respect, her absolute freedom of action and to be able to do whatever she wished with herself and her present or future possessions, "as if there had been no marriage" (Mill 1975, preface).

With this promise, Mill stated clearly that he wanted neither partner to suffer any loss of autonomy and their partnership to leave no traces except in their memories. Although this desire, expressed in 1851, would receive a more sympathetic reception nowadays, it still seems a Utopian aim. First, the form that domestic relationships can be changed neither by decree nor because the proposed changes seem attractive. The division of labor between the sexes outside the home still exists, even if the balance has changed to a certain degree, which continues to affect the relationship between partners. Partners are not entirely the masters of their own domestic fates. Second, every autonomy theory is limited when it comes to putting it into practice. A home is not just a space, otherwise it would turn into a hotel (and who would be the manager?). This constraint is evident from a prenuptial quiz published in *Cosmopolitan*—a magazine one would normally put among the partisans of the new matrimonial doctrine.[13] By answering eleven questions a woman could determine whether "the wonderful man already in her life and in her bed would be any use to her once they were married." The form the questions take reveals dual expectations. First, there is a complete rejection of marital tyranny (women refuse to be stifled by male despotism). At the same time, the closeness of the relationship must be maintained (their love must not face too much competition from other relationships—with parents or friends—or from the need for personal space). The tension between autonomy and fusion, between partners as individuals and as a couple, between "me" and "us," is experienced by all couples, whatever their professed philosophy of relationships may be. Contradictions often crop up most around the question of sexual fidelity. Even in the communes set up after 1968, adultery was a problem (Mauger and Fossé 1977). Theoretically jealousy is ruled out since the idea of partners as "possessions" is unacceptable. Adultery takes on a positive character: it is a step away from the narrow concept of a partnership towards the new "liberated" couple that should be prepared to accept new liberated relationships. Nonetheless, as E. G. Belotti writes, "the traditional scenario, with its gang of vaudeville characters that has been momentarily consigned to the wings, finally wins" (1981, 133). If the couples in an "open relationship in which the partners allow each other to have other sexual relationships, and where nevertheless their own relationship remains the special one" are most unlikely to remain together, is it not perhaps because the definition of what constitutes a "special relationship" is somewhat vague? To use Erving Goffman's expression: what is it that is renounced in a conjugal relationship that is "the symbol and the very substance of the relationship" (1973b)?

Lack of understanding and communication seem to top the list of accusations leveled at partners (Kitson and Sussman 1982). A look at the themes of the letters addressed to "problem pages" in popular magazines also shows that the question that crops up most frequently concerns the failure to express feelings of love: "He no longer tells me he loves me. In our better moments I sometimes say to him, 'Do you love me?' But he just waffles and avoids the issue. It spoils the moment. Then he's cross and I'm upset."[14]

Emotional and professional investments

Creating a partnership based on love and keeping it going demands a great deal in time spent together and in communicating feelings to the other partner, which can hamper a partner's attempt to increase the value of his or her capital resources to the maximum. Love has a price, as R. Sheckley (1980) points out in *Le robot qui me ressemblait (The Robot That Looked Like Me)*, a story of a man who, although extremely busy and with little time to spare, wishes to marry. Charles employs the services of an intermediary who has the reputation of being highly skilled at arranging marriages. The latter learns of a young woman, Elaine, who is available, but who insists on being courted strictly by the book; in other words, at least three evenings a week for two months. Charles refuses to go along with this; he would lose 17 percent of his income if he spent his time in what he considers to be ridiculous, boring, and unproductive activities. Not wishing to abandon his marriage plans, however, he orders a unique robot that resembles him in every detail. He programs it to pay court to Elaine and supervises the operation by films of the meetings taken by the robot. Two months later Charles programs his robot to ask Elaine to marry him and to end the courtship period. When the robot does not return, a concerned Charles meets Elaine and discovers that she too led an extremely busy life and since she could not fit the meetings into her schedule had also hired a robot, identical to herself. The two robots had eventually fallen in love and fled to another world. Completely astounded by these events, Charles and Elaine promise to devote "an extra hour a day—seven a week in total—to each other."

Those who decide to enter into an emotional relationship end up putting in a fair amount of overtime on their partners. Men seem to have more difficulty than women in adjusting to these emotional constraints. They feel uncomfortable when called upon to express their feelings, unlike women, who tend to get carried away by "romantic notions" (Raffin 1982). In terms of sexual identity socialization handicaps women at work and men in romance. Even so, romance requires a relationship input. Each partner needs to set aside a certain amount of energy to invest in the emotional side of the relationship. This syphoning off of emotion can mean that there is less energy available to direct towards other objectives, particularly careers. Conversely, certain investments in the labor market (or in sports or clubs) can result in a restriction in the amount of time and emotion devoted to one's partner. Nevertheless, all this interaction between the actors cannot be explained by social value alone. This interaction is evident in the search for balance between the individual's emotional obligations and the imperatives of success. In the same way, achieving the best possible returns on her capital via her husband is not necessarily compatible with a woman being "happily married." An excessive investment by her husband in his work can cause emotional upsets and be regarded almost as a form of adultery. This view is shared by one of the women writing to a magazine's advice columnist. She says that her husband's "aim is to succeed": "What has a man to offer his family when he works at least eleven hours a day and comes home exhausted and weighed down with problems? We're just stuck. The only thing we ever talk about is his problems at work. This house is like a hotel... I gave up working to look after the home and the children. That suits him fine. He is capable of providing for his family by himself, he says. So, I stay home; I've got plenty to do and I don't get bored. Even so, I know I can't stand any more of this miserable existence; this is not the kind of life I want!"[15] Those who claim to be "very happily married" seem to be in those relationships where the man professes to attach greater importance to his family life than to his work (Bailyn 1970). A happy marriage is not only related to the extent to which cultural capital is protected, but it also depends on the amount invested in the family by both partners.

The wishes expressed by John Stuart Mill are unrealistic since they do not take into account the inevitable implications of two people living together in marriage. In practice, behaving as if nothing had happened would not affect each partner's social capital, but by making it seem as if the other partner was transparent, invisible even, he or she would be offended. Strangely enough, the effects would be similar to the highly criticized situation where a wife, by her devotion and self-denial, becomes invisible in her husband's eyes.

Conclusion

THE underlying approach to this analysis is based on a somewhat jaundiced view of the world. It is no coincidence that the readers of the first edition—particularly if they were not sociologists—who were less dismissive of this approach to marriage, were often those who had experienced divorce or separation. These men and women, no doubt because they had found themselves in a position where they had had to draw up a balance sheet of their own marriage, were more ready to accept what seemed others to be a systematic attack on married life and too crude a sociological "reduction." These reactions highlight a very important aspect of the way in which marriage functions: the nature of the exchanges that take place between husband and wife are not normally made explicit.

Self-interested calculations are seldom present in a happy marriage, as this letter to a magazine from a woman reader implies: "There is a problem that really disturbs me. It's my husband's attitude. He's more than just careful with money. I can't buy anything without consulting him first, and I have to explain every purchase I make. And yet I'm not a spendthrift. There is another problem, but it's my fault this time: I'm very possessive and go through torments when my husband attends certain social functions organized by his company without me. I nag him about it and make him account for every minute." There is no way of knowing who started calculating first, but the result was that the other partner replied in kind. This couple was so busy making entries in their notebooks that they did not have time to appreciate or love each other. Each partner suspects the other of having a good time without him or her. Behind this story of wasting time or money is a denunciation of personal self-interest.

If married life is to remain enjoyable, perhaps partners should not be too explicit about their system of exchanges and should insist on their own personal enjoyment only with discretion. This does not mean that love does not count the

204

cost, as the saying goes, but that the weighing of the cost should be kept private and that one should not give the impression that he or she is keeping a tally (Kaufmann 1992). After moments of marital friction, we discover that everything has been noted down and remembered. In love, blindness and leaving things unsaid go together. Marriage is most satisfying if it is played without either partner knowing the rules, except for the rule that requires silence about the rules.

A partner's wish to add everything up, for everything to be quite clear, is a way of saying that he or she wants to be sure that nothing is lost, that nothing is given unknowingly. To do that is to show the self-interested side of one's nature in the context of a relationship that is, by general consent, supposed to be without self-interest. In the continuing history of courtly love, conjugal love requires proof of a particular skill on the part of its adepts, that of knowing how to give of their time, money, and attention so that a partner feels appreciated as an individual and so that they will receive the same in return (de Singly 1990).

Love is not a contract

The things that remain unsaid reinforce love and its particular place in our individualistic society. This is why sociologists were mistaken when in the 1970s they predicted that there would be an increase in marriage contracts. It seemed evident at the time that the equal sharing of work, whether professional or domestic, would lead men and women to define precisely the services rendered and received. Those couples who did this were looked upon as representative of the future: "A growing number of people, of all age groups, considered this procedure to be a precondition of the formulation, or the continuation of the typical marriage relationship of the future" (Sussman 1975). The "hunger for equality" would lead couples to "set down in writing the terms by which they felt bound to each other." Note was also made "not only of the sharing of the possessions acquired before or during the marriage, their management, and the financial arrangements necessary in the event of death or divorce, but also the arrangements to be made in the event of them having to move and the sharing of child-rearing and domestic tasks between the marriage partners" (Weitzman 1974, 173).

But it did not happen like that: there turned out to be very few takers for a contract in which the type and extent of tasks would be spelled out. The people who favored this self-management model did not translate their concerns about the equality of exchanges into a contractual relationship since they were as concerned as those who were in favor of the communal model about maintaining their personal image, and harmony within their marriage. These errors with regard to predicting the future arise from the underestimation of the virtues implicit in marriage. All partners—whether they are married or living together—must be able to believe, and make others believe, that they are motivated by feelings other than self-interest. They need to show their partners and those around them at all times that their motto is not "for better but not for worse."[1]

"It is so nice to be loved for yourself"

This return to an element that sociological analysis normally excludes—love—has the advantage of setting the limits of a work that has been written to measure the profits and losses of marriage. Excluding the love factor for too long can in turn lead to a new kind of blindness that hides the love found in relationships that can only exist without self-interest and that ignores the effects of this inevitable lack of self-interest.

A marriage is not an enterprise like any other, despite what Bertrand Lemennicier would have us believe. Here, in this book, I have shown how analogy does not equal reality. It is not true that "an individual acts in the same 'rational' manner whether he is choosing between two brands of yogurt, two makes of car, two political programs, or two women" (Lemennicier 1988, 15). It is possible that we might be "blind" in not going for the best value when buying a car or yogurt, but we cannot help but be blind when we fall in love. In fact, one's partner can be considered a product whose function, ideally, is to guarantee that the buyer is not simply a portfolio of shares in the job market hopefully to preserve his or her social value within the marriage partnership.

In a marriage an individual is no more or no less irrational[2] or self-interested[3] than in any other situation, but he or she needs to defend as much as possible what one might call his or her "humanity." It is simply the vague, unstructured conditions under which the choice of partner is made, and in which marriage exists, that create the relative autonomy that affection needs to operate within a social context. In other words, marriage gives each partner the social benefits that come from feeling loved and wanted. This is the point that the Count makes in *The Barber of Seville*. He is loved by Rosina, who does not know how wealthy he is: "It is so nice to be loved for oneself!" he exclaims.[4] By this reintroduction of the effects of love, we can understand how it is that in contemporary societies in which the distinction between the two dimensions of personal identity—capital resources and personal qualities—has been increasingly stressed, the symbolic devaluation of the institution of marriage has not been accompanied by a similar devaluation in the idea of "togetherness." This latter concept, despite the price paid particularly by women in terms of their social and cultural capital, is the best way to protect the partners' human interests and the construction of their personal identities (de Singly 1992a).

Postscript: Twenty Years Later

THIS book is an account—in the strict sense of the term—of the way in which men and women managed their social and cultural interests within their marriages during the 1970s. This method of acquiring an understanding of the reality of married life is equally valid in analyzing marriage partnerships in the 1990s, despite the women's liberation movement after 1968, the massive entry of women onto the labor market, and the consequent demands for domestic tasks to be shared. These elements have not destabilized to a sufficient degree the objective and subjective mechanisms that lead to the loss in value of women on the labor market and that result in women being more dependent on marriage than men.

Good intentions are not enough to transform the fundamentally social relationship between the sexes. At the end of the nineteenth century August Strindberg intimated as much in his short story "Dissensions." He recounts the story of a young man and woman who wanted to break away from the tradition that assigned different activities on the basis of gender and who wanted both sexes to receive the same education so that they would have "the same interests" and thus have a marriage of true minds. But force of habit and acceptance of social constraints resulted in the young couple behaving like everyone else. The young woman

> saw that she was not moving at the same pace as her husband. They were like two racehorses. They had been weighed before the start of the race and their weight had been the same. They had promised to run at the same pace; everything had been so finely calculated that they ought to have finished the race together and left the course together. But now the husband was already a good length ahead of his wife. If she did not hurry she would be left behind... And that is exactly what happened.

This is also what is happening in France at the end of the twentieth century. Despite all the changes that have taken place within the family over the past two decades (de Singly

1993), there has been no reduction in the unequal cost of marriage for men and women. Generally speaking, the price of being married, in terms of investment in the labor market, is still higher for a woman than for a man. Moreover, the data relating to working women and mothers does not indicate that there is equal involvement in the labor market between husbands and wives. The figures showing a lessening gap between the number of women having a job as compared to men must not be too hastily interpreted as meaning that there is equality of the sexes in the workplace.

Since, moreover, increasing numbers of marriages have broken up during the last twenty years—a situation that has revealed the price that has to be paid for marriage—women have had more opportunity to discover the social and economic drawbacks associated with a commitment to setting up a home. Marriage has increasingly become an emotional relationship rather than a union of two families, but even so the division of labor between the sexes has not improved as far as women are concerned. In the 1990s more women than ever are suffering from the negative effects of marriage in spite of their increased presence in the workplace. Moreover, their jobs have had to take second place behind their husbands'. The mismatch between the two recent changes in the relationship of marriage partners—the greater importance attached to love and changes in the sharing of tasks—has affected women more than it has men. In general men have been less affected by the increasing instability of marriage and relationships in modern society; the constraints of domestic tasks leave them with more independence, even though separation of the partners makes it hard to maintain close relationships with their children (Bertaux and Delcroix 1991; Sullerot 1992; de Singly 1993c).

The situation of highly qualified women has improved over the past two decades, however, and certainly in comparison with less well-educated women. While the importance attached nowadays to individual independence and to marriages based on love has increased at all social levels, class differences have become less significant (see chap. 6). The demands made by marriage increasingly have to be reconciled with women's demands for autonomy. However, women with more substantial academic capital pay a lower price for this new type of conjugal life, which has nonetheless a greater destabilizing effect on marriage. The cost of managing their own accounts and the changes in the relationship between the sexes are borne more heavily by women with little in the way of cultural or economic resources. This social "revolution" has put educated men and women more on a more equal footing while at the same time it has widened the gap between educated women and their less well-educated sisters.

Women always pay a higher price for marriage

Are marriage partners so alike today that an outsider cannot distinguish between them (Badinter 1986)? If the differences between the sexes have faded over the past twenty years, then the approach employed in this book can now be classified as being of no more than historical interest. However, before consigning it to the archives, perhaps we should examine a little more closely the assertion that the conflict of interests between the sexes has now disappeared. Could it be that we have been the victims of a collective illusion and have been led to believe by the considerable body of opinion on the changes that have taken place with regard to sexual identity, the malaise now affecting men, and the great success of the women's (feminist) movement that the problems associated with marriage now are simply the result of people falling out of love? But what if over two decades very little has in fact changed, despite (or perhaps because of) appearances? If today we wish to know whether a married woman's (or cohabitant's) academic capital is managed in the same way as that of a married man (or cohabitant), we simply have to draw up a balance sheet of her accounts. Perhaps embarking on a marriage partnership has other effects apart from emotional dependence on one's partner.

Statistics have the reputation of merely confirming what everybody already knows. Nevertheless, existing data on the returns from academic qualifications and the use of an individual's time during the course of a day clearly show that marriage is not a "painless" experience. During this period, in which we have been led to believe that the "traditional" marriage model has been dealt a deadly blow, women continued to take responsibility for most of the domestic tasks and to spend less time on their careers.

The differences in returns from academic qualifications brought to light by the INSEE inquiry on training and professional qualifications (1985) confirmed fully the findings of the research conducted in 1970 (see chap. 3).[1] The twelve tests comparing married women with both single women and married men all reveal a loss in value of a married woman's academic capital. A female high-school graduate with no other qualifications has less than a one-in-ten chance of becoming a senior executive if she is married, whereas a married man with the same academic capital has more than a one-in-three chance of achieving that position. The six tests comparing married men with single men show that the former are always at an advantage. A comparison between single men and single women reveals that the men are better off in four cases to two (see Appendix 1).

The continued existence of this inequality springs from the imbalance in the division of labor between marriage partners. In fact, according to the Timetable Study carried out by INSEE (1985–86), working wives with two children do two-thirds of the household and child-rearing tasks and less than half of the paid work undertaken by both partners (Roy 1990; Chaudron 1991). While fathers with two children (and a working wife) spend two-and-a-half times more of their time on their professional activities than on their domestic activities, their wives spend their time equally between the two. In families where both partners work, the women invest more of their time in household and child-rearing tasks, whereas men devote more of their time to their work.

Gradual exclusion

The changing of the barriers separating men and women— with the latter only rarely excluded from the possibility of working, even after they have had children—has only made a slight difference to differentiation between the sexes. The continued existence of the division of labor according to gender and its harmful effects on women has gone almost unnoticed because of the extensive debate on the changes that has taken place. Paradoxically the effect of this debate has been to maintain the status quo. Many commentators ask the purpose in continuing to draw attention to inequalities between men and women, and the domestic realities that cause them, since today "all women have a job." Such an assumption is wrong for two reasons: in the first place, the number of women going out to work depends to a very great extent on the number and age of their children. Second, and more important, it fails to take account of the different levels of involvement by women in the labor market. Thus more than six out of ten mothers with one child, four out of ten with two children, and one in ten with three children are in full-time employment.

It almost appears as if sex differences within a marriage have suffered the same fate as class differences in French schools: the right to make a particular choice at a given moment in time—entry into the seventh grade for working-class children, when to have children for women—has been replaced by a process of exclusion that is all the less obvious for being a gradual one. This happens at school with the differentiation between courses for potential graduates and dropouts and the hierarchy of importance given to courses; within the domestic arena it is present in the distinction between full-time and part-time work. Part-time work, which increased during the 1980s and which was mainly destined for women (Maruani and Nicole 1989), can be seen as a compromise that seemed to satisfy the demands of women who wanted to have a paid job without questioning to any great extent the division of labor between the sexes and the primacy given to the man's career. The younger generation also approves of this situation, having internalized the differences between fathers and mothers. Eight out of ten school children of twelve years of age believe that it is more acceptable for a father to work full-time, compared with one in ten, who favor the mother. They see mothers as working part-time.[2]

New justifications

The separation between the sexes has changed its form. Doubtless in order to make this change acceptable, both partners have made a slight modification in the amount of time devoted to work, with working mothers with two children fitting their domestic tasks into a shorter period of time, while fathers have increased their involvement in domestic tasks and child-rearing activities.[3] But over the past twenty years there has been a particularly noticeable change in the reasons given for the division of labor. Marriage as an institution has become devalued because it is seen as a game whose rules are too rigid, forcing women to do dishes because they are women and men to change the light bulbs and stay late at the office because they are men. People who live together prefer another board game in which the team somehow has to manage to carry out the same tasks without giving the impression of playing the same game time after time.

The situation resulting from this new set of rules strangely resembles the one produced by the traditional sex roles, but the players feel that there is a greater element of risk to their emotional relationship. This illusion comes about thanks to a slight generation gap: today a man need only carry out some task his wife's father would never have done or that his mother-in-law normally did and for him not to demand something of his wife that the men of the previous generation would have demanded for the couple to believe—at least before the magic has worn off—that they have succeeded in revolutionizing marriage (Kaufmann 1992). There is a slight difference between theory, which advocates the sharing of tasks, and reality, which shows no evidence of it, although the fifteen extra minutes a day that a man devotes to household tasks over a period of fifteen years, even if they do not promise a wonderful future, at least suggest that things are better now than in the past.

Another justification—the compromise that a mother has to make between her job and looking after her family in the interest of her children—was given new currency during this period. The guilty feelings of working mothers were worsened by the increased stress placed on the development of the child (encouraged by a growing interest in applied psychology) and at the same time on the importance of academic success (in turn more difficult to achieve with increasing competition). Bringing up a child successfully became a much more complicated business requiring, according to the psychology fraternity, prolonged and careful attention from the person best fitted to do the job, namely the mother. Mothers internalize more readily than fathers the idea that they are mainly responsible for bringing up their children. As a consequence they modify their career commitments to fit in with their parental duties. This is why, even in a family where both parents are allowed to be absent from work to look after a sick child, it is the mother who undertakes that task more often than her partner. Both partners manage to find good reasons to justify this, usually the fact that the father's job has priority

and that the mother's presence at such a time is more benefi-
cial (de Singly 1993a).

Even though the fact that women go out to work is no longer
openly questioned, it nonetheless continues to remain under
threat indirectly as soon the questions of the division of labor
or the extension of part-time work during prolonged periods
of high unemployment are raised. The demands made by "parental" responsibilities in child-rearing (a new way of saying
"maternal" responsibilities) represent a real and at the same
time ideological barrier to women having a job (de Singly
1992b).[4] A human resources management model would undoubtedly propose that women spell out contractually which
category they wished to be in with regard to the management
of their capital. Some could opt for a career but would have
to commit themselves entirely to their jobs; others could
choose a mixture of outside work and work inside the home
of looking after their children while realizing that they would
receive no promotion in their jobs (Schwartz 1989). The first
category of women would be in the fast track, like married or
single men; the second category would trundle along comfortably in the slow lane. With this in mind some psychologists
advise women not to get too involved with their jobs so as to
be able to devote themselves to their children at home and
to be more attentive to their needs. This recommendation
unintentionally helps us to better understand how the entry
and continued presence of women in the labor market are
no indication of an equality of opportunity between men and
women in the workplace. The long-term interests of the
mother are hardly taken into account when the social and
political interests of the child are being considered. A child is
quite obviously a possession that needs to be watched over
carefully, but does this mean that all the sacrifices have to be
made by one parent?

The greater costs paid by less well-educated women

A comparison of the price paid for marriage by women in
1970 and 1985 (See Appendix 1)[5] reveals that out of the six
levels of academic qualifications that were examined, three
had the same level of inequality, two had increased inequality,
and one had reduced inequality. For women who were at least
high-school graduates there was no increase in the cost of

marriage (two cases of the cost remaining unchanged and one reduced). For women with little academic capital marriage involved an increased cost (two increases and one unchanged). Thus the women with the most substantial academic capital were able, in comparison with other women, to enter into marriages where the subsequent cost was somewhat reduced.

Out of marriage, into poverty

Inequality of opportunity between the sexes and between social classes has to be considered together. Indeed, even if today's ideal family, with its insistence on individual independence, has become more widespread in our society, in practical terms it is not without problems for some of its participants. The increased value attached to autonomy and to the principle of emotional and psychological satisfaction has rendered marriage more unstable. The reduction in the number of marriages that stay the course produces, in turn, effects that are quite unexpected. Even though women are now able to assert their independence to a greater degree as a result of their increased involvement in the labor market, they still do not have—and those with little academic capital even less—the opportunity to end their marriages without paying a high price. Some divorced women plunge into a poverty spiral. According to F. Schultheis (1991), the logical consequence of individual autonomy, "the social trend liberating women from patriarchal ties," the changes in the law with regard to individual rights within the family whereby "women and children are freed from quasi-feudal domination by the pater familias" results in academically less well-endowed women paying "the price for actual equality and freedom." "While couples belonging to the new middle class are all in favor of the changes in legislation affecting marriage relationships (since they have an opportunity not only to contract a 'good' marriage, but also to arrange a 'good divorce,' where they remain 'good friends' and continue to exercise joint control over their children), the consequences of these changes are not at all the same for women from less privileged socioeconomic groups" (Schultheis 1991, 38).[6]

In fact, the cost of divorce is even greater for working-class women, for whom the chances of finding paid work with decent pay levels are low. If we take accommodation as an example, we can see that for women executives their marital situation has little bearing in this area, whereas "for women plant workers, on the other hand, what happens to their marriages determines to a large extent their living conditions, and only remarriage enables them to reestablish the level of accommodation that they had previously" (Festy and Valetas 1990, 302). These women, probably just as much as the others, believe in the new principles of individual freedom and take just as much advantage of the French laws making divorce easier to obtain, even if they do not possess sufficient social and economic resources to deal with the consequences.

Marriage to the state

From the 1970s on, marriage became "risky" in that it resulted in the feminization of poverty and the pauperization of single-parent families. To counteract the effects linked to changes in the law and the effects of the spread of the individuality model, France also intervened at another level, that of social benefits. It offered help, particularly by means of welfare checks (law dated 22 December 1984), to single mothers who were not receiving financial support from their ex-husbands; it also instructed the Family Allowance Department to take action to recover money not paid by the husbands.

In welfare-state societies, the system "helps to compensate for the risks and genuine inequalities arising in part from the actions of its alter ego, the state" (Schultheis 1991). It protects individuals from the effects of the postmodern family and the fragility of marriage, as one can see in a comparison of the social policies of different countries (Lefaucheur 1992). We see that in the United States, Canada, and the United Kingdom, among single-parent families "the percentage of poor people is three to four times higher than among married couples with dependent children. The risk increases even more among the young: 60 percent to 80 percent of single parents under the age of thirty are below the poverty line." In other countries, like France and Germany, "the chances of single parent families being beneath the poverty line is less . . . and the protection provided by welfare payments is by no means negligible, since it removes from below the poverty threshold around half of those who were under the poverty line" (before receiving welfare). In the more northern European countries such as Sweden or the Netherlands, welfare payments to protect individuals from the effects of divorce are even more effective: they reduce by at least two-thirds the number of single-parent families under the poverty line (Lefaucheur 1992, 428).

Women with poor educational qualifications are, in a way, "married to the welfare state" (Lefaucheur 1992, 424), one that guarantees them certain resources that would otherwise be provided by their husbands or cohabitants. Their relative independence within their private lives cannot be divorced from their dependence in other types of relationships, particularly in the social sector. The freeing of women from the conjugal yoke has resulted in the creation of new risks for marriage relationships that are not shared equally by both partners. The extension to women of the process of individualization that men had previously negotiated successfully can have the effect, particularly among women with insubstantial cultural capital resources, at some time or other in their lives of considerably reducing their standard of living.

The negative aspects of the negotiations that took place between the sexes from 1970 to 1980 and largely within the middle and upper classes were suffered mainly by the economically poorest women (de Singly 1993d). They paid the highest price in that they were least able to cope with the negative effects associated with the achievement of personal autonomy.

Appendix 1
Professional Returns on Academic Capital According to Sex and Marital Status in 1970 and 1985

Table 1
Probability of Achieving Executive Status in Terms of
Qualifications, Sex, and Marital Status in 1970

	Probability of becoming a senior executive			Probability of becoming a senior or junior executive		
	University degree	DEUG	High-school graduate	CAP	CEP	No qualifications
Married man	90	43	32	31	14	4
Single man	79	29	17	21	5	1
Single woman	83	21	8	42	13	5
Married woman	79	6	9	25	5	2
Married man	90	43	32	31	14	4
Married woman	79	6	9	25	5	2
Single man	79	29	17	21	5	1
Single woman	83	21	8	42	13	5

Source: Previously unpublished data from INSEE, FQP study, 1970, employed people aged 35–52

N.B. Among those who have continued their studies until at least university degree level, 90 percent of married men and 79 percent of married women reach senior executive status.

Table 2
Probability of Achieving Executive Status in Terms of
Qualifications, Sex, and Marital Status in 1985

	Probability of becoming senior executive			Probability of becoming senior or junior executive		
	University degree	DEUG	High-school graduate	CAP	CEP	No qualifications
Married man	86	43	37	34	24	9
Single man	67	33	21	20	8	4
Single woman	76	14	17	28	20	7
Married woman	74	13	9	18	10	2
Married man	86	43	37	34	24	9
Married woman	74	13	9	18	10	2
Single man	67	33	21	20	8	4
Single woman	76	14	17	28	20	7

Source: INSEE, FQP study, 1985, employed people aged 35-52

Appendix 2
Returns on Academic Capital According to Sex and Educational Level of Partner

Table 1
Probability of Achieving Executive Status for a Married Man in Terms of Age
When His Studies Ended and Age When His Partner's Studies Ended

Age when female partner's studies ended	Male partner's chances of achieving executive status (percentage)	
9–14	5	
15–19	16	
	(for men who ended studies at 14 or under)	
9–14	6	
15–19	23	
	(for men who ended studies at 15)	
9–14	13	
15–19	33	
	(for men who ended studies at 16)	
	Male partner's chances of achieving executive status (percentage)	
	Senior executive	Junior executive
15–19	18	36
20–24	38	45
	(for men who ended studies at 19)	
15–19	22	38
20–24	51	32
	(for men who ended studies at 20–24)	
20–24	83	15
25–29	84	8
	(for men who ended studies at 25–29)	

Source: Previously unpublished data from INSEE, FQP study, 1970, employed married men aged 35–52

N.B. A man whose studies ended at age 16 achieves executive status in 13 percent of cases if his partner finished her studies at 14 and in 33 percent of cases where the partner ended her studies between 15–19

Table 2

Probability of Achieving Executive Status for a Married Woman in Terms of Age
When Her Studies Ended and Age When Her Partner's Studies Ended

Age when male partner's studies ended	Female partner's chances of achieving executive status (percentage)	
9–14	2	
15–19	8	
	(for women who ended studies at 14 or under)	
9–14	3	
15–19	13	
	(for women who ended studies at 15)	
9–14	4	
15–19	17	
	(for women who ended studies at 16)	
	Female partner's chances of achieving executive status (percentage)	
	Senior executive	Junior executive
15–19	8	45
20–24	6	73
	(for women who ended studies at 19)	
15–19	4	63
20–24	16	69
	(for women who ended studies at 20–24)	
20–24	60	40
25–29	70	19
	(for women who ended studies at 25–29)	

Source: Previously unpublished data from INSEE, FQP study, 1970, employed married women aged 35–52

Notes

Acronyms Used in Notes and Bibliography

CERC Centre de Recherches sur les Revenus et sur les Coûts

CNAF Caisse Nationale d'Allocations Familiales

CNRS Centre Nationale de la Recherche Scientifique

CREDOC Centre de Recherches pour l'Etude et l'Observation des Conditions de Vie

FQP   Enquête Formation Qualification Professionnelle

INED   Institut National des Etudes Démographiques

INETOP Institut National d'Etude du Travail et de l'Orientation Professionnelle

INSEE Institut National de la Statistique et des Etudes Economiques

Preface to the American Edition

1. On the other hand, in the United States there is considerable research linking the family and health to the family and individual development, particularly with regard to depression among married couples and the effects of divorce on children such as academic achievement, well-being, and growth. In France, research in this area is not very well developed, with many sociologists subscribing to the belief that this is one way, albeit an indirect one, of reinforcing the institution of the family. For a review of this area of study in France see de Singly 1991.

Introduction

1. *La Vie*, no. 1952, 27 January 1983, 48.
2. *La Vie*, no. 1957, 3 March 1983, 37.
3. Balzac 1982, 97.

4. See *thèse d'Etat* "Fortune et infortune de la femme mariée" by F. de Singly, University of Paris René Descartes-Sorbonne, 1984, 2 vols., 1034 pp.

INTRODUCTION TO PART 1

1. Pope Pius XI, Encyclical *Casti Connumi*, 31 December 1930, in *Les enseignements pontificaux: Le problème féminin*, edited by Moines de Solesmes (Paris: Desclée & Co., 1953), 15–19.

CHAPTER 1. THE HUSBAND AS MANAGER OF HIS WIFE'S CAPITAL

1. Institut national de la statistique et des études économiques.
2. See Davis and Robinson 1988 and Simpson, Stark, and Jackson 1988.
3. Out of a sample of children whose parents had graduated from the Ecole Normale Supérieure, scarcely one-third reached the same academic level as their parents (Fourastié 1970, 534).
4. The four hundred ads studied were published in *Le Chasseur Français* in 1978–80. See de Singly 1984b, 523–59.
5. Unlike Taylor and Glenn 1979.
6. "The women who push their husbands," in *Elle*, March 1976.
7. Cf. chapter 6.
8. J. R. Leselbaum, "Aimez-le, aidez-le," In *Les Informations*, no. 1271 (22 September 1969): 23.
9. INSEE, *Formation et Qualification Professionnelle (FQP)* survey, 1970.
10. *Time* Magazine, 13 January 1986; *Libération*, 1 January 1986.

CHAPTER 2. THE CREATION OF A NEW CAPITAL RESOURCE—CHILDREN

1. In this chapter, in conformity with various studies, I take as my indicator of the child's cultural capital either his or her school performance or intellectual level as measured by tests. This choice in no way signifies a belief in "natural" intelligence; rather, it is based on the observations whereby schools and intelligence tests recognize performances of the same type.
2. Certain historians such as Shorter (1977) have seen the child as being too exclusively a form of emotional capital.
3. Only the creation of the child's cultural capital is dealt with in this way; the various means by which the child can subsequently catch up after failure at school are excluded. Cf. Thélot 1982 and Pitrou 1977.
4. Secondary application of data from Sewell and Shah 1968b.
5. Secondary application of data from the INSEE *FQP* study, 1977.
6. This process does not necessarily take place only after the socialization of the child has ended. The parents can benefit from some of the child's academic or cultural resources at the time they are being acquired. This is no doubt one of the ways in which parents can feel they are "staying young."

7. In their typology of services rendered by the child to his parents Schnaberg and Oldenberg (1975) do not include a reference to this reverse socialization process.

8. Cf. chapter 9.

CHAPTER 3. WORK AS AN UNCERTAIN INVESTMENT

1. D. Ménager, "Mom, Drop the Duster," *Panorama*, 1979.

2. Secondary application of data from the INSEE study, *Emploi du temps*, 1974–75.

3. Secondary application of data from the INSEE *FQP* study, 1970. Cf. de Singly 1982b.

4. INSEE, *Taxable Income* study, 1975.

5. The cost of marriage is defined by the correlation between the chances of gaining an executive position by a married woman and those of a married man with the same qualifications. The benefits of marriage are related to the correlation between the chances of achieving an executive position by a married man and those of a single man (or a married woman).

6. Married women are also less likely to join trade unions. Cf. Maruani 1979.

7. Secondary application of data from the INSEE *FQP* study, 1970.

8. The case of women who return to work after being widowed or divorced will be studied in chapter 5.

9. Secondary application of data from Roux 1969.

CHAPTER 4. DIRECT AND INDIRECT INVESTMENT

1. Data from INSEE study, *Emploi du temps*, 1974–75.

2. National conference, "Recherches et familles," Paris, 1983.

3. INSEE study, *Revenus fiscaux des ménages*, 1975.

4. INSEE study, *Familles*, 1982.

5. INSEE, *Population Census*, 1982.

6. Ibid.

7. This holds even for those children who themselves become blue-collar workers since they have a greater professional or matrimonial value than other laborers whose fathers are also laborers. See de Singly and Thélot 1986.

8. INSEE study, *Familles*, 1982.

9. Secondary application of data from Tabard et al. 1982.

10. More precisely, the relationship with the wife's job constitutes one aspect of the way the marriage is perceived.

11. Depending on the precise moment in an individual's life or marriage, the amount of capital he or she possesses and the type of work performed, one view can dominate the other. For examples see Pitrou et al. 1983.

CHAPTER 5. AN INITIAL BALANCE SHEET OF THE EFFECTS OF MARRIAGE

1. Secondary use of data from the INSEE study (*Familles*, 1975) on nearly five thousand widows and seven thousand divorcees married for a second time. Cf. de Singly 1983.

2. By definition, academic capital does not lose value. The awarding of a diploma or degree permanently recognizes a certain level of competence: one continues forever to be a high-school graduate.

3. These inventories were accomplished with the help of sociology students from the University of Nantes in France. Each couple, who answered a long questionnaire containing several questions on each book, whenever possible had to be culturally or socially dissimilar and to possess at least fifty books. See de Singly 1984b, 2:891–909.

4. The husband claims to have liked comic books "for as long as I can remember"; the wife "since we've been married."

5. How else can one describe those books (novels for the most part), which are not a part of "high" culture?

6. It is more a question of shared activities becoming individual activities, thanks to consumer goods like VCRs. Cf. Baboulin, Gaudin, and Mallein 1983.

7. Secondary application of INSEE's *FQP* study, 1970, using a subgroup of married women between the ages of 35 to 52.

8. But the cost can also be perceived by the social actors as an exclusive effect of widowhood, however.

9. We can estimate the changes partially, particularly because the capital that belongs exclusively to the husband, which could be used to meet the family's needs, is not accounted for by the wife, who is partly ignorant of its existence.

10. In a standard study she would probably be classified as a working widow (clerk), whereas previously she would have been classified as a housewife and put in the senior executive category because of her husband's job.

11. Her cultural criteria in choosing her friends were only apparent during the interview, when she stated that she did not like "manual laborers."

CHAPTER 6. TWO MODELS: CONJUGAL COLLECTIVITY AND FEMALE AUTONOMY

1. In France, the law authorizing divorce by mutual consent took effect in July 1975.

2. A total of 693 people were interviewed in 1980 by sociology students from the University of Nantes (France). Only the interviews with people in the 25 to 40 age group have been examined in this chapter. Cf de Singly 1984b.

3. We must distinguish between the "intellectual" and the "economic" groups in the middle classes: executives in the private sector are more "communistic" than workers in the public sector, such as state-employed teachers.

4. *Ouest-France*, the "Wife and Family" column, September 1982.

5. What happens in practice is less significant than the views people hold. A woman who has a job but who is against the idea in principle will be in favor of conjugal collectivity, whereas a nonworking wife who nonetheless supports the principle of working wives will be for a relationship based on autonomy.

6. Roman Catholics and people who are not critical of society opt for a fusion-type relationship in marriage, whereas people with no religious faith

and those who are critical of society prefer self-management. Competition between partners for further education serves as an example of this: half of the Catholics, one-quarter of the others, half of those satisfied with the functioning of society, and one-third of those critical of it would give priority to the husband.

CHAPTER 7. THE BENEFITS OF A "GOOD" MARRIAGE

1. Throughout this chapter descriptive adjectives such as "good," "bad," and "well" reflect current societal values, not higher philosophic standards.

2. Secondary application of data from INSEE study *Pays de Loire* ("Women's employment"), 1972. Cf. de Singly 1980.

3. Molière, *Georges Dandin or the Confounded Husband,* 1668.

4. Secondary application of data from INSEE study "Family budgets," 1979, on 5,252 households in which the reference person is employed. Cf. Glaude and de Singly 1986.

5. Secondary application of data from INSEE *FQP* study, 1970, on employed married men and women aged 35 to 52.

6 Census of state and local government employees, Coll. D. 46–46, INSEE, Paris, 1976.

7. For individuals who continued their studies until the age of nineteen, this index is 0.37 for those men and women who married down; 0.63 for ordinary marriages; and 0.97 for good marriages.

8. Secondary application of data from Mueller, Parcel, and Pampel 1979.

CHAPTER 8. CELIBACY: THE HARMFUL EFFECTS OF SUBSTANTIAL ACADEMIC CAPITAL

1. INSEE, *Population Census,* 1982.

2. According to Courgeau and Lelièvre (1986), there is nonetheless "an effect specific to agriculture" with regard to marriage.

3. Secondary application of data from INSEE *FQP* study, 1970, based on workers aged 35 to 52.

4. INSEE, *Population Census,* 1982.

5. INSEE *FQP* study, 1970, workers aged 35 to 52.

6. Women born between 1940 and 1944, INSEE, *Familles* study, 1975. Cf. Desplanques 1987.

7. Duteil 1979. The agency she went to advised her to omit any references to her doctorate "because it would put most men off."

8. This commercial also pays tribute to marriage. Obviously a middle-aged woman has to be married!

9. Civil status.

10. Balzac's term ("l'âge anti-matrimonial"): "The younger Latournelle had the courage to marry a girl who had reached the 'unmarriageable age' of 33" (*Modest Mignon,* 1844).

11. Based on the range of ages of single people (between 19 and 80 years) in the French population (INSEE, *Population Census,* 1975) compared to the readership of *Chasseur Français* (drawn from a survey of 860 ads in the October 1979 issue).

12. INSEE study, *Familles,* 1982.

13. A difference of more than one year is considered to show inequality of age. See Deville 1972.

14. C. Ullin, "Qu'est-ce qui empêche les filles de se marier?" *Femmes d'Aujourd'hui,* no. 1362, May 1977.

CHAPTER 9. LIVING TOGETHER: A LESS COSTLY MARRIAGE

1. Harriet Taylor, *The enfranchisement of women,* quoted in M-F. Cachin, preface to Mill 1975.

2. However, no study on the extent of these risks has been undertaken.

3. INSEE study, *Familles,* 1982.

4. Ibid.

5. Study, *Phosphore,* on four thousand high-school students in 1985, carried out by M. Bozon, O. Galland, and F. de Singly. According to the SOFRES-*Madame Figaro* poll (January 1990), 58 percent of the boys and 44 percent of the girls between the ages of 13 to 17 wish to get married eventually.

6. Unpublished study, extract from a series of 42 interviews with co-habitants, Nantes, 1984.

7. INSEE study, *Emploi du temps,* 1985. Cf. Audirac 1986.

8. INSEE study, *Emploi du temps,* 1984. Cf. Galland 1985.

9. Secondary application of data from INED study, *Les jeunes de 18 à 25 ans,* 1978. Cf. Gokalp 1981.

10. INSEE study, *Familles,* 1982.

11. In 1989, of the 30- to 34-year-old women who were living with a man, 23 percent of those employed as executives and 12 percent of the blue-collar workers were living together outside of marriage (Thave 1991, 71).

12. With marriage having lost its significance of previous decades, at the end of the 1980s it took on new meaning among the younger generation, whose marriages were closer to cohabitation than to traditional unions.

13. *Cosmopolitan,* April 1982.

14. *Femmes d'Aujourd'hui,* February 1977.

15. Ibid.

CONCLUSION

1. Evelyne Sullerot's thesis (1984) is wrong: cohabitants do not wish to seem motivated by individual self-interest any more than do married couples.

2. Bertrand Lemennicier's version: "It is obviously more difficult for the individual to master his 'irrational' behavior (that is, his passions and his instincts) when it is a question of choosing a wife than it is when choosing a job or clothes" (15).

3. A version that might be deduced from the anti-utilitarian point of view.

4. Beaumarchais, *The Barber of Seville* (1775). The theater—particu-larly Marivaux and Beaumarchais in the eighteenth century—and the novel in the nineteenth century played important roles in the dissemination of

the idea of romantic love. Through the techniques of deceit and disguise, they presented the separation of the two interests—utilitarian and humanitarian reason.

POSTSCRIPT: TWENTY YEARS LATER

1. Thanks are due to Alain Chenu for doing the calculations on the 1985 *FQP* study.

2. Results taken from a study on young secondary school students' reading habits (de Singly 1989).

3. From a study on the political uses of the concept of "compromise" between work and family responsibilities. See Commaille 1993 and de Singly 1993a.

4. An ideology does not have to be true for it to be believed: the children of working mothers are not "handicapped" (Spitze 1988; Menahem 1988; Vallet 1989).

5. The comparison of the price paid by women for marriage between 1970 and 1985 was carried out by the author from data on the chances of succeeding to the position of "executive" (junior and senior for those with little academic capital; senior only for the rest) of married men and women. Cf. Appendix 1.

6. The setting up of a new model: "successful divorce." See Théry 1993.

Works Cited

Acker, J. 1973. Women and social stratification: A case of sexual sexism. *American Journal of Sociology* 78 (4): 936–45.

Acock, A. C., and V. L. Bengtson. 1978. On the relative influence of mothers and fathers: A covariance analysis of political and religious socialization. *Journal of Marriage and the Family* 40 (3): 519–30.

Allen, S. M., and R. A. Kalish. 1984. Professional women and marriage. *Journal of Marriage and the Family* 46 (2): 375–82.

Almquist, E., and S. Angrist. 1970. Career salience and atypicality of occupational choice among college women. *Journal of Marriage and the Family* 32 (2): 242–49.

Aneshendel, C. S., and B. C. Rosen. 1980. Domestic roles and sex differences in occupational expectations. *Journal of Marriage and the Family* 42 (1): 127–31.

Aubret-Beny, F. 1978. Pratique éducative des parents et autres caractéristiques culturelles et démographiques du milieu familial en relation avec le niveau intellectuel des élèves de cours préparatoire. In *Enquête nationale sur le niveau intellectuel des enfants d'âge scolaire,* edited by INED-INETOP, 3:257–90. Paris: Presses Universitaires de France.

Audirac, P. A. 1986. La cohabitation: Un million de couples non mariés. *Economie et Statistique* 185:13–33.

Baboulin, J.-C.; J.-P. Gaudin; and P. Mallein. 1983. *Le magnétoscope au quotidien.* Paris: Aubier.

Badinter, E. 1986. *L'un est l'autre.* Paris: Editions O. Jacob.

Bahr, S. H. 1979. The effect of welfare on marital stability and remarriage. *Journal of Marriage and the Family* 41 (3): 553–60.

Bailyn, L. 1970. Career and family orientations of husbands and wives in relation to marital happiness. *Human Relations* 23 (2): 97–113.

Balzac, de Honoré. 1982. *Modeste Mignon* (1844). Paris: Editions Gallimard.

Barrère-Maurisson, M.-A. 1982. Les incidences de la crise économique sur le couple et la famille. *Dialogue* 77:71–81.

Barrère-Maurisson, M.-A., et al., eds. 1984. *Le sexe du travail: Structures familiales et système productif.* Grenoble: Presses Universitaires de Grenoble.

Barthes, R. 1970. *L'empire des signes.* Geneva: A. Skira.

Barugh, G. K. 1972. Maternal influences upon college women's attitudes toward women and work. *Developmental Psychology* 6:32–37.

Battagliola, F. 1984. Employées et employés: Trajectoires professionnelles et familiales: In *Le sexe du travail,* edited by M.-A. Barrère-Maurisson et al., 57–70. Grenoble: Presses Universitaires de Grenoble.

———. 1988. *La fin du mariage?* Paris: Syros/Alternatives.

Baudelot, C., and O. Choquet. 1981. Du salaire au niveau de vie. *Economie et Statistique* 39:17–28.

Baudoin, E. 1931. *La mère au travail et le retour au foyer.* Paris: Bloud and Gay.

Beaumarchais, P.-A. 1976. *Le barbier de Séville* (1775). Paris: Hachette.

Becker, G. S. 1974. A theory of social interactions. *Journal of Political Economy* 82 (6): 1063–93.

———. 1981. *A treatise on the family.* Cambridge: Harvard University Press.

Béjin, A. 1982. Le mariage extra-conjugal d'aujourd'hui. *Communications* 35:138–46.

Belotti, E. G. 1981. *Courrier du coeur.* Paris: Editions des Femmes.

Benham, L. 1974. Benefits of women's education within marriage. *Journal of Political Economy* 82 (2): S57-S71.

———. 1975. Non-market returns to women's investment in education. In *Sex discrimination and the division of labor,* edited by C. B. Lloyd, 293–309. New York: Columbia University Press.

Bensaume-Vincent, B. 1981. A l'ombre du génie: Etre femme de Pasteur. *Penelope* 4:9–12.

Bernard, J. 1972. *The future of marriage.* New York: World Publishing Co.

Bertaux, D., and C. Delcroix. 1991. Des pères face au divorce: La fragilisation du lien paternel. *Espaces et familles* 17:7–108.

Bloch, L., and M. Glaude. 1983. Une approche du coût de l'enfant. *Economie et Statistique* 155:51–67.

Blood, R. O., and D. M. Wolfe. 1960. *Husbands and wives.* Glencoe, Ill.: Free Press.

Blunden, K. 1982. *Le travail et la vertu.* Paris: Payot.

Boltanski, L. 1969. *Prime éducation et morale de classe.* Paris-The Hague: Mouton.

Boudon, R. 1977. *Effets pervers et ordre social.* Paris: Presses Universitaires de France.

Bourdieu, P. 1974. Avenir de classe et causalité du probable. *Revue française de sociologie* 15 (1):3–42.

———. 1979. Les trois états du capital culturel. *Actes de la Recherches en Sciences sociales* 30:3–6.

Bourdieu, P., and J.-C. Passeron. 1964. *Les héritiers.* Paris: Editions de Minuit.

———. 1970. *La reproduction.* Paris: Editions de Minuit.

Bourdieu, P., and M. de Saint-Martin. 1978. Le patronat. *Actes de la Recherches en Sciences sociales* 20–21:3–82.

Bourgeois, F.; J. Brener; D. Chabaud; A. Cot; D. Fougeyrollas; M. Haicault; and A. Kartchevsky-Bulport. 1978. Travail domestique et famille du capitalisme. *Critique de l'Economie politique* 3:3–23.

Bozon, M., and F. Heran. 1987–88. La découverte du conjoint. *Population* 6:943–86, and 1:121–50.

Bozon, M., J. Laufer, F. de Singly, and C. Villeneuve-Golkalp. 1994. Rapport de l'enquête sur la place et le rôle des femmes en France. Fourth World Conference on Women, Ministère des affaires sociales, de la santé, et de la ville, Paris.

Brangeon, J.-L., and G. Jegouzo. 1974. Célibat paysan et pauvreté. *Economie et Statistique* 58:3–18.

———. 1978. La condition sociale du petit paysan. In *Données sociales,* 381–400. Paris: INSEE.

Bubeck, D. 1995. *Care, gender, and justice.* Oxford: Oxford University Press.

Burguière, A. 1972. De Malthus à Max Weber: Le mariage tardif et l'esprit d'entreprise. *Annales ESC* 27 (4–5): 1128–38.

Cacouault, M. 1984. Diplôme et célibat: Les femmes professeurs de lycée entre les deux guerres.

Canceill, G. 1984. Revenu professionnel, formation et situation familiale. In *Données sociales,* 496–501. Paris: INSEE.

Cardinal, M. 1978. *Une vie pour deux.* Paris: Grasset.

Castel, R. 1981. *La gestion des risques.* Paris: Editions de Minuit.

Castel, R., and J.-C. Passeron, eds. 1967. *Education, développement et démocratie.* The Hague: Mouton.

Cave, F. 1981. *L'espoir et la consolation.* Paris: Payot.

Chabaud-Richter, D.; D. Fougeyrollas-Schwebel; and F. Sonthonnax. 1985. *Espace et temps du travail domestique.* Paris: Librairie des Méridiens.

Chalvon-Demersay, S. 1983. *Concubin, concubine.* Paris: Le Seuil.

Chaudron, M. 1983. Heur et malheur de la cuisinière. *Les Temps modernes* 438:1349–59.

———. 1991. Vie de famille, vie de travail. In *La famille: L'état des savoirs,* 133–44. Paris: Editions La Découverte.

Cherlin, A. 1980. Postponing marriage: The influence of young women's work expectations. *Journal of Marriage and the Family* 42 (2): 355–65.

Clerc, P. 1964. La famille et l'orientation scolaire au niveau de la sixième. *Population* 4:627–72.

Collange, C. 1979. *Je veux rentrer à la maison.* Paris: Grasset.

Commaille, J. 1978. *Le divorce en France.* Paris: La Documentation française.

———. 1981. Les stragégies de divorce. Paper read at the International Sociological Association, Louvain.

———. 1993. *Les stratégies des femmes.* Paris: Editions La Découverte.

Commaille, J., and F. de Singly, eds. *La famille européenne: La question familiale dans l'Union Européenne.* Paris: Editions L'Harmattan.

Courgeau, D., and E. Lelièvre. 1986. Nuptialité et agriculture. *Population* 41 (2):303–26.

Crozet, C. 1972. *Marianne ou les autres.* Paris: Gallimard.

Davis, N. J., and R. V. Robinson. 1988. Class identification of men and women in the 1970s and 1980s. *American Sociological Review* 53:103–12.

Delly. 1982. *Une femme supérieure.* Paris: Gautier-Languereau.

Delphy, C. 1974. Mariage et divorce: L'impasse à double face. *Les Temps modernes* 29:333–34, 1815–29.

———. 1977. Les femmes dans les études de stratification. In *Femmes, sexisme et société*, edited by A. Michel, 25–38. Paris: Presses Universitaires de France.

Desplanques, G. 1984. La mortalité masculine selon le milieu social. In *Données sociales*, 348–58. Paris: INSEE.

———, 1987, *Cycle de vie et milieu social.* No. D117. Paris: INSEE.

Deville, J.-C. 1972. *Structures des familles.* Paris: INSEE.

Dixon, R. 1971. Explaining cross-cultural variations in age at marriage and proportions never marrying. *Population Studies* (July): 215–18.

Dorin, F. 1984. *Les jupes-culottes.* Paris: Flammarion.

Dowling, C. 1981. *The Cinderella complex.* New York: Summit Books.

Durkheim, E. 1969. *Le suicide.* Paris: Presses Universitaires de France.

Duteil, M. 1979. *Le marché de la solitude.* Paris: De Noël.

Elder, G. H. 1969. Appearance and education in marriage mobility. *American Sociological Review* 34 (August): 519–33.

Elena, Gabriella, Giorgo, Silvia, and Luisa. 1974. *Etre exploitées.* Paris: Editions des Femmes.

Engels, F. 1954. *The origins of the family, private property, and the state* (1884). Paris: Editions Sociales.

Ernaux, A. 1974. *Les armoires vides.* Paris: Gallimard.

———. 1984. *La place.* Paris: Gallimard.

Etaugh, C., and J. Malstrom. 1981. The effect of marital status on personal perception. *Journal of Marriage and the Family* 43 (4): 801–5.

Fagnani, J. 1986. La durée des trajets quotidiens: Un enjeu pour les mères actives. *Economie et Statistique* 185 (February): 47–55.

Farge, A., and C. Klapisch-Zuber, eds. 1984. *Madame ou mademoiselle?* Paris: Editions Montalba.

Ferber, M., and H. Huber. 1979. Husbands, wives, and careers. *Journal of Marriage and the Family* 41 (2): 315–25.

Ferree, M. M. 1990. Beyond separate spheres: Feminism and family research. *Journal of Marriage and the Family* 52 (November): 866–84.

Festy, M., and M.-F. Valetas. 1990. Contraintes sociales et conjugales sur la vie des femmes séparées. In *Données sociales*, 301–5. Paris: INSEE.

Finch, J. 1983. *Married to the job: Wives' incorporation in women's work.* London: G. Allen & Unwin.

Flamenco, A. 1967. L'instruction et le choix du conjoint. In *Education, développement et démocratie*, edited by R. Castel and J.-C. Passeron, 137–49. The Hague: Mouton.

Flandrin, J.-L. 1975. *Amours paysannes.* Paris: Gallimard.

Folk, F., and A. H. Beller. 1993. Part-time work and child care choices for mothers of preschool children. *Journal of Marriage and the Family* 55 (February): 146–57.

Fourastié, J. 1970. Une enquête sur la scolarité d'instituteurs et de normaliens. In *Population et l'enseignement*, 532–38. Paris: INED.

Fraisse, G. 1992. De la destination au destin: Histoire philosophique de la différence des sexes. In *Histoire des femmes*, edited by G. Duby and M. Perrot, 4:57–85. Paris: Plon.

———. 1993. Sur l'incompatibilité supposée de l'amour et du féminisme. *Esprit* (May): 71–78.

Galland, O. 1985. Jeunes: Marché scolaire, marché du travail, marché matrimonial. In *Les jeunes et les autres*, edited by F. Proust, 217–40. Paris: Ministry of Research and Technology.

Garbe, C. 1993. Les femmes et la lecture. In *Identité, lecture, écriture*, edited by M. Chaudron and F. de Singly, 187–212. Paris: Editions Centre G. Pompidou/BPI.

Gertrude. 1979. Postface à quelques préfaces. *Questions féministes* 6:23–33.

Giddens, A. 1992. *The transformation of intimacy*. Cambridge: Polity Press.

Gilligan, C. 1982. *In a different voice*. Cambridge: Harvard University Press.

Girard, A. 1962. *La réussite sociale en France*. Paris: Presses Universitaires de France-INED.

Girard, A., and H. Bastide. 1963. La stratification sociale et la démocratisation de l'enseignement. *Population* 3:435–72.

Giroud, F. 1982. *Le bon plaisir*. Paris: Hachette.

Glaude, M., and F. de Singly. 1986. L'organisation domestique: Pouvoir et négociation. *Economie et Statistique* 187:3–30.

Glenn, N. D. 1975. The contribution of marriage to the psychological well-being of males and females. *Journal of Marriage and the Family* 37 (3): 594–600.

Glenn, N. D.; S. K. Hoppe; and D. Weiner. 1974. Social class heterogamy and marital success: A study of the empirical adequacy of a textbook generalization. *Social Problems* 21 (4): 539–50.

Glenn, N. D.; A. Ross; and J. Tuly. 1974. Patterns of intergenerational mobility of females through marriage. *American Sociological Review* 39:683–99.

Glick, P. C., and A. J. Norton. 1971. Frequency, duration, and probability of marriage and divorce. *Journal of Marriage and the Family* 33:307–17.

Goffman, E. 1973a. *La présentation de soi*. Paris: Editions de Minuit.

———. 1973b. *Les relations en public*. Paris: Editions de Minuit.

Gokalp, C. 1981. *Quand vient l'âge des choix*. Paris: Presses Universitaires de France-INED.

Gotman, A. 1988. *Hériter*. Paris: Presses Universitaires de France.

Guillaumin, C. 1978. Pratique du pouvoir et idée de nature. *Questions féministes* 2:5–39.

Hannan, M. T.; N. B. Tuma; and L. P. Groeneveld. 1978. Income and independence effects on marital dissolution: Results from the Seattle and Denver income maintenance experiments. *American Journal of Sociology* 84:611–33.

Hardy, T. 1981. *Les petites ironies de la vie* (Life's Little Ironies, 1894). Paris: Editions Gallimard.

Hiller, D. V., and W. W. Philliber. 1986. The division of labor in contemporary marriage. *Social Problems* 33:191–201.

Hoffman, L. W. 1974. Effects of maternal employment on the child: A review of research. *Developmental Psychology* 10 (2): 204–28.

Hogan, D. P. 1980. The transition to adulthood as a career contingency. *American Sociological Review* 45 (2): 261–76.

Houseknecht, S. K.; S. Vaughan; and A. Statham. 1987. Singlehood and the careers of professional women. *Journal of Marriage and the Family* 49 (2): 353–66.

Huet, M. T.; Y. Lemel; and C. Roy. 1982. Les emplois du temps des citadins. In *Archives et Documents*. Paris: INSEE.

Huppert-Laufer, J. 1982. *La féminité neutralisée*. Paris: Flammarion.

INED. 1970. *Population et l'enseignement*. Paris: INED.

INED-INETOP. 1973, 1978. *Enquête nationale sur le niveau intellectuel des enfants d'âge scolaire*. Vols. 2–3. Paris: Presses Universitaires de France.

Jorgensen, S. R. 1977. Social class heterogamy, status striving and perceptions of marital conflict: A partial replication and revision of Pearlin's contingency hypothesis. *Journal of Marriage and the Family* 39 (4): 653–61.

Julia, D. 1981. La naissance du corps professoral. *Actes de la Recherche en Sciences sociales* 39:71–86.

Kaufmann, J.-C. 1992. *La trame conjugale: Analyse du couple par son linge*. Paris: Editions Nathan.

Kellerhals, J.; N. Languin; J.-F. Perrin; and G. Wirth. 1985. Statut social, projet familial et divorce. *Population* 6:811–28.

Kellerhals, J.; J.-F. Perrin; G. Steinhauer-Cresson; L. Voneche; and G. Wirth. 1982. *Mariages au quotidien*. Lausanne: Editions P.-M. Favre.

Kitson, G. C., and L. A. Morgan. 1990. The multiple consequences of divorce: A decade review. *Journal of Marriage and the Family* 52 (November): 913–24.

Kitson, G. C., and M. B. Sussman. 1982. Marital complaints, demographic characteristics and symptoms of mental distress in divorce. *Journal of Marriage and the Family* 44 (1): 87–101.

Knibiehler, Y. 1984. Vocations sans voiles, les métiers sociaux. In *Madame ou mademoiselle?* edited by A. Farge and C. Klapisch-Zuber, 163–76. Paris: Editions Montalba.

Knibiehler, Y., and C. Fouquet. 1977. *Histoire des mères*. Paris: Editions Montalba.

Korenman, S., and D. Neumark. 1991. Does marriage really make men more productive? *Journal of Human Resources* 26 (2): 282–307.

Lafitte-Houssat, J. 1979. *Troubadours et cours d'amour*. Paris: Presses Universitaires de France.

Lagarde, F. 1981. *Liaison activité féminine-fécondité: Un essai de chiffrement*. Paris: Direction de la Prévision.

Langevin, A. 1980. Mutants, mutantes? Des raisins encore verts. *Autrement* 24:51–59.

Laurents, A. 1978. *Le tournant de la vie.* Paris: Editions Menges.

Lautrey, J. 1980. *Classe sociale, milieu familial, intelligence.* Paris: Presses Universitaires de France.

La Varende. 1959. *Un sot mariage.* Paris: Hachette.

Lefaucheur, N. 1982. *Enquête explorateur sur les conséquences financières du décès du chef de famille.* Paris: CERC.

———. 1992. Maternité, famille, Etat. In *Histoires des femmes,* edited by G. Duby and M. Perrot, 5:411–30. Paris: Editions Plon.

Lemennicier, B. 1980. La spécialisation des rôles conjugaux, les gains au mariage et la perspective du divorce. *Consommation* 1:27–71.

———. 1982. Les déterminants de la mobilité matrimoniale. *Consommation* 2:25–58.

———. 1988. *Le marché du mariage et de la famille.* Paris: Presses Universitaires de France.

Leprince-Ringuet, T. 1985. *Il faut que je rentre.* Paris: Buchet-Chastel.

Léridon, H., and C. Villeneuve-Gokalp. 1988. Les nouveaux couples. *Population* 2:331–74.

Leroy, S. *C'est dur la solitude.* Paris: R. Laffont.

Lery, A. 1984. Les actives de 1982 n'ont pas moins d'enfants que celles de 1968. *Economie et Statistique* 171–72:25–34.

Lessing, Doris. 1963. Room 19. In *A man and two women: Stories.* New York: Simon and Schuster.

Lloyd, C. B., ed. 1975. *Sex discrimination and the division of labor.* New York: Columbia University Press.

Long, L. H. 1974. Women's labor force participation and the residential mobility of families. *Social Forces* 52 (March): 342–48.

Lopota, H. Z. 1979. *Women as widows.* New York: Elsevier.

Luce, D., and H. Raiffa. 1957. *Games and decisions.* New York: Wiley.

Luhmann, N. 1982. *Liebe als Passion.* Frankfurt: Suhrkamp Verlag.

Mahoney, E. R., and J. G. Richardson. 1979. Perceived social status of husbands and wives: The effect of labor participation and occupational prestige. *Sociology and Social Research* 63 (2): 364–74.

Marceau, J. 1978. Le rôle des femmes dans les familles du monde des affaires. In *Les femmes dans la société marchande,* edited by A. Michel, 113–24. Paris: Presses Universitaires de France.

Mallet-Joris, F. 1977. *La maison de papier.* Paris: Grasset.

Martin, T. W.; K. J. Berry; and R. B. Jacobsen. 1975. The impact of dual-career marriages on female professional careers: An empirical test of a Parsonian hypothesis. *Journal of Marriage and the Family* 37 (4): 734–42.

Maruani, M. 1979. *Les syndicats à l'épreuve du féminisme.* Paris: Editions Syros.

———. 1985. *Mais qui a peur du travail des femmes?* Paris: Editions Syros.

Maruani, M., and C. Nicole. 1989. *Au labeur des dames*. Paris: Syros/ Alternatives.

Marx, J. H., and S. L. Spray. 1970. Marital status and occupational success among mental health professionals. *Journal of Marriage and the Family* 31 (February): 110–18.

Mauger, G., and C. Fossé. 1977. *La vie buissonnière*. Paris: Maspero.

Mauger, G., and C. Fossé-Poliak. 1983. Les loubards. *Actes de la Recherche en Sciences Sociales* 50:49–67.

———. 1986. De la cohabitation chez les jeunes de milieux populaires, 1975–1985. *Dialogue* 92:76–87.

Maupassant, G. de. 1957. La dot (1884). In *Toine*. Paris: Editions M. Gonon.

McDonald, G. W. 1980. Family power: The assessment of a decade of theory and research, 1970–1979. *Journal of Marriage and the Family* 42 (4): 841–54.

Menahem, G. 1988. L'activité professionnelle des mères a augmenté les chances de réussite de leurs enfants. *Economie et Stastistique* 211 (June): 45–48.

Michel, A. 1974. *Activité professionnelle de la femme et vie conjugale*. Paris: Editions du CNRS.

———. 1977. *Femmes, sexisme et société*. Paris: Presses Universitaires de France.

———, ed. 1978. *Les femmes dans la société marchande*. Paris: Presses Universitaires de France.

Mill, J. S. 1975. *L'asservissement des femmes* (The subjection of women, 1869). Edited by M.-F. Cachin. Paris: Payot.

Mincer, J. 1978. Family migration decisions. *Journal of Political Economy* 36 (5): 749–73.

Moen, P., and D. I. Dempster-McClain. 1987. Employed parents: Role strain, work time, and preferences for working less. *Journal of Marriage and the Family* 49 (August): 579–90.

Molière. 1964. *Georges Dandin ou le mari confondu* (1668). In *Théâtre complet*, 411–29. Paris: Le Seuil.

Monnier, A. 1977. *La naissance d'un enfant*. Paris: Presses Universitaires de France-INED.

Moscovici, S., ed. 1972. *Introduction à la psychologie sociale*. Vol. 1. Paris: Larousse.

Mueller, C. W., and B. G. Campbell. 1977. Female occupational achievement and marital status. *Journal of Marriage and the Family* 39 (3): 587–93.

Mueller, C. W.; T. L. Parcel; and F. C. Pampel. 1979. The effect of marital dyad status inconsistency on women's support for equal rights. *Journal of Marriage and the Family* 41 (4): 779–91.

Neill, A. S. 1960. *A radical approach to child rearing*. New York: Hart Publishing.

———. 1970. *Freedom, not anarchy*. Paris: Payot.

Niemi, B. 1975. Geographic immobility and unemployment. In *Sex discrimination and the division of labor*, edited by C. B. Lloyd, 61–89. New York: Columbia University Press.

Nussbaum, M. 1993. Justice pour les femmes. *Esprit* (May): 54–70.

Okin, S. M. 1992. *Justice, gender and the family.* New York: Basic Books.

Orwell, G. 1933. *Down and out in Paris and London.* New York: Harcourt Brace and Co.

Paolucci, B. 1978. Le développement des ressources humaines dans les familles américaines. In *Les femmes dans la société marchande,* edited by A. Michel, 97–111. Paris: Presses Universitaires de France.

Parsons, T. 1955. *Eléments pour une sociologie de l'action.* Paris: Plon.

Parsons, T., and R. Bales. 1955. *Family, socialization, and interaction process.* Glencoe, Ill.: Free Press.

Pearlin, L. I. 1975. Status inequality and stress in marriage. *American Sociological Review* 40 (3): 344–57.

Pillorget, R. 1979. *La tige et le rameau.* Paris: Calmann-Lévy.

Pitrou, A. 1977. Un processus de récupération du statut social: Le cas des cadres non-diplômés. *Sociologie du Travail* 19:1–22.

Pitrou, A.; F. Battagliola; M. Buisson; N. Rousier; J. Ruffier; and Y. Toussaint. 1983. *Trajectoires professionnelles et stratégies familiales.* Paris: CNRS.

Pohl, R.; J. Soleilhavoup; and J. Ben-Rezigue. 1983. *Formation, mobilité sociale, salaires.* Paris: INSEE.

Polachek, S. W. 1975. Discontinuous labor force participation and its effect on women's market earnings. In *Sex discrimination and the division of labor,* edited by C. B. Lloyd, 90–123. New York: Columbia University Press.

Pope Pius XI. 1930. Encyclique *Casti Connumi,* 31 December. In *Les enseignements pontificaux: Le problème féminin,* edited by Moines de Solesmes, 15–19. Paris: Desclée and Co.

Proust, F. 1985. *Les jeunes et les autres.* Paris: Ministry of Research and Technology.

Radloff, L. 1975. Sex differences in depression: The effect of occupation and marital status. *Sex Roles* 1:249–65.

Raffin, T. 1982. La naissance de l'amour conjugal: Etude du "Petit echo de la mode." Master's thesis, University of Nantes.

Rawls, J. 1973. *A theory of justice.* Oxford: Oxford University Press.

Richardson, J. G. 1979. The wife's occupational superiority and marital troubles: An examination of the hypothesis. *Journal of Marriage and the Family* 41 (1): 63–72.

Ritter, K. V., and L. H. Hargens. 1975. Occupational positions and class identifications of married working women: A test of the asymmetry hypothesis. *American Journal of Sociology* 80:934–48.

Romains, Jules. 1975. *M. Le Trouhadec saisi par la débauche* (1924). Paris: Editions Gallimard.

Ronsin, F. 1980. *La grève des ventres.* Paris: Aubier.

Ross, P. A. 1981. Marital differences in occupational distribution and attainment: A twelve-nation study. Paper delivered at the annual meeting of the Population Association of America, Washington, D.C.

Rothschild, N. de. 1984. *La baronne rentre à cinq heures.* Paris: J.-C. Lattès.

Roussel, L., and O. Bourguignon. 1979. *Générations nouvelles et mariage traditionnel.* Paris: Presses Universitaires de France-INED.

Roux, C. 1969. Aspects professionnels de la reprise d'activité des femmes mariées. *Revue française des Affaires sociales* 23 (1): 33–74.

Roy, C. 1990. Dix ans après, les nouveaux pères existent-ils? *L'Ecole des Parents* 2:37–42.

Roy, C., and H. Rousse. 1981. Activités ménagères et cycle de vie. *Economie et Statistique* 131:59–67.

Rubin, Z. 1968. Do American women marry up? *American Sociological Review* 33:750–60.

Sandis, E. E. 1970. The transmission of mother's educational ambitions, as related to specific socialization techniques. *Journal of Marriage and the Family* 32 (2): 204–11.

Schnaberg, A., and S. Oldenberg. Closing the circle: The impact of children on parental status. *Journal of Marriage and the Family* 37 (4): 937–53.

Schultheis, F. 1991. La famille, le marché et l'Etat Providence. In *Affaires de famille, affaires d'Etat*, edited by F. de Singly and F. Schultheis, 33–42. Nancy: Editions de l'Est.

Schwartz, F. N. 1989. Management women and the new facts of life. *Harvard Business Review* (1): 65–76.

Schwartz, O. 1990. *Le monde privé des ouvriers.* Paris: Presses Universitaires de France.

Segalen, M. 1980. *Mari et femme dans la société paysanne.* Paris: Flammarion.

Sennett, R. 1979. *Les tyrannies de l'intimité.* Paris: Le Seuil.

Sewell, W. H., and V. P. Shah. 1968a. Parents' education and children's educational aspirations and achievements. *American Sociological Review* 33 (April): 191–209.

———. 1968b. Social class parental encouragement and educational aspirations. *American Journal of Sociology* 73 (March): 59–72.

Sewell, W. H.; R. H. Hauser; and W. C. Wolf. 1980. Sex, schooling and occupational status. *American Journal of Sociology* 86 (3): 551–83.

Sheckley, R. 1980. *Le robot qui me ressemblait.* Paris: R. Laffont.

Shihadeh, E. S. 1991. The prevalence of husband-centered migration: Employment consequences for married mothers. *Journal of Marriage and the Family* 53 (May): 432–44.

Shorter, E. 1975. *The making of the modern family.* New York: Basic Books.

———. 1977. *Naissance de la famille moderne.* Paris: Le Seuil.

Simmel, G. 1981. *Sociologie et épistémologie.* Paris: Presses Universitaires de France.

Simpson, I. H.; D. Stark; and R. A. Jackson. 1988. Class identification processes of married working men and women. *American Sociological Review* 53:284–93.

Singly, F. de. 1976. Un cas de dédoublement littéraire. *Actes de le Recherche en Sciences sociales* 6:76–85.

———. 1977. Mobilité féminine par le mariage et dot scolaire. *Economie et Statistique* 91:33–44.

———. 1980. Richesses scolaires de la femme et appropriation maritale de sa force de travail. Paper delivered at the French Sociological Society's conference "Travail des femmes et institutions familiales," Nantes.

———. 1981a. Le mariage informel. *Recherches sociologiques* 12 (1): 61–90.

———. 1981b. La ponctuation du temps domestique. *Dialogue* 72:53–56.

———. 1981c. Le pouvoir de la communication conjugale. *Dialogue* 74:91–105.

———. 1982a. Attention! Travaux sur l'intelligence. *Commentaire* 19:495–99.

———. 1982b. Mariage, dot scolaire, et position sociale. *Economie et Statistique* 142:7–20.

———. 1982c. Un nouveau mariage de raison. *Dialogue* 77:57–70.

———. 1983. Le second mari. *Population* 38 (1): 9–27.

———. 1984a. Accumulation et partage des ressources conjugales. *Sociologie du Travail* 26 (3): 326–45.

———. 1984b. Fortune et infortune de la femme mariée. Thèse d'Etat, University of Paris V-Sorbonne. 2 vols.

———. 1984c. Les manoeuvres de séduction: Une analyse des annonces matrimoniales. *Revue française de Sociologie* 25:523–59.

———. 1987. Théorie critique de l'homogamie. *L'année sociologique* 37:181–205.

———. 1989. *Lire à 12 ans.* Paris: Editions Nathan.

———. 1990. L'homme dual. *Le Debat* 61:138–51.

———. 1992a. Le célibat contemporain. In *La nuptialité,* edited by T. Hibert and L. Roussel, 75–87. Paris: Presses Universitaires de France-INED.

———. 1992b. Travail des mères et contradictions sociales. In *Développement de l'enfant et engagement professionnel des mères,* edited by J. Cohen-Solal, 95–103. Paris: Editions STH.

———. 1993a. *Parents salariés et petites maladies d'enfant.* Paris: La Documentation Française.

———. 1993b. Les rivalités entre les genres dans la France contemporaine. In *Femmes et histoire,* edited by G. Duby and M. Perrot, 131–45. Paris: Editions Plon.

———. 1993c. The social construction of a new paternal identity. In *Fathers in families of tomorrow,* 42–75. Copenhagen: European Commission, Danish Ministry of Social Affairs.

———. 1993d. *Sociologie de la famille contemporaine.* Paris: Editions Nathan.

———, ed. 1991. *La famille: L'état des savoirs.* Paris: Editions La Découverte.

Singly, F. de, and C. Thélot. 1986. Racines et profils des ouvriers et des cadres supérieurs. *Revue française de Sociologie* 27 (1): 47–86.

Smith, T. E. 1981. Adolescent agreement with perceived maternal and paternal educational goals. *Journal of Marriage and the Family* 43 (1): 85–93.

Sofer, C. 1982. Essai sur la théorie économique de la division du travail entre homme et femme. Ph.D. diss., University of Paris-Dauphine, 1982.

Solé, J. 1984. *L'amour en Occident.* Brussels: Editions Complexe.

Spitze, G. D. 1988. Women's employment and family relations: A review. *Journal of Marriage and the Family* 3:595–618.

Spitze, G. D., and L. J. Waite. 1981. Wives' employment: The role of husbands' perceived attitudes. *Journal of Marriage and the Family* 43 (1): 117–24.

Stafford, R.; E. Backman; and P. Dibona. 1977. The division of labor among cohabiting and married couples. *Journal of Marriage and the Family* 39 (1): 43–57.

Still, A. 1976. *Roman-Songe.* Paris: Julliard.

Strindberg, A. 1986. Dissensions (1884–85). In *Marié!*, 115–28. Arles: Actes-Sud.

Suaud, C. 1978. Consécration religieuse et professionnalisation féminine en milieu rural. *Cahiers du Gespro* (Nantes) (1): 3–37.

———. 1982. *L'art de cultiver sa retraite.* University of Nantes.

Sullerot, E. 1984. *Pour le meilleur et sans le pire.* Paris: Fayard.

———. 1992. *Quels pères? Quels fils?* Paris: Fayard.

Sussman, M. 1975. Marriage contracts: Social and legal consequences. *Marriage, Divorce, and the Family Newsletter* 1:7.

Tabard, N., and P. Clapier. 1979. *Influence du travail féminin sur les budgets familiaux.* Paris: CREDOC.

Tabard, N.; M. F. Valetas; P. Clapier; and H. Kleinmann. 1982. *Fécondité et conditions de vie.* Paris: CREDOC.

Taylor, C. 1992. *Multiculturalism and "the politics of recognition."* Princeton: Princeton University Press.

Taylor, P. A., and N. D. Glenn. 1979. The utility of education and attractiveness for females' status attainment through marriage. *American Sociological Review* 41 (June): 484–98.

Thave, S. 1991. Célibataires mais pas seuls: Evolution récente des cohabitations de célibataires. In *La nuptialité,* edited by T. Hibert and L. Roussel, 59–74. Paris: Presses Universitaires de France-INED.

Thélot, C. 1982. *Tel père, tel fils?* Paris: Dunod.

Théry, I. 1993. *Le démariage: Justice et vie privée.* Paris: Editions O. Jacob.

Thompson, L., and A. J. Walker. 1989. Gender in families: Women and men in marriage, work, and parenthood. *Journal of Marriage and the Family* 51 (November): 845–71.

Thomson, E. 1980. The value of employment to mothers of young children. *Journal of Marriage and the Family* 42 (3): 551–66.

Treiman, D., and K. Terrell. 1975. Sex and the process of status attainment: A comparison of working women and men. *American Sociological Review* 40:174–200.

Udry, J. R. 1977. The importance of being beautiful: A re-examination and racial comparison. *American Journal of Sociology* 83 (July): 154–60.

Valetas, M. F. 1982. *Le nom de la mère.* Paris: CREDOC.

Vallery-Radot, R. 1915. *Madame Pasteur.* Paris: Flammarion.

Vallet, L. A. 1986. Activité professionnelle de la femme mariée et determination de la position sociale de la famille. *Revue française de Sociologie* 27:655–96.

———. 1989. Activité professionnelle de la mère et ambition scolaire de l'enfant. Paper delivered at the First Annual Conference on the Family Group, Rennes, France.

Vernier, B. 1977. Emigration et déréglement du marché matrimonial. *Actes de la Recherche in Sciences sociales* 15:31–58.

Veron, J. 1984. Mariage, famille et réussite sociale des femmes en France. Paper delivered at the second "Les familles d'aujourd'hui" symposium, International Association of Francophone Demographers, Geneva.

Weber, M. 1971. *Economie et Société.* Vol. 1. Paris: Plon.

Weitzman, L. J. 1974. Legal relation of marriage: Tradition and change. *California Law Review* 62 (4): 1169–1288.

———. 1985. *The divorce revolution: The unexpected social and economic consequences for women and children in America.* Glencoe, Ill.: Free Press.

Wells, H. G. 1983. *Love and Mr. Lewisham* (1899). Oxford: Oxford University Press.

Zick, C. D., and K. R. Smith. 1988. Widowhood, remarriage and changes in economic well-being. *Journal of Marriage and the Family* 1:233–44.

Index